VISIBLE SPEECH

THE ONENESS OF VISIBLE SPEECH

fɔˠ s k ɔˠ ænds ɛ vn j i r z ɔ g o

four score and seven years ago

фор скор энд сэвэн йирз эго

फ़ोरॱ स्कोरॱ रण्ड सैविन यौअर्स अगो
fora   skora   eṇḍa saivina yīarsa ago

휘 스코어 앤드 세븐 이어스 아고
h ŏ s kh ŏ ae d se bŭ i ŏ j a g
w ŏ ŭ o ŏ   nŭ   n   ŭ   o

f r s k r a n d s w n y r z a g o

قُورْ إِسْلُورْ كَنْرَ سَعَنْ يِبْرَشْ رُقَفْ
ogaʃ   sri:ynafas   dnaʃ   roksiʃ   rof

フォアー スコア アンド セブン イヤーズ アゴー
foā   sukoa   ando   sebun   iyāzu   agō

fo lyr sy guo lyr a dde sievie yilyrssy eggo

pu ar es ku ar an de se ba an yi ir iz a gu

佛爾斯國爾恩得色文伊爾斯阿鈎
fo er si guo er en de se wen yi er si a gou

VISIBLE SPEECH

THE DIVERSE ONENESS
OF WRITING SYSTEMS

JOHN DeFRANCIS

UNIVERSITY OF HAWAII PRESS

HONOLULU

oging-in-Publication Data

rse oneness of writing systems / John

Bibliography: p.
Includes index.
ISBN 0–8248–1207–7
1. Written communication. 2. Writing. I. Title.
P211.D36   1989   89–4708
411—dc19   CIP

Frontispiece: The rendition of "four score and seven years ago" in a number of different scripts illustrates the fact that English, like any other language, can be written in any script, though with widely varying degrees of simplicity and closeness of fit between sounds and symbols. For identification of scripts and discussion see pages 248–251.

∞™ *The paper used in this publication meets the minimum require-ments of American National Standard for Information Sciences—Permanence of Paper for Printed Library Materials*
ANSI Z39.48–1984

*There are no pure systems of writing
just as there are no pure races in anthropology
and no pure languages in linguistics.*

—I. J. Gelb

CONTENTS

FIGURES

PREFACE

This book is the first general study of writing by a specialist in Chinese. As such it provides a corrective to the seriously flawed views of the Chinese system of writing that have permeated previous studies and offers a more clear-eyed perspective from which to examine writing in general.

Such a corrective is long overdue. For more than four hundred years, ever since Westerners first came in contact with the characters that make up the Chinese system of writing, descriptions of this writing have been distorted by a fixation on its exotic secondary features. At one level the system has been misrepresented as "pictographic" or "ideographic," while at a more sophisticated level it has been misrepresented more subtly. All levels of misrepresentation are to be found in the recent spate of publications that touch on the subject.

To me this sudden upsurge is something like the proverbial last straw. The cumulative effects of a professional lifetime in which I have had to put up with error about Chinese have finally propelled me to take up arms against the misrepresentation of its system of writing. It is simply intolerable that Chinese writing continues to be misrepresented as "pictographic," a level of intellectual muddle-headedness on a par with discoursing about astronomy in terms of astrology. It is also intolerable that the nature of writing—of all writing—continues to be misunderstood in large part because of the misrepresentation of Chinese.

More is at stake here than a mere academic matter regarding the nature of Chinese in relation to other forms of writing. Notions about Chinese have a direct bearing on many specific areas of thought and action. Error about the Chinese system of writing can subtly lead to bias against the Chinese people themselves. The fact that Chinese characters lack the alphabetic feature of Western scripts has been used to support the argument that Chinese think differently and so were unable to match Western initiative in developing abstract theoretical science. Western phonetic alphabets are analytic systems that represent basic sounds; ergo, Westerners developed analytic thought while Chinese failed to do so—because of their peculiar script. The view of Chinese as a nonphonetic system of writing has been used to buttress the demand that children should be taught to read by "the whole word" method rather than that of "phonics." The Chinese, it is argued, go directly from print to meaning via their "ideographic" script; ergo, printed words in English should be learned as semantic wholes rather than as combinations of letters representing sounds. The nature of the script has also been cited in recent computer hype touting the expenditure of billions of dollars to endow computers with artificial intelligence. Chinese characters supposedly represent graphic units of information that are mechanically processed by the mind without any intervention of spoken language; ergo, intelligent computers can be developed which will process these units with even greater efficiency than can the human mind.

In the face of such weighty matters it is essential that we get our facts straight about Chinese in particular and about writing in general. This is no easy thing to do, since the misunderstanding is pervasive, deep-seated, and often impervious to rational discussion. The issues involved are complex, in part intrinsically so, but also in large part owing to obfuscation by those who cannot see the forest for the trees or cannot separate myth from reality. Although these matters are complex in detail, they can nevertheless be simplified considerably, even if not really made simple, by reduction to their essential aspects. It is the aim of this book to provide such an exposition, one which, while based on sound scholarship, will attack the issues in language comprehensible to nonspecialist readers. Technical terms have been kept to a minimum. These are explained, as nontechnically as possible, in the glossary.

Although Chinese has provided the springboard for this exposition, the focus is on the much broader applicability to writing in general. As the table of contents makes clear, most of the discussion will be devoted to other systems of writing. Apart from providing the impetus for the work as a whole, Chinese will receive special attention only because misconceptions regarding that system continue to underlie much of the misunderstanding of writing in general.

ACKNOWLEDGMENTS

In writing this book I have been heavily indebted to many people who have provided assistance of various kinds.

It gives me much pleasure to extend my heartfelt thanks to my colleagues J. Marshall Unger, professor of Japanese at the University of Hawaii, Robert Sanders, professor of Chinese at Ohio State University (formerly at the University of Hawaii), and Björn Jernudd, a specialist in language planning formerly attached to the East-West Center. These friends entered into a great many fruitful discussions regarding virtually every aspect of the book and provided incisive comments on various drafts of the work.

I am grateful to the two outside readers for the University of Hawaii Press who gave the manuscript a meticulous reading and in their reports to the Press made numerous valuable suggestions for improvement. One of them, S. Robert Ramsey of the Department of Hebrew and East Asian Languages and Literatures at the University of Maryland, has sent me additional helpful comments. James D. McCawley, professor of linguistics at the University of Chicago, has also provided a number of much-appreciated notes on some three-fourths of the book from a background that includes teaching a course on writing systems.

I owe a special debt to several scholars who gave critical readings to the sections in this book dealing with writing systems in which I am not expert. In view of my sharp criticism of the pervasive misconceptions regarding my own field of specialization, namely Chinese, I have been particularly anxious to see to it that in every case my discussion of a specific writing system has been checked by a specialist in that field. It should be emphasized, however, that these scholars, and all those who have been kind enough to review my work, are in no way responsible for any errors of fact, interpretation, or formulation that may remain in the book. My material has gone through successive revisions, the reviewers are busy people who have seen only one of the many drafts, and I may not have fully understood the purport of some suggested emendations, or may not have chosen wisely among the sometimes disparate views that specialists have presented regarding many aspects of writing. I hope, however, that I have done justice to the invaluable help of the following scholars in the areas indicated:

Arabic, Hebrew, and Phoenician: Roger Allen and other members of the Department of Oriental Studies, University of Pennsylvania.

Egyptian: David Silverman of the Department of Oriental Studies, University of Pennsylvania.

English: Judy Kellog, Department of English, University of Hawaii.

Greek and Latin: Alfred Burns, professor emeritus of Classics, University of Hawaii.

Korean: Ho-min Sohn and Gerald Mathias, Department of Asian Languages and Literatures, University of Hawaii.

Mayan: Lyle Campbell, professor of anthropology and linguistics, SUNY Albany.

Sumerian: D. O. Edzard, Institut für Assyriologie und Hethitologie, Universität München, and Renee Gallery, who describes herself as "Former Assyriologist."

Yi: Yin Binyong, Chinese Academy of Social Sciences.

It is a pleasure also to acknowledge the help of several nonacademic readers who checked on the readability of the manuscript from the viewpoint of The General Public.

I also express my deep appreciation to the many individuals, among them the librarians at the University of Hawaii and other institutions, who provided miscellaneous help, such as tracking down elusive bits of information in not readily accessible sources.

Finally, more than a word of thanks is due to my long-suffering colleagues, who were repeatedly called upon to rescue me from my embroilments with a stupid word processor that refused to make any allowances for my ineptness.

I
WRITING IN COMMUNICATIVE CONTEXT

1.

Kinds of Communication

Imagine, as in science fiction time-travel, that when Lincoln delivered his Gettysburg Address, his remarks were taken down verbatim by an international corps of stenographers that included an Egyptian scribe of the third millennium B.C. and some American scientific linguists of today. Apart from the Americans present, none of the stenographers understood a word of English. They had, however, been trained to take dictation, even in a language they did not understand, by noting the sounds in their own speech that most closely approximated the sounds they were hearing, and then writing down these approximations in their own traditional scripts. Relying solely on this training, they wrote down Lincoln's opening words in the various ways illustrated by the frontispiece of this book.

Apart from the diversity of symbols used in these scripts, one of the things that may strike the reader's attention and raise some eyebrows is the existence of some clearly pictographic symbols among the welter of strange signs. Aren't such symbols supposed to represent meanings and not sounds? Don't they stand in a class apart from phonetic writing, of which our own alphabetic letters are an example? How is it possible to speak of a oneness in all this diversity?

These queries raise the basic question as to just what constitutes writing and what we mean by the term. A full answer to this question will take up most of this book. We can start by placing writing in its broader context and by introducing some key terms and concepts.

Definitions and Dichotomies

One useful way to look at writing is to view it within the total framework of human communication. In this context speech must be placed first among the various modalities, followed by writing and, much farther behind, other means which, taken together, use all of our five senses. Some of the last are of only marginal utility, as in the case of smell. But that it too can serve a communicative function is illustrated by the story, perhaps apocryphal, of two opera stars who had to sing a tender love duet with their faces close together. Offstage antipathy needed no words when it could be conveyed by the overwhelming smell of garlic plentifully ingested by one of the singers just before the performance.

More important in the overall picture is the generalized use of supplements to communication that have in recent years received attention under such topics as body language, kinesics, and proxemics. Proxemics concerns how close people come to each other in the course of conversation. Kinesics involves the physical movements that accompany speech; it is a supplementary form of communication distinct from sign language.

A full discussion of communication should consider all these aspects. In our case, however, we will look at these matters only insofar as they have a bearing on writing. As we shall see, there is a complex relationship between writing and some other mediums of expression.

In approaching writing and related modalities it should be carefully noted that there are two main schools of thought whose adherents might be labeled inclusivists and exclusivists on the basis of their support for one or the other of two definitions of writing:

> Inclusivists: Writing includes *any* system of graphic symbols that is used to convey *some amount of thought.*
>
> Exclusivists: Writing includes *only* those systems of graphic symbols that can be used to convey *any and all thought.*

The inclusivist definition of writing includes such limited systems as mathematical notation and chemical formulas. It also includes petroglyphs, Amerindian pictographs, and international symbols such as those for "No Parking" and "No Smoking." The exclusivist definition of writing excludes these symbols on the grounds that while they permit partial expression of thought, they are far too limited and cannot be expanded into complete systems that would enable us to write a poem or a philosophical treatise or a manual on how to operate a word processor. Exclusivists point out that not all the sounds we produce are music, and not all the motions we make are dance. So why then must all the marks we make be considered writing? Just as all that glitters is not gold, so all that's written is not writing.

It appears that we can distinguish between *partial writing* and *full writing* by how much of human thought they can represent. These terms can be defined in this way:

> Partial writing is a system of graphic symbols that can be used to convey only some thought.
> Full writing is a system of graphic symbols that can be used to convey any and all thought.

Inclusivists believe that both partial and full writing should be called writing. Exclusivists believe that only full writing deserves this label. The failure to agree, or even to note that there is a fundamental difference of opinion, is one of the main sources of confusion in discussions of writing.

In a way it doesn't much matter which definition we adopt, *so long as we do not confuse the two.* This means in particular that we should not unthinkingly assume that there is a relationship between partial writing and full writing, or that the former represents an early stage of the latter. In some cases elements of partial writing are part of a broader full system of writing. Thus an ordinary text in English can contain numerical and other special symbols (e.g., "The book costs $19.95"). In other cases partial writing represents a dead-end system that stands completely apart and has nothing to do with full writing. Only superficially do the two have any resemblances. At a more basic level they are essentially unrelated, since they are based on fundamentally different and opposing principles. This is the case with Amerindian pictographs (see detailed discussion in chapter 2), as opposed to Chinese characters and other full systems of writing. Confusion and error often arise from overlooking these facts.

The attempt of the exclusivists to restrict the definition of writing to full writing parallels the attempt of scientific linguists to restrict the definition of language to speech. Neither appears to have much chance of success. People insist on calling all sorts of things writing, and even many linguists refer to "spoken language" and "written language." Bowing to these realities, I shall extend the use of *language* to include "written language," "sign language," and even "touch language," and shall apply the dichotomy of partial and full to all.

The same dichotomy applies to all forms of human communication.

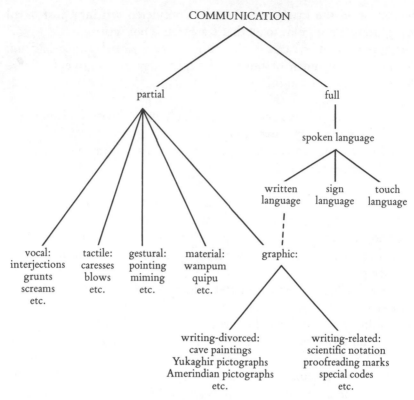

Figure 1. Communication Classification Scheme

Figure 1 provides a graphic overview of all communication from this perspective. It shows the two main branches, partial and full, of the communication tree. Full communication starts with spoken language. This leads into three other modes of full communication. Partial communication possibly involves all our senses, but the branches depicted are limited to those of real importance. Even so, our communication tree is limited since there are many more forms of communication than those dealt with here. A more comprehensive and detailed classification would also have to take care of such exotic forms as drum and whistle surrogates for speech (Umiker 1974).

The various modes of communication are not mutually exclusive. Scholars sometimes read papers containing diagrams and charts to academic audiences who follow the oral presentation from written handouts and slides. One can point and shout at the same time. And it is possible for full communication to make use of the partial modes, especially those of the same modality. Thus materials written in standard orthography frequently contain charts, mathematical notation, and other graphic symbols. Despite these mixtures and overlaps, the various mediums retain their distinctive identities.

Figure 1 supports my central thesis that all full systems of communication are based on speech. Further, no full system is possible unless so grounded. Most of the book is devoted to discussion of writing systems within the framework of this thesis, but I begin by highlighting spoken language, the primary medium of communication, and its role in touch language and sign language.

One of the main objectives of this introductory section, and of the next chapter, is to loosen the mind-set that predisposes people to accept without question the concept of full communication divorced from speech. Unquestioned preconceptions have led many people, including otherwise careful scholars, into uncritical acceptance of specific claims for such full communication that a bit of investigation and the application of common sense would have shown to be dubious if not outright fraudulent. This mind-set is particularly apparent in the area of writing, but it manifests itself in the general underestimation of the role of spoken language in all forms of human communication.

Spoken Language

As human beings we are unique in the way we think and express our thoughts in speech. Our ability to think is superior to and qualitatively different from the instinctual behavior of animals in general. The same is true of spoken language as compared to human and non-human vocalizations that fall far short of full speech. Dogs answer when their masters whistle and growl menacingly if strangers intrude. We instinctively express pain with groans, grief with sobs, joy with other sounds. But only full spoken language enables us as human beings to express any and all thought.

Full spoken language is the defining characteristic of the human species. Other species can be defined by other, more limited, communicative abilities—bats by their ability to produce and detect sonar, bees to perform dances that communicate elaborate messages, and so on through the gamut of our coinhabitants on planet earth. In all of these cases the medium is unalterably part of the genetic make-up of the species. The same is true of language in human beings.[1]

It can hardly be accidental that speech was the most fully developed means of communication of *Homo sapiens.* It was, to be sure, not the sole means of communication, nor was it the first to emerge. The prevailing view among students of the subject is that in the first few million years of their existence our ancestors communicated chiefly by gestures. These were supplemented by such vocalizations as grunts and screams, gross acoustic signals that were all that could be produced—given the still undeveloped state of the vocal tract, the higher neural programs which control the anatomy, and the social organization that would require a more advanced means of exchanging information. The spiral of evolutionary progress in all these related and mutually reinforcing areas eventually led, some 50,000 years ago, to the emergence of speech as the dominant medium among the multimodal channels of communication (Hockett 1978; Wang 1979).

The switch in channels that resulted in the ascendancy of speech, and the significance of all this in human evolution, are vividly summarized in the following statement that concludes a review of literature dealing with the origins of language:

> Consider, now, that hand-carrying, hunting, and tools and technology . . . gave the hands many things to do. As time passed there was more and more to communicate about, and an ever larger number of occasions when the hands were much too busy to be used even for vitally important semaphor. As a ridiculously trivial example, imagine two or three folks gathered around a heavy object to lift it; when all are ready, how can the leader's hand signal *"Now!"?* So, more and more it was necessary for our ancestors to eke out their lives with grunts, and more and more it was crucial for the grunts to be specific and unambiguous.
>
> That could easily have led nowhere (and for many homonid groups doubtless did), for in organic evolution there is never any advance guarantee that selection will successfully adapt a species to the environmental and social demands it faces. In fact, however, it led to the birth of true language, because here we are [Hockett 1978:300–301].

Yes, here we are, at the top of the heap, thanks in large measure to the fact that full speech enabled our ancestors to out-communicate rivals who had only gestures and rudimentary grunts at their command. Speech was a major factor leading to the ascendancy of the human animal in the process of natural selection, and today speech, supplemented by other modalities, continues to be the primary means of communication. All human communication is based on one of the several thousands of spoken languages now in existence.

All these languages possess two essential design features that distinguish speech from other vocalizations. The specific details of these design features differ from language to language.

One design feature is an inventory of basic distinctive sounds that linguists refer to as *phonemes*. For example, four such basic sounds are contained in the English word conventionally spelled "Fred." The unconventional spelling "Phred" of the *Doonesbury* comic strip illustrates the point that the same basic sound can be represented by different individual symbols or combinations of symbols. Phonemes, and the symbols used to represent them, are the basic building blocks used to form words, sentences, and extended discourse.

Languages vary widely in the number of these basic sounds, from around 20 for Hawaiian and Japanese, to about 40 for English, and over 60 for several languages spoken in the Caucasus. One of the largest numbers of phonemes is found in the language spoken by a branch of the Southeast Asian people variously known as Hmong or Miao or Meo. The White Meo language has no fewer than 80 phonemes—57 consonants, 15 vowels, and 8 tones (Heimbach 1966, 1:8–17).

The second essential design feature of spoken language is the stringing together of the phonemes, and the words and other extensions, in various sequences that are peculiar to each individual language. Thus English and Korean permit the sequence *pap,* with a *p* in both initial and final position in a word, whereas Mandarin Chinese and Japanese limit the use of *p* to initial position, as in *pa.* The principal word order of English is subject-verb-object (SVO), whereas in Japanese it is subject-object-verb (SOV), and in Pharaonic Egyptian it was verb-subject-object (VSO). Within individual languages, variations in sequencing of linguistic items are related to variations in meaning. In English, *pat* has one meaning, *tap* another, and *apt* still another. The same is true of *John loves Mary* and *Mary loves John.*

Speaking a particular language involves emitting from the mouth a series of sounds whose sequence follows the rules peculiar to the individual language. When our ears hear speech they receive the sounds in the same order in which they came from the speaker's mouth. The ability to process speech by ear and by mouth is normally acquired in early childhood and is an accomplishment that surely ranks among the marvels of human achievement.

All languages are alike in enabling their speakers to express all their thoughts. In contrast to the widespread notion that some languages are primitive and rudimentary, linguists insist that all languages are complex systems that can be adjusted to enable their speakers to express any thoughts they want to. Languages differ not so much in their ability to express thought as in the strategies they employ for doing so. But such differences in strategy, that is differences in pronunciation, vocabulary, and sentence structure, are of quite secondary importance compared to the ability of every language to function as an effective medium of communication among the members of a given speech community.

The language of which we have the earliest knowledge, that of the Sumerians some 5,000 years ago, had a complex grammar with ten cases for nouns and distinctions of tense, number, and person for verbs (Thomsen 1984:88). It had a vocabulary rich enough for extensive economic records, and literary output that included poetry, epic tales, and even library catalogues (Kramer 1963). For obvious reasons the vocabulary did not cover the area of nuclear power. But if the Sumerians had needed to talk about this and other areas, they could have adjusted their language to enable them to do so.

This potential applies to all forms of speech current and past. Eskimo is rich in specialized terms for various kinds of snow, deficient in vocabulary for nuclear power, but capable, like Sumerian, of enrichment in this area. English is strong in the nuclear area, poor relative to Eskimo in regard to snow, but capable of making all sorts of fine distinctions either by combining several words to form a phrase (e.g., "hard-packed snow"), or creating simple new words if repeated usage warrants it. English is also "underdeveloped" relative to Chinese in that its ambiguous "uncle" must be expanded into such roundabout expressions as "father's elder brother" for the more specific *bóbo* and "husband of one's maternal aunt" for the terser *yífu.*

While no one would really consider English to be an inferior language because it is lacking in the areas indicated, many would not hesitate to bestow this label on language systems that do not measure up to the presumed superiority of English. This is particularly the case with languages that lack writing or with socially restricted languages such as English-based pidgins and dialect variations. The fact of the matter is that Hawaiian Pidgin English, to take one example, despite its simplified grammar and vocabulary limited by use in certain areas of discourse, is as rule-governed and as full of potential for expansion as any more fully developed language.

One of the best examples of linguistic adaptability is that of Navaho, a language spoken by American Indians in Arizona and New Mexico. It cannot be expected that the language of a mere 50,000 people inhabiting a desert area remote from the sea would be particularly well adapted to discourse on intricate problems of maritime warfare. Yet during World War II American armed forces in the Pacific theatre made use of several hundred Navaho speakers to transmit open messages, without time-consuming resort to encoding and decoding, confident that Japan and other Axis powers lacked personnel capable of handling this language (Kahn 1967:550).

The foregoing discussion is not meant to suggest that there are no differences among languages in their immediate ability to handle all areas of knowledge. Apart from making a point against linguistic snobbery and provincialism, it is meant primarily to stress the fact that all spoken languages are capable of adapting to express their speakers' thoughts now or in the future, as their areas of experience and knowledge expand. And the equal capacity of all languages to meet any present or future demands placed upon them in turn is stressed to provide a perspective from which to view past and present efforts to tackle the problem of how to express thought by other means.

Touch Language

One of these other means is touch language. What we might call *partial touch language* is very widely used, is indeed universal. But such a partial means of communication can convey only a few messages. A caress says one thing, a punch in the nose says something else. Both can convey their general message without recourse to speech, but neither can convey the detail expressible by other means.

There are two kinds of touch language capable of expressing any and all thought. One is the system developed primarily for blind people who can hear and speak. For these blind there is available the Braille system of touch reading and writing based on characters made up of raised dots similar to the one through six dots on dominoes. The sixty-three possible permutations of these dots represent numerals, letters, punctuation marks, and other symbols. Special six-key Braille typewriters provide a means for the blind to express themselves in writing as well as for the production of reading materials in the system.

Braille is readily adaptable to any spoken language or to any system of writing based on an alphabet or simple syllabary. Such adaptation is necessary because it is difficult, if not impossible, to use traditional orthographies directly in embossed form, for ordinary graphic symbols are generally too complex for even especially sensitive fingertips to be able to discriminate. This is true for English as normally written, and it is even more true for such complex nonalphabetic systems as Chinese characters. For the Chinese blind the Braille technique has been adapted to the simple Pinyin system of alphabetic transcription based on the Roman alphabet. All adaptations of the Braille system are based either directly or indirectly on a spoken language, be it English, Chinese, or any other. The complete dependence of this touch language on spoken language is thus quite clear.

Another category of touch language capable of expressing any and all thought is best illustrated by the case of Helen Keller. The moving story of how this was achieved has been told in general terms (Keller 1959; Lash 1980). There is, however, a dearth of detailed linguistic analysis comparable to that done on a massive scale for spoken languages and on a fairly extensive scale for sign languages. Nevertheless it is crystal clear that "Keller touch language" was directly tied to the English language, was indeed a sort of tactile dialect of English based on finger spelling, that is, on spelling the letters of our alphabet with tactile equivalents.

Moreover, it should be stressed that Helen Keller was not born deaf and blind, but became so afflicted at the age of 19 months, and apparently retained some residual memory of speech throughout the years that intervened until she learned touch language. In her own words,

> I am told that while I was still in long dresses I showed many signs of an eager, self-asserting disposition. Everything that I saw other people do I insisted upon imitating. At six months I could pipe out "How d'ye," and one day I attracted every one's attention by saying "Tea, tea, tea" quite plainly. Even after my illness I remembered one of the words I had learned in those early months. It was the word "water," and I continued to make some sound for the word after all other speech was lost. I ceased making the sound "wah-wah" only when I learned to spell the word [Keller 1959:17].

Even though Helen Keller could not hear speech, or see a written text, she was able through touch to achieve an astonishing mastery of the English language that was far superior to that attained by others with similar afflictions, or for that matter even by persons endowed with all their senses. She even learned, though on a considerably lower level, to express herself in speech. Despite her own exceptional abilities, it was possible for her to achieve all that she did only because of the devoted help of her almost equally remarkable teacher, Annie Sullivan, who herself was able to achieve what she did only by using her native English language to develop a full touch language.

The same is true of whatever ability to communicate is achieved by other deaf-blind. In point of fact, literature on this subject is scant and unclear, in part because of the wide range of persons placed in this category—the congenitally deaf-blind, the adventitiously deaf-blind, those with varying degrees of deafness and blindness, those with other physical and mental impairments. Thus one source notes that "as a result of the Rubella epidemic during the mid-sixties, some 6,000 children were born deaf-blind, many with additional handicaps" (HKNC 1964). On the other hand, it has also been stated that total absence of auditory and visual abilities with deaf-blind children is rare (Stremel-Campbell and Matthews 1987:141).

It appears, moreover, that there is a relative absence of systematic research expressly aimed at communicative problems of young children with the dual impairment of deaf-blindness (Bullis 1987). Despite this dearth of research literature, accounts of work involving the deaf-blind in the United States make it abundantly clear that all attempted methods of communication, from physical contact to electronic aids, are ultimately based on spoken English and have been developed by persons in full command of the language in all its forms.

It could not be otherwise. That a full language based on touch could be developed by two Helen Kellers, that is, by two people as divorced from spoken language as she was, seems utterly out of the question. However fascinating the Keller touch language is in itself, it has little bearing on our present problem except for its illustration of the close connection between that medium of expression and the medium represented by spoken language.

Sign Language

More relevant, and therefore deserving of a bit more consideration in the present study, is communication by physical movements of the body, chiefly the hands, and chiefly as practiced by the deaf among themselves and with hearing people. There are some half a million profoundly deaf people in the United States (Bellugi and Klima 1975: 174). The major medium of communication of these people is some sort of sign language.

An all-encompassing view of gestural communication reveals that here, too, there is a dichotomy of partial and full systems. In all cultures miscellaneous gestures are used to convey certain ideas. For rival members of the Montague and Capulet houses the gesture of biting one's thumb could be an insult serious enough to provoke a fight (*Romeo and Juliet* I.i). Most gestures of this sort are culture-specific. The same gesture of rubbing the two forefingers against each other means "shame on you" to some Americans, but "sharpen a pencil" to a Chinese. Miming gestures, on the other hand, can be more general. Thus making motions of putting something in one's mouth and chewing is likely to be generally interpreted as having to do with eating.

The gestures just noted must be sharply distinguished from the more extensive and systematic gestures that make up what are usually called sign languages. Complete sign languages are capable of conveying any and all thought, from everyday matters to abstract scientific topics. They do so by a complex system of gestures that involves other parts of the body besides the hands and conveys grammatical as well as lexical information. As one writer notes regarding American Sign Language (Ameslan or ASL):

> There can be no doubt that in ASL the hands carry only part of the language signal. In addition to the hands, the signer's facial expression, posture, and movement of the head and body are all significant. Further, a specific combination of head position and facial expression forms a grammatical signal of subordination and marks relative clauses in ASL [Liddell 1978:88].

Just as there are many kinds of spoken languages, so are there many kinds of sign languages. These are, for the most part, mutually unintelligible. That is to say, sign language is not a single system, a visual lingua franca which can be automatically understood by those who see it. The major reason for this is that while some signs are iconic, that is, based on miming the shape of an object or the representation of an action, many have lost their iconicity or never had any in the first place. Most signs, regardless of their origin, are conventional gestures that need to be learned, just like conventional sound sequences in spoken languages.

Sign languages can be classified chiefly in two ways. One is by the people who use them, which leads to such designations as British Sign Language, French Sign Language, and Chinese Sign Language. Another basis of classification is the degree to which they are related to spoken language.

Although users of British Sign Language and American Sign Language may speak a common language, the two systems are for the most part mutually incomprehensible, since they differ far more than does the speech of the two groups of signers. In addition to using different gestures for the same concept, a situation which parallels universal differences among spoken languages, they also use the same sign for different concepts. This phenomenon is also well known in natural languages, as in the case of English versus French, which have in common written expressions that are known to the teaching profession as *faux amis* 'false friends.' A case in point is *fat* meaning 'obese' in English and 'conceited' in French. An example of a false friend in American and Chinese sign languages is the gesture made by pointing the right thumb at one's chest; it means 'myself' in ASL but 'teacher' in CSL (Klima and Bellugi 1979:152).

The typological classification of sign languages is complicated by several factors. One is that the several varieties of sign languages used in the United States differ in the extent to which they are deliberately or unconsciously related to spoken English. Another is that scholars disagree about the extent of the relationship between sign and speech. Some view sign languages as rudimentary systems that merely mimic speech. Others claim full comprehensiveness and complete autonomy (Baron 1981).

Of the half-dozen or so varieties of sign language used in the United States, most are in fact deliberately based on the grammar of spoken English, and all make use of finger spelling, either as the primary technique or as a supplementary device, especially in the production of proper names (Wilbur 1976). However, supporters of the most important of the sign systems, namely American Sign Language, which is used by more than half of American signers, assert that it has its own grammar and its own system of signs (Klima and Bellugi 1979; Baron 1981).

My own view of the matter is that the truth lies somewhere

between the opposing claims of complete dependence and complete autonomy. Those scholars are certainly in error who claim that American Sign Language is a rudimentary variety of English with necessarily limited vocabulary and even more restricted rules of grammar. Words are added at will in ASL, in the main not by adding a host of completely new and unrelated signs but by the more transparent technique of compounding (e.g., combining the signs for 'eat' and 'sleep' to form the word for 'home'). If frequently enough used, these multiple-sign combinations tend to coalesce into one-sign simplifications (Klima and Bellugi 1979:198), a process roughly akin to the change in pronunciation from *can not* to *can't* in spoken English. One factor favoring such a simple means for greatly increasing the lexicon, and for making other linguistic distinctions, for example, in the area of grammar, is the almost infinite number of signs that can be made by varying the hand configurations, as well as the hand, face, head, and body movements. Another factor, which seems to be generally overlooked, is the cumulatively greater visual discriminatory power that is probably developed by those deprived of the sense of hearing as compensation for their loss and as a necessary result of using signs in communication.

Apart from the matter of vocabulary, other aspects of ASL, including the equivalent of grammatical rules, are also far more complicated than they appear to casual observers. The overall result is a highly sophisticated system that can be labeled as rudimentary only out of ignorance or because literal translations into spoken language convey a misleading impression of primitiveness, masking the underlying complexity.

Yet it also appears that adherents of ASL, out of an understandable desire to counter mistaken views of its restricted nature, exaggerate its independence from speech. The development of ASL, which historically is derived from a French system of sign language, owes much to the aid of hearing people. In the first stage the system consisted only of some rudimentary gestures, which were initiated by the deaf themselves. In the second stage some hearing persons, first in France and then in the United States, stepped in and expanded these rudimentary signs into a full system influenced by their own speech. In the third stage the deaf took over from their hearing allies and further adapted the system as they saw fit, as for instance by telescoping multiple gestures into simpler signs, while still preserving features to facilitate signing interchange with less adept hearers.

Speech further influences ASL because most signers are readers of standard English, and some are also speakers of the language. Signing is often accompanied by actual or mimed speech for lipreading by deaf interlocutors. New words are frequently brought into sign directly from the standard written form by the device of finger spelling (Klima and Bellugi 1979:331; Siple 1978:5). One ASL supporter notes that "Proper names are of course fingerspelled, and must be fingerspelled during an introduction, even if the person has a 'name sign'." He further notes that "ASL borrows linguistic forms and patterns from English" (Battison 1978:96–101). Many English metaphors are taken over into ASL (Frishberg 1981:60–69). Grammatical patterns are influenced by, if not identical with, those of the spoken language. American Sign Language roughly follows the SVO order of spoken English. Japanese Sign Language, on the other hand, roughly follows the SOV order of that language (Fischer 1978:317).

The fact that ASL is heavily influenced by spoken English is surely indicated by the following literal rendition of a sentence, recorded on television for study purposes, that contains fourteen signs and two finger-spelled words:

> tomorrow morning I group friend together-will-go to *ocean city* for interview and find place sleep

Or, more freely:

> Tomorrow morning I am going to *Ocean City* with some friends to look for summer jobs and a place to stay [Stokoe 1975:219].

Apart from the finger spelling of "Ocean City" and the almost one-to-one correspondence of the other lexical items, the relationship of the signed sentence to spoken English is also indicated by its word order and by the fact that the signer could be lipread as saying "and."

In contrast, the same sentence spoken in Chinese would be something like the following:

> Míngtian zǎoshang wǒ yào gēn jǐge péngyyou dào Ocean City qù zhǎo xiàtian de gōngzuò, yě zhǎo zhù de dìfang.

> Tomorrow morning I will with several friend to *Ocean City* go find summer job, also find reside place.

The order of the Chinese Sign Language equivalent for this sentence, I have been informed, "basically" follows that of speech, and this is generally true, although there are "often" differences between the two, the amount of difference being inversely proportional to the educational level of the signers. Here, and in signing generally, the Chinese deaf must also use lipreading. Use of the Chinese Finger Alphabet, created by Zhou Youguang and Shen Jiaying in the early 1960s on the basis of the new Pinyin transcription system, is an additional feature of signing in Chinese (Shen Jiaying and Zhou Youguang, personal communications, 1/6/87 and 1/14/87).

In short, sign language is not a single universal system of communication. It is not totally independent of the language of the people who use it, nor does it seem that such an independent system is even possible. It is a moot question whether the deaf might have been able, or in the future might be able, to develop a full system on their own, for it would be hard to imagine a practical test situation in which the deaf have no interaction with the hearing.

In any case, while ASL and other sign languages are undoubtedly full systems of communication, there is no clear evidence that a full system of sign language completely independent of speech has ever existed, though American Plains Indian Sign Language has often been advanced as a candidate. Knowledge is lacking about the origins of PSL, "a sign system used by a hearing population that, at least originally, seems not to have shared a common language" (Baron 1981: 219–220). It is also not clear how extensive an area of thought could be handled by such a system of signs. A leading authority on sign language, expressing both his own views and those of the prominent linguist Carl Voegelin, states that there is question

> whether the 'sign talk' of the Plains ever functioned as a complete language. . . . Its use was confined to situations of fairly limited and predictable contexts. Its users always had their native languages in which to express things not covered by the sign lexicon and grammar, so that matters of moment could be referred to an interpreter or translator. That some ideas were not completely expressible has been admitted by advocates of 'the sign language' as a medium for global understanding [Stokoe 1974:355].

Of the many possible explanations for the origins of this partial sign language, the least likely is that some monolingual speakers of different languages bumped into each other in the plains, sat down together, and improvised a mutually comprehensible system without any recourse to speech. A more likely scenario is that some among them learned at least a smattering of each others' spoken language and used this knowledge to help fix the meaning of new or existing gestures. The gestures, according to some authorities (Mallery 1893:637–648; Taylor 1975:335), were extensively used even among speakers of the same language.

Such a use of speech-based communication to elaborate a new system of communication among speakers of different languages has much in common with the way Esperanto was created as a workable system of international communication that, without being anyone's native language, is clearly dependent on the known languages on which it is based.

An even better analogy, which has actually been advanced to explain the evolution of sign languages generally, involves the development of what is usually referred to as Hawaiian Pidgin English (Fischer 1978). This originated in the plantations of Hawaii from the need for communication between English-speaking overseers and imported laborers speaking Chinese, Japanese, Korean, and other languages. What evolved was a serviceable pidgin that was originally nobody's first language but became the first language of immigrant offspring. Second-generation speakers expanded the rudimentary pidgin into a full-fledged language of a type that linguists refer to technically as a *creole.*

That the American Plains Indian Sign Language represents a sort of visual pidgin that evolved from a mixture of speech and sign appears to be the most plausible explanation of its origin. The same applies to other, more fully developed systems of sign language, which were minimally speech-based in respect to word order and generally relied heavily on visual representation of phonemes, so that those systems used in the United States might well be called American Creole Sign Languages.

Those who believe that full sign language totally divorced from speech is possible will have to come up with something more persuasive than unsupported conjectures regarding the unique inventiveness of American Plains Indians or partisan defenses of sign languages generally. That spoken language is indispensable to sign language must be acknowledged as a basic fact, as it has in the case of of touch language.

2.

What Is Writing?

The role of speech in writing is a subject of even greater debate than it is for sign language. A great deal of the controversy is due to disagreement as to what constitutes writing. It is therefore essential that we apply the dichotomy partial/full to written language as well.

In chapters 3 through 5 I take up in detail the different relationships between sounds and symbols as I describe the workings of various full systems of writing. In this chapter I concentrate on driving home the distinction between "partial" and "full" writing by stressing some overlooked aspects of the former that severely limit its ability to express thought.

Limited Symbols for Limited Use

In the seventeenth and eighteenth centuries Western intellectuals were much taken with the idea of creating a universal language based on scientific principles similar to those which they thought underlay the Chinese system of writing. In their view, Chinese characters constituted "the pictorial algebra of the sciences and the arts" and as such convey ideas directly to the mind without the intermediary agency of speech (Amiot 1776:282–285). Leibniz and many other outstanding thinkers of those centuries devoted much effort to developing scientifically worked out schemes for a "Universal Language" and a "Universal Writing" that would be better adapted to expressing the rapidly expanding scientific knowledge than imprecise and ambiguous natural languages (Knowlson 1975; Slaughter 1982).

Despite the complete failure of these attempts, people still like to imagine that it is possible to create a universal system of writing capable of expressing thought unmediated by any particular language.

20

Thus the well-known anthropologist Margaret Mead has called on scholars to join in creating "a written form of communication independent of any languages of the world" and adapted to "high-level philosophical, political, and scientific communication." For such a system, she said, the Arabic numeral system provides a partial model, and the Chinese system of writing "the most complete model" (Mead and Modley 1968:62).

Instead of an all-embracing universal system of writing capable of covering all areas of "high-level" communication, what has actually been created is a number of limited systems that are generally restricted to certain specific areas. There are many such systems, some highly specialized, others aimed at the general public. Among the latter are symbols designed to meet the needs of international travel, such as those in widespread use in airports and railway stations and on highways. Well-known examples are arrows to indicate directions to take, crossed knife and fork to indicate a restaurant, suitcase and key to indicate baggage lockers, a telephone to indicate the location of that instrument. Often the symbols are combined with letters or words, as in the case of a black "5T" enclosed in a red ring with a slash to indicate "No entry for vehicles exceeding five tons laden weight."

Some of the signs that have been mentioned are iconic, more or less close replicas of the things depicted, but most are highly stylized. As one study of graphic symbols for international communication points out, such image-related symbols cannot be assumed to be simple, self-explanatory, universal, or timeless. For example, the use in some countries of the silhouette of a steam locomotive to mark a railroad crossing might be understood by people accustomed to travel by electrified trains as marking instead the location of a museum devoted to transportation. The symbols have to be learned, and many are effective only "with limited audiences in limited geographical areas and within a limited historical period" (Modley 1966).

Much effort is expended to make these symbols more effective. Research toward this end has been conducted by various organizations seeking standardization of the symbols, for example, the United Nations, the International Civil Aviation Organization, and the International Union of Railways.

Narrower in scope than the foregoing symbols are those developed for use in specialized fields such as chemistry, astronomy, engineering, and other areas of science and technology. Music has its own notation. So have the publications field and the academic world: communication between authors, editors, and typesetters is carried out in part by the use of proofreading marks. The need for secrecy has led to the creation of codes of various kinds in which symbols sometimes replace words in conventional orthography.

The most widely used of all partial systems is the Arabic numerals. These are, of course, only a small part of the system that has been developed for the mathematical sciences. But even this system, elaborate as it is, has limitations in its use and its universality. A leading historian of the subject has written at length about the difficulty in reaching agreement on standardizing the symbols. He also stresses the difficulty in agreeing on how much notation "in purely ideographic form" should be used in preference to ordinary language (Cajori 1928, 1:426–431; 1929, 2:343–350).

Attempts to express all mathematics in symbolic form have invariably failed. A glance through the literature, a typical example of which is presented in figure 2, reveals its hybrid style; special symbolization is only a partial means of expressing thought even in the area of mathematics. The same applies to all other fields of symbolization based on nonphonetic principles.

Despite their common limited nature, there is an important difference between the symbols presented above and those discussed in the following sections. The systems treated so far were all created by literates as signs for concepts they had largely managed to represent in their conventional orthographies. The symbols were by no means entirely divorced from specific forms of speech.

Numerical symbols are the best example of the special status of this group of signs. They contrast sharply with the numerical records of prewriting peoples, which matched pebbles or scratches on bones with objects being counted: one sheep, one pebble; one sheep, one pebble; . . . one sheep, one pebble, no more. Only after people developed writing did they give evidence of more advanced numerical thinking by devising symbols such as the Sumero-Akkadian left-pointing wedge for 'ten' (Friberg 1984:113).

Although some symbols created by literates have entered into international usage, they are not as divorced from speech as we often think they are. Thus the symbol "2" is language-free only if completely devoid of context. But in specific uses such as "2e" and "2nd," we have to pronounce the former as French *deuxième* and the latter as English *second*.

What this means is that the partial systems discussed in this section

A natural question in the study of geometric operators is that of how much information is needed to estimate the eigenvalues of an operator. For the square of the Dirac operator, such a question has at least peripheral physical import. When coupled to gauge fields, the lowest eigenvalue is related to chiral symmetry breaking. In the pure metric case, lower eigenvalue estimates may help to give a sharper estimate of the ADM mass of an asymptotically flat spacetime with black holes. We use three tools to estimate the eigenvalues of the square of the (purely metric) Dirac operator: the conformal covariance of the operator, a patching method and a heat kernel bound.

I. A lower bound. Let V be a vector bundle associated to the $SO(n)$ (Spin(n)) frame bundle of a compact n-dimensional oriented (spin) Riemannian manifold X, with a positive-definite inner product $\langle\ ,\ \rangle$. For each metric g, let $T_g\colon C^\infty(V) \to C^\infty(V)$ be a geometric elliptic symmetric differential operator of order $j < n$. If $g' = e^{2\sigma}g$ is a conformally related metric, suppose that $T_{g'} = e^{-j\sigma}e^{-(n-j)\sigma/2}T_g e^{(n-j)\sigma/2}$. Let $\lambda_1^2(g)$ denote the lowest eigenvalue of T_g^2.

PROPOSITION 1. (i) *If T_g is invertible then $\exists c > 0$ s.t. $\forall g' \in [g]$, (the conformal class of g),*

$$\lambda_1^2(g') \geq c^{-2}(\operatorname{Vol} g')^{-2j/n}.$$ (1)

(ii) *Suppose that a multiple mV of V contains a trivial subbundle of real dimension $> n$. Then the best constant $\tilde{c}$ in (1) is*

$$d \equiv \sup_{f\neq 0}\left|\int \langle f, T_g^{-1}f\rangle\, d\operatorname{vol}\right|\Big/\|f\|^2_{2n/(n+j)}.$$

Proof. (i) Let ψ range through $C^\infty(V)$. Then

$$\lambda_1^{-1}(g') = \sup_{\psi\neq 0}\left|\int \langle \psi, T_g^{-1}\psi\rangle\, d\operatorname{vol}'\right|\Big/\int \langle\psi,\psi\rangle\, d\operatorname{vol}'$$

$$= \sup_{\psi\neq 0}\left|\int e^{n\sigma}\langle\psi, e^{-(n-j)\sigma/2}T_g^{-1}e^{(n+j)\sigma/2}\psi\rangle\, d\operatorname{vol}\right|\Big/\int e^{n\sigma}\langle\psi,\psi\rangle\, d\operatorname{vol}$$

$$= \sup_{f\neq 0}\left|\int \langle f, T_g^{-1}f\rangle\, d\operatorname{vol}\right|\Big/\int e^{-j\sigma}\langle f,f\rangle\, d\operatorname{vol}.$$

Figure 2. The Hybrid Style of Mathematics
A typical example of mathematical literature, showing that even in this area, perhaps the most abstract of all writing, extensive communication is impossible without ordinary language. Reprinted with permission from John Lott, "Eigenvalue Bounds for the Dirac Operator," *Pacific Journal of Mathematics* 125 (1) (1986):117.

should be considered as part of full writing systems—in some cases, perhaps, of all writing systems, in other cases only of those systems whose speakers have adopted the symbols. In this respect they are quite different from other partial systems, despite their apparent surface similarity.

A Yukaghir Love Letter

The above title has been attached by several writers to the item depicted in figure 3, which first came to my attention in a book by a British linguist, Geoffrey Sampson (1985:28–29), in which it is described as "a copy of a letter sent by a girl of the Yukaghir tribe of north-eastern Siberia to a young man." Presenting the "letter" as an example of written communication which is "not in any sense dependent on spoken language," Sampson invites the reader "to see whether he can guess independently something of the message it contained." Adding "I imagine that he will have little success," Sampson then goes on to present the content of the message in considerable detail, as follows:

> The conifer-shaped objects . . . are people. The second from the right is the writer (the row of dots represents plaited hair and thus shows that she is a woman); the next one leftwards, the recipient of the letter, was previously her lover, but has now gone off to live with a Russian woman (plaited hair, together with a skirt with panniers distinguishing Russian from Yukaghir costume). The Russian woman, naturally, has broken up the relationship between writer and addressee (line from head of the Russian woman cutting through the lines joining the two Yukaghir); nevertheless, the new *ménage* is stormy (crisscross lines linking the two). The writer is unhappy (crossed lines) alone in her house (the rectangular enclosing structure), and she is still thinking of the addressee (curly tendril reaching toward him). On the other hand the addressee should bear in mind that there is another young man at home (far right) sending a tendril toward her. If the addressee wants to act on the message, he had better hurry before his new household has children (two small conifers on the left).

I was piqued by Sampson's presentation of this item. As he correctly surmised, I was unable to guess anything of the message it contained. But I wondered how he had succeeded, ostensibly independently,

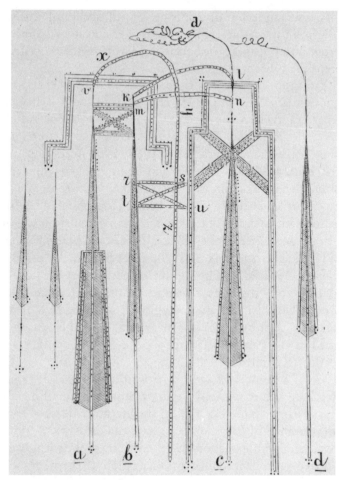

Figure 3. A Yukaghir Love Letter (from Shargorodskii 1895: follows p. 148)

where I had failed so miserably, in deciphering something belonging to what he describes as "*semasiographic systems* . . . of visible communication . . . which indicate ideas directly," in contrast to systems "which provide visible representations of spoken-language utterances." Sampson does not provide so much as a footnote to tell us the secret of his success in interpreting the message. Indeed, he does not even tell us where he found the original of his illustration.

The search for a solution to the mystery of the Yukaghir "love letter" has turned out to be a fascinating bit of scholarly detective work.

The story is worth recounting at some length, for it will throw a great deal of light on the nature of systems that "indicate ideas directly." It will throw an even more embarrassing light on scholarly treatments that accept the concept of such systems of writing.

The Yukaghir are settled fishers and reindeer herders scattered throughout a large area in the lower reaches of the Kolyma and other rivers that empty into the Arctic Ocean in the Yakut Autonomous Soviet Socialist Republic. The area has the dubious distinction of having some of the harshest weather in the world. According to Waldemar Jochelson, a Russian linguist and ethnographer who spent three years among the Yukaghir, the average temperature is $-18°$ for the year and can sink to below $-70°$ in winter (Jochelson 1899:49).

Jochelson estimates that the total Yukaghir population was 700 people when he was there in the 1890s (Jochelson 1899:49). There were only 288 Yukaghir speakers in 1970, according to the census of that year (Comrie 1981:281). The figures reflect in part the acculturation of the Yukaghir by the more advanced Yakuts and Russians. Jochelson already describes them as "true polyglots," speaking two or more languages besides their own (Jochelson 1928:57). That language is generally placed in the Paleo-Siberian group—a geographic, not a genetic, classification (Kreinovich 1968:435).

A check of a number of works on writing, several of which I had consulted long before without paying attention to anything about the Yukaghir, turned up the fact that in the literature devoted to writing, the item presented by Sampson is perhaps the most widely cited example of written communication divorced from spoken language. More than a dozen works reproduce an illustration of the item, sometimes with only passing reference to it among the examples of such writing, occasionally with explanations as to its meaning, generally with a citation to the source from which it was taken. None, however, provide any really illuminating analysis of the issues involved in this type of communication. With rare exceptions, those who summarize its message fail to inform us how, exactly, they came by their understanding, leaving open the possibility that they may have copied only the illustration and arrived independently at an understanding of its contents, as one ordinarily does in reading a foreign language.

Did the authors all understand the meaning of the illustration merely by looking at it? This possibility will, I believe, be accepted only by those readers of this book who arrive at the same intepretation as Sampson's before looking at his presentation. Others may suspect

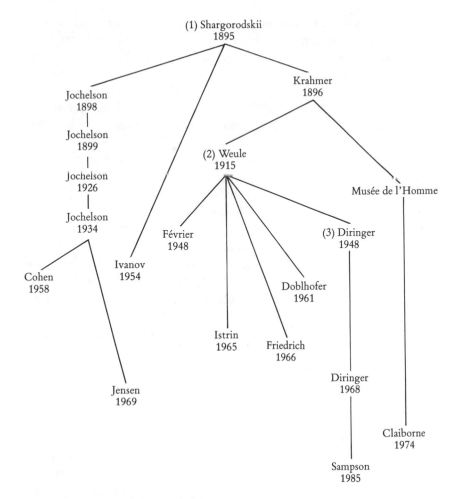

Figure 4. Lineage of the "Yukaghir Love Letter"
Note: Numbers in parentheses indicate different graphic versions.

(as I did) that these works are merely handing on hearsay. So who received it from whom? And how did the whole business get started in the first place?

In attempting to answer these questions I have had to call on far-flung friends and fellow academics, especially librarians, to serve as assistant sleuths in gathering information and tracking down clues and leads. Working backward from a late source to an earlier one, I was finally able to construct a family tree going back to a nineteenth-century Russian by the name of S. Shargorodskii (figure 4).

Shargorodskii is an intriguing figure about whom we would like to know more. According to his friend Waldemar Jochelson, Shargorodskii was sent to Siberia as a political exile (Jochelson 1926:445). So was Jochelson himself, after he took part in revolutionary activities against the Tsarist regime as a Narodovolets, a member of a radical organization called Narodnaya Volya (People's Will) that included a terrorist wing responsible for the asassination of Tsar Alexander II in 1881. Jochelson was sentenced in 1885 to ten years of exile in Siberia (Isayev 1977:247; *New York Times,* November 2, 1937). In the course of his banishment Jochelson, like a number of other exiled political activists, became an ethnologist specializing in the area of Siberia that had become familiar from his years of forced residence there.

We are not informed of Shargorodskii's transgression against the government of the Tsar, but it was probably of a serious nature, for the place to which he was banished was in the area that has been described as "a place of exile for the most dangerous and desperate political prisoners in the hands of the Tsar" (Mowat 1972:230, 238–239). Shargorodskii spent the years 1892 and 1893 in the Yukaghir village of Nelmenoye in the Kolyma River area near the Arctic Ocean. The village was probably very small, for Jochelson, in reporting on his linguistic and ethnographic work during his stay among the Yukaghir, notes villages of only half a dozen or so huts (Jochelson 1926: 435, 438).

Like Lenin and other political exiles to Siberia, Shargorodskii was apparently able to turn his enforced stay to good account, for in 1895 he published in the journal *Zemlevedenie* (The study of the earth) a ten-page article entitled "On Yukaghir Writing." Accompanying the article are six photographic reproductions of the more elaborate examples of such writing. The ones which he numbered 3 and 5B are reproduced as our figures 3 and 4, respectively.

Three years after the appearance of Shargorodskii's article, Jochelson published one more example of such writing (Jochelson 1898); he subsequently reproduced this in other publications (1899, 1926). The seven items published by these two Russians appear to be all that have ever appeared in print.

In 1896, the year immediately following the appearance of Shargorodskii's original article, a virtually full translation into German was published by a certain General-Major Gustav Krahmer in the geographical journal *Globus.* In reproducing Shargorodskii's six illustrations, Krahmer designated them as *Briefe* 'letters,' although Shargorodskii himself had referred to them only with general or noncommittal Russian terms meaning "writings" and "figures."

In a footnote Krahmer indicates that his work is based on Shargorodskii's article. Jochelson in several of his publications also refers to and cites his friend's original contribution, as does another Russian writer, S. V. Ivanov, who reproduces three of Shargorodskii's illustrations and Jochelson's addition (Ivanov 1954). These three appear to have been the only ones to make direct use of Shargorodskii's work. All other writers on the subject apparently relied on later works which must be considered as second-, third-, or fourth-hand sources.

In 1914 an exhibition was held in Leipzig under the auspices of the Museum for Ethnological Studies. Included in the exhibition was a section entitled "Forerunners of Writing in the Past and the Present." At the request of visitors to the exhibition, the director of the museum, Karl Weule, published a little booklet briefly explaining the items in the section on writing (Weule 1915). It includes a number of illustrations based on "original drawings" by an artist named Paul Lindner. One of the illustrations presented by Weule, who, since he also refers to it as a "letter," probably got it from Krahmer, appears with the caption "Yukaghir Love Letter" and a brief explanation of its meaning. Thus the original illustration (our figure 3) emerged in a second, very slightly different version with an eye-catching title that helps explain the attention it has been given.

Weule's popular booklet went through twenty editions, and Lindner's drawing became the most copied version of the Yukaghir "letter," appearing in works on writing that were published in English (Doblhofer 1961, translated from the German), French (Février 1948), German (Friedrich 1966), and even Russian (Istrin 1965), the last making use of a Russian translation of Weule's booklet rather than relying directly on Shargorodskii.

Apart from these, there were other descendants of Krahmer's work. The Musée de l'Homme in Paris has on display and in its archives illustrations of the Yukaghir productions "based on Gustav Krahmer" (Mme. Laurence Delaby, Département d'Asie, Musée de l'Homme, personal communication). Claiborne (1974) reproduces from the museum collection a version of the Yukaghir "letter" that is identical to our figure 3.

In contrast to Shargorodskii, who appears not to have published anything on the Yukaghir beyond his 1895 article, his friend Jochelson wrote prolifically on the subject in Russian, German, and English.

Jochelson's work is the source for the reproduction by Jensen (1969) of an illustration identical to ours. Marcel Cohen, in his important study of writing (1958), one of three or four basic works on the subject, also relied on Jochelson to reproduce not the usual illustration chosen by most writers, but one that Jochelson and Shargorodskii both designate as No. 5 (not shown here).

There is an element of uncertainty about the source for the illustration in David Diringer's *The Alphabet,* perhaps the most widely read work in English on writing. It appears to be based on Weule, though the evidence is circumstantial. Diringer first published a book on the alphabet in Italian in 1937. It contains extensive bibliographical references, Weule among them, and numerous illustrations, but none related to the Yukaghir. However, some of the illustrations he does include are specifically noted as "based on Weule" (Diringer 1937:49, 66, 71–72).

Diringer's subsequent works in English omit the extensive bibliography and notes of the earlier work. The two-volume edition of *The Alphabet* published in 1968 has figure 3, but without any explanation (1968, 2:17c). His earlier one-volume edition (1948) has both the illustration and an explanation of what he labels the "Sad love-story of a Yukaghir girl" (1948:35). The illustrations in both editions are identical. In the later edition it appears on a page with several other items, with the note "drawing by Kadma Diringer."

This drawing, by Diringer's daughter, represents a third version of the letter. Although it is presumably based on Paul Lindner's second-hand drawing, the copy is very poor, for the proportions of the original are distorted and a whole central section is omitted. In the explanations given by Shargorodskii (1895:142) and Jochelson (1926:449), the section omitted in the Diringer drawing receives specific mention in their interpretations. Yet Diringer failed to note the discrepancies, presenting instead a sketchy summary that is similar in its essentials to other renditions. Finally, the Yukaghir illustration in Sampson (1985: 28) is identical with the third-hand version introduced by Diringer.

We now come to the crucial question concerning the Yukaghir illustration: How do we, or any of those who cited it and provided explanations, know what it means? To give an authoritative answer to this we have to go back to Shargorodskii, for apart from Jochelson, Krahmer, and Ivanov, who cite their predecessor, the others fail to make clear exactly how they arrived at their understanding.

During his two-year stay in the village of Nelmenoye, Shargorodskii informs us, he came to have a close relationship with the Yukaghir and won their trust, so that they ceased to look upon him as a Russian against whom they should be on guard. He joined the young people in their rare days of leisure, when they would come from neighboring villages to attend a day-long dance in one of the huts.

As the young people assembled for the dance, a girl might take a piece of fresh birch bark and start carving with a very sharp knife. The others gathered around and watched the progress of the carving. There was much banter, and guesses were made as to who was being depicted and what was being said. Incorrect guesses were met with derision by the carver, so that eventually (by a process of elimination, as in the game of "Twenty Questions"), all present would arrive at an understanding of the contents.

Shargorodskii adds that while those present at the dances were all acquainted with each other and were quite familiar with the personal relationships involved, so that they could easily deduce the contents of the carved accounts, outsiders would remain in the dark. Thanks to his good relationship with the Yukaghir, he himself was not only able to attend the dances and observe the goings-on, but he also had information from the young men that made it easier to understand the carved "messages." Even some of the girls, who were supposed to be reticent in speaking about their feelings, as the boys were permitted to do, told him what was being conveyed on the birch-bark carvings, a means of expression exclusive to young women.

The contents of the compositions, Shargorodskii continues, were limited to affairs of the heart. One of the greatest concerns of Yukaghir girls was the fact that while they were tied down by continual work, such as fishing in the summer and gathering fuel in the winter, the boys had frequent opportunities to go to Russian settlements for various purposes. The young women worried about their menfolk falling prey to the attractions of Russian women.

The importance of the facts just mentioned is underscored by their reiteration in the work of Jochelson. He stresses that only a few Yukaghir made use of these birch-bark compositions (1898:287). Reproducing an illustration which he numbers 152 (our figure 3), he adds:

> The Yukaghir, particularly young men, often and for various purposes go to Sredne-Kolymsk. These journeys arouse the jealousy of the young girls because they think that the Russian women whom the

young men meet are much more handsome and attractive than they themselves. They are afraid that the Russian women will alienate their affections. When a young Yukaghir once gets to town, he tries to stay there as long as possible, in order to obtain news, for the more news he can tell on his way back home the more welcome he is. . . . The longer the boy is absent, the more jealous the girl becomes; then she cuts a letter on birchbark saying how sad she is. In this way originate compositions like our figure 152 [Jochelson 1926:449–450].

In short, the notorious "love letter" and others like it are nothing more than the semiritualized product of these Yukaghir party games. They must not be thought of as real letters posted to someone who would read them as we do our mail. The Russian observers make clear that the compositions were primarily vehicles whereby young women could publicly express their feelings on the single theme of love and separation in a socially acceptable form before a small circle of friends gathered together to dance and have fun. If the "letters" were sent anywhere, it was not by the girls to their boyfriends, but by visiting Russians to the Museum for Anthropology and Ethnology of the Academy of Sciences in St. Petersburg (now Leningrad), where, Jochelson notes, the only surviving copies of the originals were to be found (Jochelson 1926:445).

In the accounts of Shargorodskii and Jochelson, the only original sources of information about the Yukaghir, these birch-bark compositions comprise one of three kinds of "writing." A second kind consisted of local small-scale maps that were drawn by men to indicate travels for hunting and other purposes. The conventions governing these maps must have been quite clear to the men concerned, because topological and other features such as rivers and dwellings were clearly depicted with only a few different symbols.

The same is true of the third type, individual attempts at record-keeping (see figure 5). A copy was written in Shargorodskii's presence and explained to him by a Yukaghir man who said it records having a shawl (top of illustration) made for him by a Yukaghir woman and giving as payment several different items such as a comb, tobacco, and (at the bottom) eleven buttons. We know what this memo means because its originator told Shargorodskii, who wrote the information down for us.

Leaving aside the symbols in this memo and the previously mentioned maps, the number of different symbols in the seven illustrations

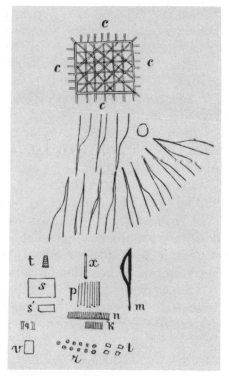

Figure 5. Yukaghir Mnemonic Notation (from Shargorodskii 1895: follows p. 148)

of Yukaghir "letters" appears to be extremely limited. There are: figures of Yukaghir men and women, Russian women, children, and complete and partial houses, together with crossed lines, criss-crossed bars, curving lines, and curlicues used to indicate relationships and feelings among individuals. The details of the actual permutations of these items are apparently only partly revealed by the sketchy summaries available to us. Nevertheless it is quite obvious that we have here a very restricted means of communication, since the total inventory of different symbols in what might grandly be called the complete corpus of Yukaghir epistolary literature amounts to a mere one to two dozen items.

The accounts of this extremely limited Yukaghir "writing" presented by Shargorodskii, and secondarily by Jochelson, make it clear that its contents were directly or indirectly conveyed to them orally by the authors themselves. And we now, like all who so uncritically seized upon and inflated the "Yukaghir Love Letter" for its heart-tugging appeal, only know its meaning because Shargorodskii recorded it for us. Were it not for the fact, documented here for the first time, that there is an unbroken line of language-mediated communication from the carver through Shargorodskii and then, among others, Krahmer, Weule, Diringer, and Sampson, the message of this so-called love letter would have been lost forever.

The way in which the meaning of the Yukaghir "letter" was actually transmitted, first to a small circle of intimates at the time of its creation and later to a worldwide audience by a succession of scholars, most closely parallels the way in which the meaning of a highly allegorical medieval painting or of a Bayeaux tapestry originated and was transmitted over time. This analogy suggests that the Yukaghir birchbark carving should be viewed as an example not of writing but of anecdotic art whose message can be understood only to the degree one is in contact with its creator or the situation or culture that produced it or someone who can interpret it for us. It is therefore appropriate that one Soviet scholar who reproduces an illustration of the carving does so in a book devoted to the pictorial arts of the peoples of Siberia (Ivanov 1954).

One would never know the truth about the "letter" from the way it has been presented by most of those who have cited it. Not that they intentionally seek to mislead readers. Rather, they themselves have been led astray by their gullibility regarding the power of pictographic writing. This leads them to forget that their knowledge of the message was not worked out through prior knowledge of the symbols and the working of the system. The process follows these steps:

1. They see some pictographic "writing."
2. They are told, or read, the meaning of the written message and perhaps of the individual symbols.
3. They forget that they have not worked out the meaning themselves and that they should check on how the message was first conveyed.
4. Forgetting the stages by which they came to understand the message enables them to claim in all sincerity that pictographic writing indicates ideas directly, without dependence on spoken language.

This then is the reality of writing that Sampson would have us believe might be capable of evolving into "a full-fledged semasiographic language rivalling English, French, and German in expressive potential" (Sampson 1985:32). It speaks volumes for the theories of writing conjured up by mind-sets that set great store on such alluring but unquestioned evidence as that of the notorious "Yukaghir Love Letter."

Amerindian Pictographs

The limited scope of pictographic representation is also illustrated by the so-called picture writing of the North American Indians. Most treatments of the subject also reveal some analytical false steps.

Amerindian pictographs can be classified into three groups. The first comprises isolated pictographs, many of them the ubiquitous petroglyphs, which even if identifiable as to subject transmit only the most meager of messages. The two most extensive studies of Amerindian picture writing, those contained in the six-volume work by Schoolcraft (1851–1857) and the 822-page classic by Mallery (1893), illustrate thousands of pictographs which convey no more information than do the isolated graffiti drawn on countless American walls. At most, isolated Indian pictographs communicate only as much as such limited symbolizations as heraldic insignia placed on coats of arms, the male-female figures seen on restroom doors, and "No Left Turn" or "Steep Incline" warnings pictured on highway signs.

As to more extensive conglomerations of pictographs, one student of the subject makes the useful distinction between mnemonic symbols, whose function is to aid the recollection of information, and notificational pictographs, whose function is to convey new information (Taylor 1975:354–356). An examination of the Amerindian pictographic "texts" contained in the works by Schoolcraft and Mallery shows that mnemonics greatly outnumber notificational pictographs.

The mnemonic function of pictographs is well illustrated by the musical notation and the chronological records of the Dakotas. Schoolcraft presents a sequence of 48 pictographs that are schematized drawings of humans, animals, and other concrete objects. These are "signs depicting the chief objects of stanzas committed to memory." Another series of 38 pictographs that serve as prompts for a chant includes one, a tree with human legs, which evokes the chanted words "I dance till day light" (Schoolcraft 1851, 1:380–381; 1852, 2:226–227, and plate 57). Such pictographs are no more informative than the depicted objects themselves. They are not writing.

As for Indian chronological records, an example frequently cited in the literature about writing is "Lone-Dog's Winter Count," shown in figure 6. According to the detailed account by Mallery, it was the custom of some Indians to depict events, mixing the historical with the personal, to form a system of chronology in which the years were reckoned by winters, each year being individualized by a specific recorded symbol. The Winter Count under discussion spanned the years 1800–1870. The first device, for the year 1800–1801, consists of 30 parallel black lines in three columns; it represents the death of that number of Dakotas at the hands of their enemies. The device for 1801–1802 is the head and body of a man covered with red blotches, and it represents the year of a smallpox epidemic. The last device is a black circle with two red stars; it refers to the solar eclipse of August 7, 1869 (Mallery 1893:266–328).

This particular winter count was painted on a buffalo robe; it was completed not long after the date of the last entry. As Lone-Dog himself explained,

> with the counsel of the old men of his tribe, he decided upon some event or circumstance which should distinguish each year as it passed, and marked what was considered to be its appropriate symbol or device upon a buffalo robe kept for that purpose. The robe was at convenient times exhibited to other Indians of the tribe, who were thus taught the meaning and use of the signs as designating the several years [Mallery 1893:266].

Another winter count presented by Mallery was the production of several generations of Indians—grandfather, father, and son. In still another, the chronicler "gathered the names of many years from the old people and placed them in chronological order as far back as he was able to learn them." In comparing the several winter counts which he encountered, Mallery found that they often corresponded, but sometimes differed, as in the sequencing of events and the topics chosen for recording. He adds that there was no fixed or uniform mode of exhibiting the order of continuity of the year-characters. They were arranged spirally or lineally, or in serpentine curves, by boustrophedon or direct, starting backward from the last year shown or proceeding uniformly forward from the first year selected or remembered. Any mode that could combine continuity and allow for regular addition seemed equally acceptable (Mallery 1893:269–270).

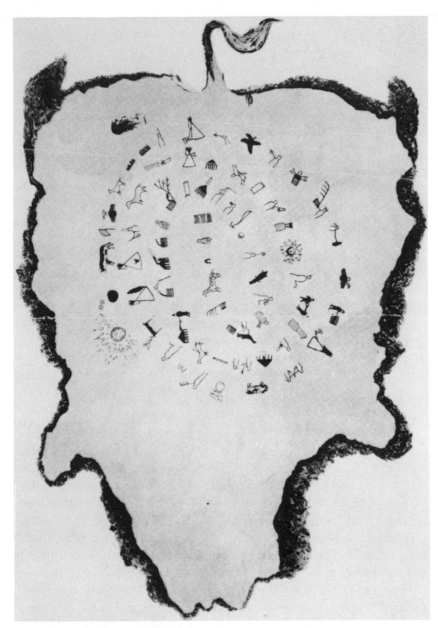

Figure 6. Lone-Dog's Winter Count (from Mallery 1893: pl. 20)

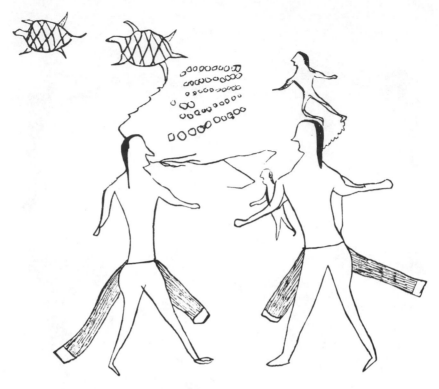

Figure 7. Letter from a Cheyenne Father (from Mallery 1893:364)

More interesting than the preceding examples of pictographs serving an obvious mnemonic function are those that embody new information, such as warnings and guidance, hunting notices, topographic information, notices of direction, and declarations of war. Brief information of this sort was conveyed either by simple pictographic symbols or by other mutually understood signs. The Natchez, for example, issued a declaration of war by pictographically depicting an attack. Indians in Florida conveyed the same message by sticking into the ground arrows to which long hairs were attached (Mallery 1893).

Pictographic messages of greater complexity are actually very few in number. There are only two or three examples, and these are repeatedly cited in the literature on writing. One (figure 7) is a letter sent by mail by a Cheyenne father called Turtle-Following-His-Wife to his son Little-Man away from home conveying the information that he was sending him $53 (represented by 53 little circles) and asking him to return home. Turtle-Following-His-Wife gave the money, together

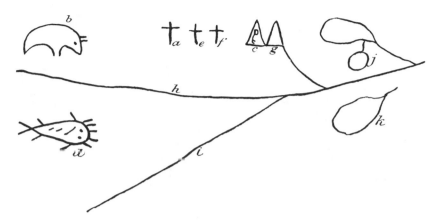

Figure 8. Ojibwa Love Letter (from Mallery 1893:363)

with an explanation of his letter to his son, to Agent Dyer, who mailed the money and a covering explanation to Agent McGillycuddy, "which enabled him to understand the pictographic letter" when it was shown to him by Little-Man with a request for the money (Mallery 1893:363–364).

The second example (figure 8) is a missive which Mallery reproduces with the caption "Ojibwa love letter." It was written, Mallery was told, by an Objiwa girl, the daughter of a shaman skilled in such matters, who "had simply acquired her pictographic skill from observation at her home." Mallery gives the following explanation of the letter:

a. The writer of the letter, a girl of the Bear totem, as indicated by that animal, *b.*

e and *f.* The companions of *a,* the crosses signifying that the three girls are Christians.

c and *g.* The lodges occupied by the girls. The lodges are near a large lake, *j,* a trail leading from *g* to *h,* which is a well-traveled road.

The letter was written to a man of the Mud Puppy totem, as indicated in *d.*

i. The road leading to the lodge occupied by the recipient of the letter.

k and *j.* lakes near which the lodges are built.

In examining *c,* the writer's hand is seen protruding from an opening to denote beckoning and to indicate which lodge to visit. The clear indications of the locality serve as well as if in a city a young woman

Figure 9. Chippewa Song-and-Dance Troupe Petition (from Schoolcraft 1851, 1: pl. 60)

had sent an invitation to her young man to call at a certain street and number [Mallery 1893:362–363].

An important characteristic of the two preceding examples of "notificational" pictography is that the messages involved a sender and a recipient who were on close terms—in one case, a father and his son, and in the other, a girl and her lover. It can hardly be doubted that what enabled the recipients of the messages to decipher them is what Mallery calls the "preconcerted" nature of the communications. That is to say, in these cases, as was probably true of all notificational pictography, there was *prior agreement* between closely connected persons as to the significance of the specific signs included in the messages sent by one to another. The examples are only a bit more elaborate than the preconcerted agreement involved in the famous "One if by land, and two if by sea" that was intended to signal the route the British redcoats were taking toward Lexington and Concord.

A seeming exception to this pattern is the frequently cited example (figure 9) that Diringer captions "ideographic document of North American Indians" (1968, 2:17) and Friedrich labels "Indian Petition to the Congress of the United States" (1966:187). Diringer provides no discussion, but Friedrich (p. 21) summarizes the content of the petition as a demand by a number of Indian chiefs for the retrocession of some fishing grounds, without, however, indicating how he came to understand the message. His treatment of the item gives the impression that it is simply a case of a somewhat unusual bit of bureaucratic paperwork in which a petition sent by a group of Indians is received and read by members of Congress.

A quite different picture emerges from the detailed account Schoolcraft gives (1851, 1:414–421). In January 1849, he says, eleven Chippewas from the Lake Superior area presented themselves in Washington with a pictographic petition in five sheets for the President of the United States. They were led by a half-breed called Martell, "who acted as their conductor and interpreter." Martell, according to Schoolcraft,

> appeared to be the master-spirit and prime mover of the visit, and of the motions of the entire party. His motives in originating and conducting the party were questioned in letters and verbal representations from persons on the frontiers. He was freely pronounced an adventurer, and a person who had other objects to fulfil, of higher interest to himself than the advancement of the civilization and industry of the Indians. Yet these were the ostensible objects put forward, though it was known he had exhibited the Indians in various parts of the Union for gain, and had set out with the purpose of carrying them, for the same object, to England. However this may be, much interest in, and sympathy for them, was excited. . . . The journey had not been authorized in any manner by the department [of Indian Affairs]. It was, in fine, wholly voluntary, and the expenses of it had been defrayed, as already indicated, chiefly by contributions made by citizens on the way, and from the avails of their exhibitions in the towns through which they passed; in which, arrayed in their national costume, they exhibited their peculiar dances, and native implements of war and music. What was wanting, in addition to these sources, had been supplied by borrowing from individuals.

From Schoolcraft's account Martell emerges as something of a con artist. There were doubts about the authority or approval of the visit on the part of both the Chippewas and the frontier officers of the government. "These very doubts led the party, under the prompting of their leader, to resort to the native pictorial art . . . to give authority to the delegates visiting the seat of government."

So it appears that Martell, as leader and interpreter to the party, helped draw up the attention-getting petition, the meaning of which he then explained orally on the numerous occasions during their seven-to-eight weeks' stay in Washington when the chiefs, in their colorful native dress, were paraded "at private houses, at levees, and places of public resort, and at the halls of Congress." Schoolcraft twice tells us very specifically that information contained in the petition was written down "from the lips of the interpreter" (1851, 1:416). In short, we understand this example of pictographic writing only because its authors provided a detailed oral explanation of it.

The conclusion is unavoidable that the "Petition" was not a genuine written communication but a stage prop designed for no other purpose than to obtain a hearing—literally a hearing—for demands that perhaps really did seek to obtain the retrocession of some land, but may have been primarily aimed at increasing the take for the troupe and its leader—what Schoolcraft delicately calls "the avails of their exhibitions."

Partial/Limited/Pseudo/Non- Writing

The revelation of how limited the foregoing examples of pictographic and symbolic writing really are may not by itself be enough to convince us all that the seventeenth- and eighteenth-century notion of "Universal Writing" has no basis in truth. People who believe that the world will end on a certain date merely come up with another date when previous predictions turn out wrong. In the case of "Universal Writing," there is always Chinese to fall back on.

One of the things that lies behind much of the belief in full writing based on the pictographic or ideographic principle is an atomistic view of how we think and how thought can be represented. Much thinking about thinking seems to consider that it is a process in which we match inner concepts with things "out there"—either real objects or pictures or symbols that evoke real or imagined entities. So a widely read eighteenth-century authority on Chinese defined Chinese characters as "images and symbols which speak to the mind through the eyes —images for palpable things, symbols for mental ones. Images and symbols which are not tied to sound and can be read in all languages" (Amiot 1776:282). From the view of mental activity manipulating such soundless symbols it is but a short step to envisaging the reduction of the symbols into minimal components that can be better processed by optical scanners connected to thinking machines using only on-off switches.

An opponent of the concept of artificial intelligence, John Searle (1980), expresses his objections by imagining the following situation: A man who knows only English is locked in a room. Under the door someone slips a newspaper article in Chinese, questions in Chinese about the article, and a long set of instructions in English explaining step by step how to compare and manipulate the Chinese characters in the article and in the questions about it. Given enough time (perhaps years!), and assuming that the instructions are complete and accurate, the man should be able to compose all the answers. However, because the instructions deal *only* with the distribution of characters, not with grammar or meaning, it is obvious that he would not be using intelligence to perform his task in the same way he would if the questions and answers were in English. By analogy, Searle argues, the mere fact that a computer program (a set of instructions) can generate correct answers to questions about newspaper articles does not prove that the program endows a computer with real understanding or intelligence, with the ability to think.

Another penetrating critic of conventional views about thinking, Hans G. Furth, presenting views closer to those of the holistic Gestalt school than to the elementaristic approach of some psychologists, insists that "thinking is always to be regarded as a generalized mode of behavior and can in no way be conceived as a simple cumulation of single events or connections" (Furth 1966:177). Noting that the congenitally deaf also show obvious evidence of intelligent behavior, he further divorces thinking from symbolic representation of any kind, even spoken language, and concludes that "thinking develops through living contact with the environment regardless of the presence or absence of a ready-made linguistic symbol system" (Furth 1966:288).

Granting that thinking can occur without speech, it still seems that, in the evolutionary progress of humankind, speech has evolved as the fullest and most efficient means of conveying thought. To a greater or lesser degree, speech underlies all full forms of sign language, and it is this which has enabled the deaf to expand their knowledge and their rudimentary gestures beyond what they could have accomplished if left to their own limited devices.

Speech also underlies all full forms of written language, in contrast to the partial systems discussed earlier. Just how the mind manipulates the symbols in these various forms of writing, or for that matter in other forms of communication, calls for much more research (which Furth persuasively stresses should pay special attention to the deaf). Surely, however, it is not by computer-like processing of atomic elements, nor by manipulating pictographs which supposedly only need to be expanded in use to become full systems of writing.

The belief that pictographs *can* be expanded in this way stems largely from the exaggerated idea of the power of pictures, as represented by the cliché that a picture is worth a thousand words. Actually, pictures are often ambiguous, especially without context, and they are not inherently self-evident. Far from being worth a thousand words, a picture often requires a thousand words to explain it.

Baron (1981:35–37) cites several examples showing how people must "learn" to see. One involves a congenitally blind man who gained sight at the age of fifty-two; it took months for him to become aware of visual details that had been thoroughly familiar to him from touch. Baron also notes "the reports of anthropologists that populations which are not accustomed to visual representations have difficulty recognizing objects—including themselves—in photographs." She quotes (from Deregowski 1973:168) the following observation involving a thirty-five-year-old member of a remote Ethiopian tribe:

> EXPERIMENTER: Points to the picture: 'What do you see?'
> SUBJECT: 'I'm looking closely. That is a tail. That is a foot. That is a leg joint. These are horns.'
> E: 'What is the whole thing?'
> S: 'Wait. Slowly. I am still looking. Let me look and I will tell you. In my country this is a water buck.'

An even more telling episode is recounted by the anthropologist M. J. Herskovitz in the following comments on the common reaction of surprise among his colleagues to the finding that people unaccustomed to photographs had difficulty in understanding them:

> I have had an experience of this kind, similar to that reported from many parts of the world by those who have had occasion to show photographs to persons who have never seen a photograph before. To those of us accustomed to the idiom of the realism of the photographic lens, the degree of conventionalization that inheres in even the clearest, most accurate photograph, is something of a shock. For, in truth, even the clearest photograph is a convention; a translation of a three-dimensional

subject into two dimensions, with color transmuted into shades of black and white. In the instance to which I refer, a Bush Negro woman turned a photograph of her own son this way and that, in attempting to make sense out of the shadings of grey on the piece of paper she held. It was only when the details of the photograph were pointed out to her that she was able to perceive the subject [Herskovitz 1959:56, cited in Segall, Campbell, and Herskovitz 1966:32].

Clearly it requires some training, which most of us acquire so early that we forget the effort involved, to see in little, two-dimensional, black-and-white pictures the multidimensional, multitextured, multisized, multicolored, and otherwise differentiated objects that are so familiar a part of our physical world. More important, it requires even more training, and considerably greater feats of memory, to recognize and reproduce pictographs and stylized symbols that stand for these familiar objects.

Evolution has endowed us with the phenomenal ability to hear and speak the names of literally thousands of things, to learn additional thousands of other words, and to master complex rules for stringing all these together into a potentially limitless number of utterances. Contrary to popular misconceptions about the matter, ordinary people command enormous vocabularies. Research has shown that five-year-old children already know five to ten thousand words, and that college graduates have vocabularies in the sixty- to seventy-five-thousand word range (Seashore and Eckerson 1940; Oldfield 1963; Hockett 1978:278).

Individual Yukaghir and American Indians, even if we view them as living in culturally limited societies, must have had spoken vocabularies measuring in the tens of thousands. The examples of their pictographic writing cited above tell us that they were able to achieve the quite unremarkable feat of memorizing a few dozen pictographic symbols of things and actions and to combine these, each in his or her idiosyncratic order, to express a few thoughts for a few contemporaries who were already privy to much of what was being conveyed. There is no evidence in their cases, and there is none in the history of human evolution, to suggest that it would be possible to extend such limited pictographic messages to cover all that the authors were able to utter. And there is no evidence that scholars far removed from the people who wrote these rudimentary messages could decipher them without the direct or indirect assistance of the people who wrote them.

Compare this with the situation in full writing systems. The Sumerians wrote on clay some 4,000 to 5,000 years ago. Up until around the middle of the last century the very existence of their writing, and even of the Sumerians themselves, had been lost to all knowledge. Today a Sumerologist like Samuel Noah Kramer can pick up a newly found tablet written several millennia ago and tell us what it says. The most dramatic example of this sort of feat involves the early stage of the decipherment of some cuneiform writing. Controversy over the validity of particular claims for decipherment was laid to rest in 1857 when the Royal Asiatic Society presented copies of a newly discovered inscription to four scholars with a request that they submit independent translations in sealed envelopes. The results showed such a degree of correspondence in the translation of the inscription, which turned out to be the annals of the Assyrian King Tiglath-Pileser I (1116–1076 B.C.), that there could be no doubt about the validity of the claims as to how that particular cuneiform system worked (Pope 1975:114–117).

There is nothing remotely comparable to this in the literature on pictographic writing. The people involved in such writing, as we have seen, were largely dependent on preconcerted agreement regarding the content. Most scholars who have written about the subject have been dependent upon a few sources going back to the time when the messages were written. Shargorodskii lived for two years among the Yukaghir and may even have known the lovelorn lass whose birchbark carving he tells us about. Mallery had extensive field experience among the Indians, was a contemporary of some at least of the authors of the pictographs he cites, talked with knowledgeable Indian agents, and specifically states that the meaning of many pictographs he interprets for us "is definitely known from direct sources" (1893:637). Schoolcraft was married to an Ojibwa woman who acted as his interpreter and doubtless helped out with some of the oral explanations to which he makes frequent reference (1851, 1:336, 350, 351, 361, 389, 390).

All this is overlooked by scholars hooked on the idea of pictographic writing. It is perhaps excusable that they sometimes fail to cite sources, or fail to check sources which would have proven untrustworthy, or otherwise fall heir to faults unavoidable in scholarly work. We all have to build on the work of our predecessors and take some things on faith. What is inexcusable is to exploit examples of pictographic writing by claiming that they represent the prototypes of full-fledged writing systems without once asking, much less answering, the crucial question, "How does the system work?" That question should constitute the very core, the very raison d'être, of any work devoted to writing. It is answered in meticulous detail in dozens if not hundreds of volumes devoted to full systems of writing.

The forthright answer to how pictographs work as a system is that they don't. Pictographic writing is not a system. It is at best exceedingly limited in what it can express and who is able to understand it. It is not protowriting nor a forerunner of full writing. And it should not be called writing without the clearly expressed reservation that it refers to a very restricted type of communication.

There is no possibility whatsoever that pictographs based on the nonphonetic principle underlying their usage by the Yukaghir and the North American Indians could evolve into a full system of nonphonetic writing. Evolutionary progress has decreed against our developing such pictographs as a full system of communication. It is too late to turn back. The same evolutionary imperative which has led to the ascendancy of speech has also decreed that it must form the basis of all full forms of communication. Among these, as history amply attests, are the diverse full systems of writing which comprise the main subject of this book.

Full/Unlimited/Real Writing

If we insist again that speech underlies all real writing, which is only that writing which permits expressing any and all thought, we need now to delve further into the relationship between the two. Here too we find a great deal of confusion and not a little disagreement— between linguists and the general public, and among linguists themselves. In coping with this situation it will be helpful to keep firmly in mind the aphorism coined by a leading student of writing that I have adopted as the motto of this book:

> There are no pure systems of writing
> just as there are no pure races in anthropology
> and no pure languages in linguistics [Gelb 1963:199].

A more frequently cited and more influential view of writing was propounded three decades before this in a book by Leonard Bloomfield that can be said to mark the founding of the American school of descriptive linguistics. Bloomfield said: "Writing is not language, but merely a way of recording language by visible marks" (1933:21).

In this pronouncement Bloomfield sought to reserve the word *language* for "speech" and relegated writing to a secondary status, as expressed particularly by his use of the word *merely.* His attitude, which was conditioned in part by a background of work with unwritten Indian languages, was also a reaction against the almost exclusive preoccupation of nineteenth-century European linguists with written materials, and against the schoolmarm tendency to base notions of correctness on stilted bookish norms. (Don't say "It's me," Johnny, say "It is I.") Bloomfield's stand helped to create a climate in which for some time most American linguists displayed a marked lack of interest in writing.

Dissenting views to the idea that writing was "merely" a way of recording speech were expressed by various scholars, more and more as time went by. One pointed out that there are differences in word order in the spoken and written domains, as in the case of spoken "two dollars and twenty-five cents" versus written "$2.25" (Edgerton 1941). Another cited puns that have to be written to be appreciated, such as "The Tax Collector, City Haul" (Bolinger 1946).

The strongest attack came from a rather remarkable group of linguists centered in Prague. Joseph Vachek, a member of the Prague School who from the 1940s on wrote most extensively on the subject, opposed what he referred to as "the often asserted inferior status of written utterances as opposed to their spoken counterparts." He propounded instead a "functional approach," in which spoken language was viewed as serving the need for immediate oral communication and written language as a means of graphic communication "in a static way, i.e. in a preservable and easily surveyable manner." Moreover, he said, "the use of the written norm for higher cultural and civilizational tasks" constituted "safe evidence of its specific status." A key aspect of this "specific status" is indicated in two successive sentences that are typical of Vachek's rather woolly argumentation. In the first he differentiates writing by referring to it as "characterized by considerable autonomy." In the immediately following sentence he drops the restrictive "considerable" and further inflates it by speaking of "this autonomous linguistic status of the written norm" (Vachek 1973).

The degree of writing's independence from speech is thus a matter of great disagreement. At one extreme is the complete dependence of writing, drawn from Bloomfield's pronouncement on the subject. At the other is the complete independence claimed by proponents of pictographic and ideographic writing. In between are all sorts of gradations based on differing evaluations of actual systems of writing.

It is probable that there would be general agreement that no system of writing ever has, or ever can, represent all the features and nuances present in oral communication. Nor does Bloomfield's use of *merely* indicate that he viewed writing as a carbon copy of speech, since he himself expressed dissatisfaction with the "inadequacies of the actual systems," that is conventional orthographies, in representing their underlying spoken languages (Bloomfield 1933:291). In essence, therefore, in stating that writing was merely a way of recording speech by visible marks, Bloomfield was saying only that writing *had* to be based on speech, not that it was an accurate representation of speech, or not even, perhaps, that it did nothing but represent speech. If this interpretation of Bloomfield's views is correct, then I think he was closer to the truth than those critics who have emphasized the divergence between writing and the strict representation of speech to the point where they even edge toward or openly embrace the concept of writing completely divorced from sound.

If all full systems of writing are based on speech, and none is possible unless so grounded, then we must examine how writing represents speech. And because writing cannot represent speech with complete fidelity, we also need to examine how and to what extent it departs from the straight and narrow path of phonetic representation. The details, since they vary from system to system, are taken up in subsequent chapters dealing with individual writing systems. Here I pave the way with some general comments.

By and large one can say that all writing systems convey meaning by two means. The first is by the use of symbols which represent sounds and function as surrogates of speech. The second is by the use of symbols that add nonphonetic information. These two together are combined in different proportions in different scripts. Together they comprise what I call the "Duality Principle" that forms the basis for all true systems of writing.

The pervasive tendency to exaggerate the nonphonetic aspect of writing leads to several related errors that can culminate in a belief in the existence of full systems of writing based on pictographs. One error is to think that pictographic symbols necessarily have a pictographic function, that is that pictographic symbols are always used to to convey whatever ideas the pictographs as pictographs may evoke. This error can be described in other words as the failure to distinguish between form and function. Because of this failure many people are blind to the significance of the epoch-making invention that marked the birth of true writing. That invention was the *rebus principle,* whereby a pictographic symbol was used not for its original meaning value but specifically to represent the sound evoked by the name of the symbol. The change in function that results from using a picture as a rebus can be illustrated by the use of a picture for a bee followed by that for a leaf to express the sounds of the word *belief.*

The two pictures involved in this simple illustration are just as much phonetic symbols, syllabic ones in this case, as are the letters in our conventional way of writing the word. One who continues to refer to them simply as pictographs misses the central point about the nature of writing and overlooks one of the greatest inventions in human history.

Pictographs used as pictographs lead nowhere. Pictographs used as phonetic symbols lead to full writing. All inventions of full writing originated from pictographs. Not all pictographs lead to writing. The history of writing is as full of dead ends as is the history of human evolution.

The rebus principle formed the basis of three systems of writing, generally thought to have been independently developed, which were created at intervals of about fifteen hundred years: first by the Sumerians about 3000 B.C., then by the Chinese about 1500 B.C., and last by the Mayas about the beginning of our era. The systems developed by these peoples were based on exactly the same basic principle despite the differences in how their symbols look.

The particular form that phonetic symbols take, whether they look like pictures or have no resemblance to anything, is a matter of quite secondary importance. Certainly, other considerations, such as aesthetics and efficiency, are also involved. But efficiency is mostly a modern concept, and it was certainly not a major concern of the specialized scribes and elitist groups that have been primarily concerned with writing. Much more basic than these matters is the ability of all phonetic symbols of whatever shape to function as the basis of full systems of writing.

In the matter of phonetic representation, *all* systems are incomplete, since they all fail to take account of some things that are present in speech. There are significant features such as intonation, stress, and tempo which are virtually never represented in standard orthographies and are dealt with, if at all, only in specialized studies by scholars. With regard to the phonetic representation that does occur, there is a very wide range of completeness and efficiency.

In general we can say that what might be called the "phoneticity" of a system of writing, that is, the detailed fit of symbols to sounds, falls within a range that theoretically extends from 1 to 99 percent. One hundred percent efficiency in representing speech can be achieved only by nongraphic means, such as tape recorders and other acoustic recording devices. Zero percent representation likewise means we are dealing with something other than writing, or, if you will, full writing, since it encompasses such pseudowriting as that of the Yukaghir and the North American Indians.

As far as real writing is concerned, the efficiency rating starts at near the top for scientific systems created by highly skilled phoneticians, such as the system called "Visible Speech" that was developed by Alexander Melville Bell. Among actually existing orthographies, Finnish ranks very high because of its close correspondence between sounds and symbols. It decreases somewhat for systems such as German, Spanish, and Russian. It drops further for French, still further for English, and even further for Chinese. An eminent Chinese linguist has suggested that English is 75 percent phonetic, Chinese only 25 percent (Chao 1976:92). Many people mistakenly think that the figure is actually zero for Chinese. This ranking, impressionistic though it doubtless is, nevertheless comprises a suggestive ranking of writing systems on the basis of their phoneticity.

Amplifying on the "Duality Principle" enunciated earlier, we can say that the poorer a writing system is in phonetic representation, the more it compensates, either by design or by historical accident, by greater use of nonphonetic devices. Some of these essentially mnemonic devices have been noted: visual puns and numerical expressions. Other devices include capitalization, grammatical hints such as punctuation, and semantic clues such as those of Chinese notoriety. Still others are the outright pictographic symbols used in Egyptian writing.

Students of writing are at odds in trying to explain these nonphonetic phenomena. At the heart of their disagreement is the question of how to relate levels of writing to levels of speech.

With respect to levels of speech, there is general agreement that utterances consist of a hierarchy of phonological units. The smallest of these is the phoneme. Various numbers of phonemes (1–2 in Hawaiian, 1–4 in Chinese, 1–7 in English) make up syllables. Various numbers of syllables make up words, phrases, sentences, and so on.

The symbols used in writing can be considered in relation to the levels of speech just mentioned. If a system of writing represents phonemes, it is said to be a phonemic system, and its symbols are collectively referred to as an alphabet. Finnish, German, Russian, English, Korean, and many other languages have phonemic or alphabetic scripts. If a system of writing represents syllables, it is said to be a syllabic system, and its symbols, which can individually be called syllabograms, are collectively referred to as a syllabary. The simple Japanese script called kana is the best-known representative of syllabic systems; it comprises a syllabary of fewer than fifty symbols.

While there is general agreement about phonemes and syllables, there is a fundamental difference of opinion as to whether or not there exist other levels of writing related to other levels of speech, such as a level for words, and still other levels for ideas expressible only in phrases or sentences. The most extensive discussion of the whole matter of levels, and of accepting additional levels besides the phonemic and the syllabic, is by a number of linguists who follow the lead of William Haas of the University of Manchester (Haas 1970, 1976, 1983). His views appear in large part to be a more elaborate and sophisticated restatement of the ideas that have led to popular acceptance of the notion that Chinese characters represent words.

Sampson follows the overall approach initiated by Haas in presenting the unique thesis that since the Korean alphabet represents some "distinctive features" below the level of the phoneme (e.g., lax versus tense for consonants, and rounded versus spread for vowels), therefore it should be set apart in its own category, which he labels "featural" (Sampson 1985:120–144). My rejection of his thesis appears in "The Forest of Family Trees," below, and in the discussion of Korean in chapter 5.

Sampson also follows Haas in elaborating on the widespread academic practice of referring to Chinese characters as logographic, that is, representing words. Here I anticipate my rejection of these ideas by stating my conviction that the notion of Chinese as belonging to levels that are variously labeled pictographic, ideographic, word-syllabic, logographic, and morphemic is in error. Sampson, Haas, and others have seriously undervalued the phonetic element in Chinese writing. As noted earlier, estimates of the phoneticity of the Chinese script range from a high of 25 percent to a low of zero. The 25 percent figure is, to my mind, much too low, and the zero estimate is based on ignorance.

Although these matters are discussed in greater detail in the next chapter, I present below, as an appetizer, a character which is used independently to represent the word *mǎ* 'horse' but is also used as a component in a compound character, where it is used solely for its sound. Joined with this *mǎ* character is another character that functions as a semantic "determinative" meaning 'female' and gives a clue to the meaning of the whole complex character.

馬 *mǎ* 'horse'

媽 *mā* 'mother'

The meaning of the complex character is not determined by the sum of the meanings of the two elements of which it is composed. That is to say, it does not mean 'female horse,' though it would be possible to invent, as is often done, a false etymology for *mā* 'mother' based on the idea of a female who works like a horse. However appealing such an etymology might be, especially to hard-working mothers, the reality is that the *mǎ* 'horse' component in *mā* 'mother' is merely a phonetic symbol, just as we might use the picture of a horse to represent the word *hoarse*. We distinguish homophonous *horse* and *hoarse* by differences in spelling. Chinese distinguishes more or less homophonous *mǎ* 'horse' and *mā* 'mother' by the device of semantic determinatives.[1]

The problem of how extensive, and how significant, these phonetic elements are in Chinese is crucially important, but here we need only note that the precise figure of phoneticity of Chinese characters is really beside the point, because even if the figure of 25 percent were to turn out to be only an educated guess needing drastic reduction, it would still be necessary to classify Chinese as a phonetic system of writing of the syllabic type. For what determines the level of a writing system is the indispensable operational unit that enables the script to function. In Chinese that unit is a graphic symbol that represents a syllable.

The concept "operational unit that enables a script to function" is essential to counter the imprecise phraseology used by most students of writing, who say that such-and-such element in writing "represents" this or that element in speech. Thus it is often said of the Korean writing system, which has letter-symbols and combines these into groups corresponding to syllables and words, that it "represents" phonemes, syllables, and words (Taylor 1980). This is true, but it is only true in the same sense that English orthography "represents" both phonemes and words.

The confusion and ambiguity inherent in the multiple use of the word "represents" can be avoided if we establish a dichotomy between two units: (1) The meaningless graphic unit that corresponds to the smallest segment of speech represented in the writing. This is the basic operational unit without which a script simply could not function. I call this unit a *grapheme*. (2) The basic unit of writing that is surrounded by white space on the printed page. I call this unit a *frame,* following the terminology suggested by William S.-Y. Wang (1981:226–228).

English graphemes are letters that either singly or in combination represent phonemes (e.g., *s, sh*). They may themselves constitute frames (e.g., *I* and *a* in *"I have a dream."*) or combine to form frames representing words. It has become the convention, especially since the advent of printing, to separate words by white space, a practice which, while not carried out with scientific accuracy or consistency, contrasts with theearlierpracticeofrunningallthewordstogether.

Chinese graphemes are characters that singly represent whole syllables. They may themselves constitute frames (e.g., the character for *mă* 'horse'), or combine with other nonphonetic elements to form more complex characters representing frames (e.g., the character for *mā* 'mother').

It is important to note that in English, apart from a few one-letter frames such as the pronoun *I* and the article *a*, frames always consist of more than one grapheme—as many as twenty-three in a long word like *disestablishmentarianism.* In addition to differing in number of phonetic components, the graphemes and frames also differ in the amount of space that they occupy. These self-evident disparities bring out in strong relief and constantly reinforce the difference between the two units in English.

In contrast, Chinese frames invariably contain only one grapheme and are so written as to occupy exactly the same amount of space as an independent grapheme (e.g., the characters for 'horse' and 'mother' cited above). These obvious but secondary similarities between the two units contribute to the general failure to make a clear distinction between grapheme and frame in Chinese, which in turn leads to the common mistake of concentrating attention on the frame as the more conspicuous and ubiquitous unit.

In all writing systems the grapheme is by far the most important of the two units. What happens beyond the grapheme is of quite secondary importance, as demonstrated by the fact that English would be able to function, though with different degrees of efficiency, whether it separated words or ran them together. The same is true of Chinese and of all other writing systems.

The ability of writing systems to function without the use of frames is well illustrated by the case of Japanese. In most Japanese publications, apart from division of text by means of punctuation marks, all the graphic symbols are strung together like a continuous string of beads without any regard to dividing them into groups on the basis of semantic considerations. Delimitation of frames is largely restricted to primers and dictionaries, where the graphic elements are grouped together, surrounded by white space, to form lexical items.

Indeed, it is probably true for all writing systems that frames are most clearly evidenced in the entries found in their dictionaries. This being so, perhaps frames might better be defined as the items occuring in lexical lists such as dictionaries, and hence might better be renamed *lexemes*—words in English (e.g., *horse, hoarse,* and *disestablishmentarianism*), and characters in Chinese (e.g., the characters for *horse* and *mother*). Dictionaries are late additions to writing systems, however, so that their lexemes play a secondary role to the more basic graphemes.[2]

English functions fairly well with its imperfect system of graphemes of the phonemic or alphabetic type. It could function also with a system of graphemes of the syllabic type, but with much greater difficulty, because its inventory of spoken syllables, over 8,000 in number, is too large to be represented simply in this way. Chinese functions, though not easily, with graphemes of the syllabic type. Its inventory of spoken syllables—only 1,277 counting tones and 398 not counting them—is small enough to be represented in this way and still allow for the cumbersome addition of semantic elements to compensate for the imperfections of the phonetic base. It could, of course, be written very simply with an alphabetic system, such as Pinyin, the auxiliary romanization scheme adopted in 1958.

Neither English nor Chinese writing, nor the writing of any other language, can function with graphemes based on any of the semantic levels—discourse, words, or even morphemes. For the number of the equivalent spoken items at the command of the average speaker of any language is so enormous that the human mind has shown no evidence of being able to represent them with graphemes of this sort, despite its ability to manipulate them by mouth and by ear.

In the light of all this it should be clear that the key question to ask about writing systems is not the ambiguous one of what they "represent" but the more precise query as to what are the basic units—the graphemes—that make the systems work. In Finnish and English, it is alphabetic symbols that represent the phonemes of these languages. In Japanese and Chinese, it is graphic symbols that represent their respective syllables. Finnish does its job with almost one-to-one correspondence between sound and symbol. English writing has poor sound–symbol correspondence but makes up for this in various ways. The Japanese kana system does its job in a fairly simple and efficient manner by its good correspondence between syllabic sounds and syllabic symbols. Chinese has even poorer sound–symbol correspondence than does English but makes up for this by various nonphonetic clues.

The parallelism between the foregoing pairs of languages leads me to set up dichotomies of "pure" phonetic writing and "meaning-plus-sound" scripts. So we have "pure" phonemic scripts (Finnish) versus "meaning-plus-sound" phonemic scripts (English) on the one hand, and "pure" syllabic scripts (Japanese kana) and "meaning-plus-sound" syllabic scripts (Chinese) on the other. In between these pairs I sandwich "pure" consonantal scripts (Arabic) versus "meaning-plus-sound" consonantal scripts (Egyptian at the time of the pharaohs).

No script with a zero phonetic component can function as a full system of writing. One with only a small percentage can. The phonetic operational unit, that is the grapheme, is the heart of the system. In the total weight of the human body, the heart counts for little. In the functions that sustain life, it counts for everything. No heart, no life. No phonetics, no writing. Weak hearts can be doctored in various ways. And so, as will be shown below, can weak phonetic systems.

The Forest of Family Trees

The failure to see that the heart of all writing systems is its phonetic base has tended to confuse people about the relationships that exist among systems of writing. We should look at a few classification schemes in order both to pinpoint previous analytical shortcomings and to suggest further lines of thought about these matters. To this end I present my own typological analysis as an aid to hacking our way through the forest of family trees that have grown up from attempts to classify systems of writing.

In approaching the classification the dichotomy between partial and full should be kept firmly in mind. In particular, it should be noted that all forms of partial writing, other than the specifically speech-related examples represented by numerical notation, do not properly belong in a discussion of writing at all. They are as out of place as, in a book on the history of automobiles, would be a profusely illustrated introductory section on "Oxcarts of the World." Oxcarts can never evolve into automobiles, or pictographs into real writing, unless they change the principles on which they are based. While it may be legitimate to discuss pictography in a comprehensive study of human communication, to include them in works devoted to writing only obscures the issue unless they are clearly and categorically dismissed as limited, dead-end means of communication.

With this reiterated caution let us now continue the communication classification scheme presented earlier in figure 1 by showing the ramifications of the written language branch in the writing classification scheme in figure 10. This classification is in line with the generally held opinion that full writing has its origins in pictures. Most pictorial representation must of course be characterized as dead end, since in only a few cases did it make the transition to full writing. Some pictorial representation led to abstract representational symbols such as the Chinese characters for "above" and "below" (originally respectively a dot above and below a horizontal line). These are dead-end symbols which are part of full writing.

The most important use of pictures, a use which marked the breakthrough to full writing, is represented in the chart by the vertical line leading from "pictures" to "rebus symbols." From the use of the rebus principle came first of all the creation of syllabic systems. Later came consonantal systems, and still later alphabetic ones.

Some comments are necessary regarding the terms used in the bottom row. I place the term *pure* in quotation marks to suggest "so-called" and to emphasize my endorsement of the Gelb quotation that there are no really pure systems of writing. The term is used in a relative sense to contrast with other terms, namely those which I have previously called by popular names but in the chart present under briefer and more technical labels. The equivalent expressions are as follows:

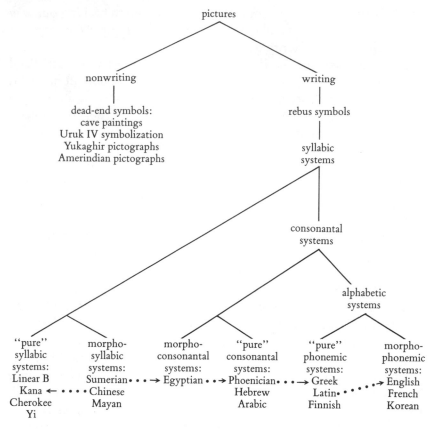

Figure 10. DeFrancis Writing Classification Scheme

"meaning-plus-sound" *syllabic* systems = **morphosyllabic** systems
"meaning-plus-sound" *consonantal* systems = **morphoconsonantal**
systems
"meaning-plus-sound" *phonemic* systems = **morphophonemic**
systems

If an inclusive term is needed for these three kinds of scripts, I suggest "morphophonic" or "morphonic" as drawing attention to the dual aspect of the systems, namely the primary phonetic aspect plus the secondary but nonetheless important nonphonetic, that is semantic or morphemic, aspect.

The typological classification represented by this terminology is fleshed out with some examples of writing systems belonging to the various types. The chart also adds a bit of genealogical information in the form of dotted lines with arrows pointing from parent to off-spring.

With all this as background, let us consider how others have dealt with the classification of writing systems. Our first candidate is one of the first scholars to write extensively about the subject. Toward the end of the last century Isaac Taylor published a two-volume history of writing in which he presented an evolutionary model consisting of a succession of five stages (Taylor 1899, 1:5–6). These stages can be summarized as follows:

1. pictures
2. pictorial symbols } ideograms
3. verbal signs
4. syllabic signs } phonograms
5. alphabetic signs

Subsequent classification schemes, as A. A. Hill points out, have been essentially the same as that presented by Taylor (Hill 1967:92).

Taylor variously characterized Chinese characters as pictographs, ideograms, and verbal phonograms. They comprised, he said, "the most notable instance of a graphic system which has never succeeded in advancing beyond the most rudimentary stage of conventionalized picture writing" (Taylor 1899, 1:25)—a characterization he also applied to Amerindian pictographs.

A somewhat similar classification, but without Taylor's crude denigration, has recently been presented by Sampson in a study whose essence is graphically summarized in a typological tree, presented in figure 11, which is adapted from his own schematic tree and from his subsequent discussion (Sampson 1985:32 and passim). On the basis of the latter, and in order to facilitate comparison with other schemes, I have slightly extended his tree by subdividing his "segmental" category into "consonantal" and "vocalic + consonantal," and by adding his examples of the various kinds of writing. The top part of the tree is explained by his statement that "We shall use the term *semasiographic systems* for systems of visible communication akin to that of the Yukaghir example, which indicate ideas directly, in contrast to *glottographic systems* which provide visible representations of spoken-language utterances" (Sampson 1985:25).

Sampson explains the dotted line as showing that the inclusion of semasiographic systems under "writing" is open to question. Re-

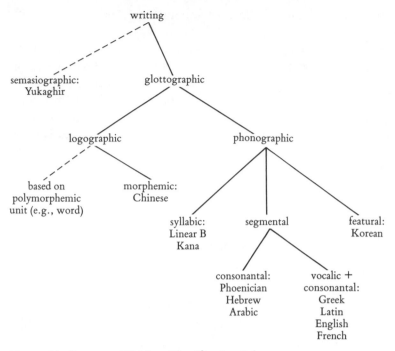

Figure 11. Sampson Writing Classification Scheme

marking that the decision "is ultimately a personal choice about how to use words," he does seem to indicate a preference for inclusion. Thus he states that "There would appear in principle to be no reason why a society could not have expanded a semasiographic system, by adding further conventions, until it was fully as complex and rich in expressive potential as their spoken language." And, he adds, while the current trend to extend the use of semasiographic symbols, such as the "give way" road sign consisting of a downward-pointing triangle, "is hardly likely to lead to the evolution of a fully-fledged semasiographic language rivalling English, French, or German in expressive potential," nevertheless "logically speaking such an outcome seems not absolutely excluded" (Sampson 1985:30–35).

The lower right branch of phonographic writing includes the familiar syllabic and segmental (i.e., phonemic or alphabetic) scripts and previously mentioned featural orthographies, of which Korean is his sole example. The lower left branch includes scripts which he calls "logographic," a term commonly used to designate writing that represents units of speech at the level of words. He urges shunning the word *ideographic,* as well as *pictographic* and *picture-writing,* as blurring distinctions which students of writing need to keep apart (Sampson 1985:35).

The solid line leading from "logographic" to "morphemic" indicates Sampson's view that such writing cannot practically represent anything more than a morpheme, the smallest unit of meaning in spoken utterances. The dotted line indicates "a hypothetical rather than an actual possibility" of a writing system with a separate symbol for every word regardless of the number of morphemes of which it is composed (Sampson 1985:39).

Apart from the named systems that I have added to his tree on the basis of his discussion, Sampson also discusses standard Japanese extensively, and Sumerian and Egyptian somewhat, as examples of "mixed" scripts.

We next consider the views of I. J. Gelb, the author of one of the most important works on the subject. He conveniently summarizes his extensive discussion in an elaborate family tree that names more than sixty different scripts and in a chart which he entitles "Stages of the Development of Writing" (Gelb 1963:x–xi, 191). These form the basis for our figure 12.

One of the main differences between Gelb and the previously mentioned scholars is that he rejects as writing what he calls "desciptive-representational" symbols, which he illustrates with the letter sent by Turtle-Following-His Wife to his son, and "identifying-mnemonic" symbols, which he illustrates with Lone-Dog's Winter Count. Such symbols, he says, never have been, and never can be, anything more than "limited systems." He adds that a system of this sort "can develop into a full system of writing only if it succeeds in attaching to a sign a phonetic value independent of the meaning which this sign has as a word. This is phonetization, the most important single step in the history of writing. In modern usage this device is called 'rebus writing' " (Gelb 1963:193–194). Gelb is the only one of the writers under discussion to stress the distinction between limited and full writing and the pivotal role of the rebus principle in the transition. His views have greatly influenced my own thinking in these matters.

The most novel classification scheme is that presented by A. A. Hill in a discussion which I have summarized, using his terminology, in the form of the tree in figure 13. His unique handling of Amerindian pictographs as writing at the discourse level is poles apart from Gelb's dismissal of such symbols as not real writing. Also novel is his use of

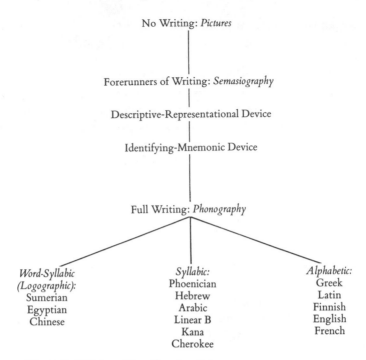

No Writing: *Pictures*

Forerunners of Writing: *Semasiography*

Descriptive-Representational Device

Identifying-Mnemonic Device

Full Writing: *Phonography*

Word-Syllabic (Logographic):	*Syllabic:*	*Alphabetic:*
Sumerian	Phoenician	Greek
Egyptian	Hebrew	Latin
Chinese	Arabic	Finnish
	Linear B	English
	Kana	French
	Cherokee	

Figure 12. Gelb Writing Classification Scheme

new labels for old concepts so as to bring out how some scripts are related phonemically. Thus *monophonemic* refers to systems in which there are separate symbols for individual phonemes; *partial phonemic* refers to systems in which single symbols represent single consonants, and only the consonants; and *polymorphemic* refers to single symbols which stand for all the phonemes in a syllable (Hill 1967).

Leaving aside the diverse terminology used by our four authors, there appear to be two main areas of disagreement and one key area on which they all agree. Sampson stands alone in his treatment of Korean, Gelb in his opposition to accepting pictographs as writing. I agree with Taylor, Gelb, and Hill on Korean, and with Gelb on pictographs.

But I strongly disagree with them all on what in my view is the major error that they all make in separating Chinese from other full systems whose phonetic base they acknowledge by such characterizations as "syllabic" or "phonemic." For all their erudition and convoluted treatment of the subject, these scholars end up with views that are remarkably similar to popular misconceptions regarding Chinese and other systems of a similar nature.

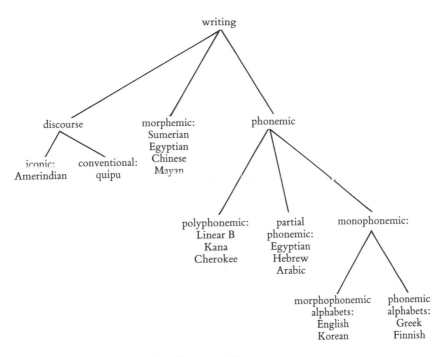

Figure 13. Hill Writing Classification Scheme

One reason for the almost universal misunderstanding stems from the predisposition to overvalue the power of pictures and the semantic value of nonphonetic symbols. This is revealed by the offhand acceptance of questionable claims for such graphic representation. Sampson presents the example of the Yukaghir love letter as his sole evidence for postulating the existence of a "semasiographic" system of writing that might rival English in expressive potential. Hill accepts that the Chippewa "Petition" was "sent" to Washington and he fails to realize that it was actually a hand-delivered sales pitch accompanied by oral explanation. Even Gelb, for all his stress on the limitations inherent in pictographic symbols, reproduces a number of Mallery's examples, including those of the Ojibwa girl and the Cheyenne father, without noting the even greater limitation implicit in Mallery's reference to the preconcerted nature of such notificational pictography.

A corollary to the overvaluation of such symbolization is the general undervaluation by these scholars, and by the public at large, of the phonetic aspect in Chinese writing. In the case of most writing systems, scholars are at pains to show how they are phonologically based and should be classified according to the smallest underlying phono-logical unit. That unit is generally recognized to be either a syllable or a phoneme. (Sampson goes still lower in the phonological scale with his featural unit for Korean.)

But when Chinese is discussed, this emphasis on the smallest phono-logical unit is suddenly abandoned, and one presumes as the basic unit a word or a morpheme. Instead of taking the grapheme, as was done for other writing systems, discussion focuses on the frame, or lexeme, as the basis for classification. Chinese characters are recognized as also representing sounds, but they are generally said to do so as a single whole, not through the use of component phonetic elements. And while it is recognized that such phonetic elements exist and enter into the composition of some Chinese characters (most of them, actually), this fact is generally dismissed because, as Sampson puts it, "there is nothing regular about this" (Sampson 1985:146)—a line of reasoning that has led a number of scholars to classify English as also "logo-graphic" or "ideographic" because of its many discrepancies in spell-ing (Kōno 1968:85; Zachrisson 1931:5).

The obfuscation could not be more complete. To cut through the misunderstanding we need to keep the principles that allow the crea-tion of full writing firmly in mind. We turn now to examine just how the ingenious creators of scripts played their variations on the single theme of phonetic writing.

II
FULL WRITING SYSTEMS

3.

Syllabic Systems

It is probably not accidental that the three seemingly unrelated inventions of writing—Sumerian, Chinese, and Mayan—which we now take up in detail, were all based on the syllabic principle. There can be little doubt that it is easier to conceptualize a syllable than to analyze utterances into their smaller phonemic units. This is especially likely to be the case if the syllabic structure of a particular language, when compared to that of other languages, possesses special features that make it easier to concentrate attention on the syllable.

Such indeed was the case for Sumerian, Chinese, and Mayan. In all these languages, more so than in English and many other forms of speech, the syllable was usually a unit of meaning. It was often even an independent word. To be sure, this semantic feature should not be exaggerated, as is frequently done by those who misrepresent the languages as "monosyllabic" in the sense of consisting exclusively of words of one syllable. It is only in relative terms that their syllables are more heavily endowed with meaning and that their words consist of one syllable.

In these languages concentrating attention on the syllable was doubtless also facilitated by the fact that the sounds making up the syllables were simpler and more restricted than in languages like English. Sumerian and Mayan syllables apparently contained a maximum of three phonemes, Chinese four or five, compared to the seven of English.

From a theoretical point of view, if the invention of writing is facilitated by the factors just mentioned, it would appear that the spread of the syllabic principle to writing other languages would also be facilitated if these borrowing languages have a restricted inventory of syllables. This is indeed the case of the two syllabic systems, Japanese and Yi, that I have chosen to represent the group of "pure" syllabic scripts. Compared to the more than 8,000 syllables of English, the approximately 800 of Yi and mere 100 or so of Japanese are simplicity itself.

The development of "simple" syllabic writing was still not an easy task, however. The creators of writing systems were not trained linguists who could undertake their task by first making an inventory of the syllables in their language and then devising a symbol to match each syllable. They had only a vague notion that a symbol could be used to represent a sound. What sounds to represent, and how to represent them, were therefore not worked out systematically but haphazardly, in a variety of ways that differed from one system to another and even within the same system.

"Meaning-plus-Sound" Syllabic Systems

Of the three systems that will be discussed first, there is general agreement that Sumerian and Chinese should be classified together. The common category to which they belong has been variously labeled. Reflecting a usage that began to receive scholarly acceptance in the thirties, Gelb (1963) refers to this category as *logographic* or *word-syllabic*. Hill (1967) and Sampson (1985) adopt the more technical term *morphemic* that has recently been preferred by academics. My own suggestion, aimed at stressing the phonetic component, is *morphosyllabic*.

There is considerably less agreement on how to handle Mayan. Gelb excludes it from this category and even considers that it and related Central American systems "do not represent full writing since even in their most advanced stages they never attained the level of development characteristic of the earliest phases of the Oriental systems" (Gelb 1963:61). Sampson states that even though the inscriptions of the Mayas are not yet deciphered, it is far from clear that Gelb is justified in denying that they constitute writing in the full sense (Sampson 1985:46–47). Although he refers to Mayan writing only in passing, Hill labels it "morphemic" along with Sumerian and Chinese (Hill 1967:95). In recent years specialists in Mayan writing have increasingly stressed its phonetic component, as indicated by the presentation of what they call "A Maya Hieroglyphic Syllabary" (Mathews 1984: 311–314). I follow them in this matter except for the abovementioned modification of the label.

Of the three morphosyllabic systems, modern scholarship stressing origins and typology goes back a century or so for Sumerian, about half a century for Chinese, and only the past few decades for Mayan. The quantity of archaeological data needed for scholarly consideration along these lines follows the same downward progression. Part of the reason for this is that climatic and other conditions were most favorable for the preservation of Sumerian and related writings, least favorable for Mayan. The Western religious and cultural preoccupation with the Near and Middle East has also tended to concentrate scholarly interest in that area. For a variety of reasons, therefore, it turns out that Sumerian not only comes first in the history of writing but ranks first in terms of scholarly attention.

Sumerian

Interest in Sumerian writing only began around the middle of the last century for the very good reason that even the existence of the Sumerians and their script was completely unknown until that time. The rediscovery of both after several millennia of oblivion comprises a fascinating chapter in the annals of modern scholarship and one of its crowning achievements (Kramer 1963; Pope 1975; Barber 1974).

This achievement cannot be viewed as merely the product of cloistered scholars poring over abstruse and exotic texts. It also involved feats of daring and endurance, the most spectacular of which was the occasion in the 1840s when the soldier-scholar Henry Rawlinson risked his life dangling by a rope three hundred feet in the air in order to copy some trilingual inscriptions carved into a sheer cliff at Behistun in what is now southwestern Iran (Kramer 1963:17).

The strange symbols of these inscriptions had first come to the attention of Europeans early in the seventeenth century when an Italian traveler brought back some inscribed bricks which he had found in the ruins of a city that he correctly identified as Babylon. Throughout the seventeenth and eighteenth centuries many inscriptions bearing these symbols found their way to Europe and became the object of scholarly attention. In 1700 an Oxford professor gave to the symbols the name *cuneiform,* from the Latin word *cuneus* 'wedge' (Kramer 1963; Pope 1975).

One of the first steps in the decipherment of the inscriptions was the discovery that there were different types of these wedge-shaped symbols that doubtless represented different kinds of writing systems. By tabulating the symbols it was determined that some inscriptions were

written in an alphabetic script since there were only forty-two different signs. Other scholars, assuming from the location of some inscriptions that they were written in Old Persian, further guessed, correctly
as it turned out, that they would contain a stereotyped pattern common to inscriptions in well-known scripts of that language; this pattern was: "A, the great king, the king of kings, the king of . . . , the
son of B, the great king . . ." (Gordon 1982:49). Following these
leads, in 1802 a German scholar named Georg Grotefend correctly
identified ten signs and three proper names. Rawlinson and other
scholars carried the work further and succeeded in the complete
decipherment of the Old Persian cuneiform inscriptions (Kramer 1963;
Gordon 1982; Pope 1975).

This success enabled scholars to try applying the values of the deciphered symbols to the same symbols as they occurred in the two other
inscriptions. The procedure involved is akin to guessing that the English pronunciation of the placename *Paris* may be at least a partial
reflection of the original French pronunciation. Taking into account
the number of different symbols contained in the inscriptions, the
scholars also proceeded on the asumption that they might be written
in syllabic scripts.

These procedures enabled the scholars to determine that the second
of the three inscriptions was written in a system consisting of 111 syllabic signs. It turned out to be a translation of the Old Persian version
into a language called Elamite, which is not related to any well known
language and appears to have had limited use, as it never became
important outside of western Iran (Gordon 1982:61–62).

Then it was determined that the third inscription was written in a
syllabic script consisting of more than three hundred signs. A major
breakthrough in the decipherment of this inscription was achieved in
1847 when the Irish scholar Edward Hincks succeeded in identifying
the first word which was not a proper name: the pronoun *a-na-ku* "I"
—practically identical with its Hebrew counterpart, *anoki*. The validity of his decipherment received dramatic confirmation ten years later
in the previously mentioned episode in which four scholars independently deciphered an inscription in the same language (Kramer 1963:
16–18; Gordon 1982:62–71; Pope 1975:114–117). Thus another cune-
iform-based script was recognized as representing a Semitic language
that was later more narrowly identified as Akkadian (or Accadian)—
also called Assyrian, Babylonian, and Assyro-Babylonia (EBMIC 1988:
192; Kramer 1963:19).

The Akkadian language turned out to be of great importance and generated enormous interest. This was due in part to its membership with Hebrew in the great Semitic family of languages. It was also due to its close connection with several other writing systems, as became apparent when huge numbers of inscriptions were unearthed in the archaeological excavations that began to proliferate in the middle of the nineteenth century.

In the course of these excavations inscriptions came to light that were written in a cuneiform script that Hincks was the first to recognize as having been devised for a hitherto unknown language. Three years later, in 1853, Rawlinson delivered a lecture in which he described the language as similar in some respects to Mongol and Manchu but having little or no resemblance to them in vocabulary. In 1869 the French scholar Jules Oppert concluded that the language also had close affinities with Turkish, Finnish, and Hungarian. He suggested calling the language, and its writing system, Sumerian, basing his conclusion on the title "King of Sumer and Akkad" found in some inscriptions dealing with early rulers (Kramer 1963:19–21).

In the decades that followed, further excavations turned up thousands of Sumerian inscriptions, the decipherment of which revealed a system of writing important in several spheres. It has the distinction of being the earliest full system of writing ever created; it formed the basis of the world's first great civilization; it served for a long time, much as Latin did later, as the medium of learned communication of diverse peoples who spoke other languages. And, finally, its cuneiform symbols were modified, as happened also in the case of the Latin script, to represent a host of different languages.

The major locale of these developments is the area lying between the Tigris and Euphrates rivers in what is now Iraq. Around 3500 B.C. the Sumerians, whose original home has been variously traced to a number of localities, including the region of the Caspian Sea, invaded and took over the land from the Proto-Euphratean people who had first settled the area a millennium or so earlier. The newcomers established themselves in city-states along the lower reaches of the two rivers, and within a few hundred years of their arrival they began to make records by pressing symbols into lumps of alluvial mud which were hardened into the bricks that have come to light in many sites throughout the area.

The dating of these sites has been much debated. Archaeologically the sequence is clear, since an uppermost Uruk I site obviously comes later than Uruk II, III, and so on. But no absolute dates can be assigned to the sites or to the texts found there since they contain no historical information that can be dated. One careful scholar has nevertheless proposed the following tentative chronology (Driver 1976:7):

Uruk IV	c. 3500 B.C.
Uruk III–II	c. 3300 B.C.
Jemdet Nasr	c. ?–2900 B.C.
Uruk I	c. 2650–2400 B.C.
Shuruppak/Fara	c. 2600–2500 B.C.
Ur	c. 2575–2475 B.C.

The Uruk IV period produced inscriptions limited to numbers and pictured objects (Driver 1976:6). Some of the latter symbols were recognizable pictures, others were highly stylized and abstract. The subject matter was temple transactions of an economic nature. This system of accountancy was a kind of shorthand that used nonphonetic symbols. For a long time, as one writer puts it, the notation was "only a means of producing catchwords for someone who was more or less familiar with the context but needed to be reminded of particular details. Not only do we find no traces of a verbal system, but there are no hints of syntactic relations" (Nissen 1986:329). The author further notes, for example, that the tablet reproduced in figure 14 may read " 'Two sheep delivered to the temple (or house) of the goddess Inanna,' or '. . . of the gods An and Inanna,' or 'Two sheep (received from) the temple/house of the goddess Inanna/the gods An and Inanna' " (Nissen 1986:329–330).

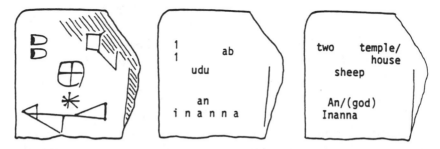

Figure 14. Sumerian Partial Writing: Uruk IV Dead-End Symbols
Pictographic and representational symbols similar in concept to the dead-end symbols of countless early cultures that never developed a full system of writing. Reprinted with permission from Hans J. Nissen, "The Archaic Texts from Uruk." *World Archaeology* 17 (3) (1986):330.

The symbols were doubtless clear enough to the temple accountants who dealt with the matters in question and would have known, for example, whether the temple was giving or receiving the items noted. But the lack of phonetic notation, of fixed serial order, and of other attributes that characterize ordinary writing would have made the message unintelligible to later readers, including modern scholars, unless they were able to work backward from later stages of such symbolization and reconstruct the pronunciation and meaning of the text.

In short, what we have here, as several writers have repeatedly pointed out, is a limited notational system whose function was largely mnemonic (Tyumenev 1969:73; Diakonoff 1975; Powell 1981). As such it was conceptually no more advanced, although more elaborate, than the Yukaghir and Amerindian mnemonic devices.

The same can be said of some other notational devices which several scholars have advanced as the precursors of the symbols discussed above and of full Sumerian writing. Much has been made of the bookkeeping practice based on clay pebbles and on clay balls with such pebbles inside and incised symbols outside, the latter being largely limited to such geometric figures as cones, spheres, and disks supposedly standing for sheep, cloth, and other commodities. These clay objects have been traced back to about 8000 B.C. and have been found throughout much of the prehistoric Near and Middle East from Khartoum to the Indus River valley (Schmandt-Besserat 1978, 1979, 1981, 1984, 1986; Powell 1981; Jasim and Oates 1986).

The claims for these objects as possible precursors to the invention of writing have been criticized as "unjustified on chronological and geographical grounds, imprecise or incorrect in terms of many of the purely formal comparisons that have been made, inadequate as an explanation of the appearance of writing, and based on an error of classification" (Lieberman 1980:339). There is, I believe, an even more fundamental error in most of the attempts that have been made to relate early notational systems to the origin of writing. The first objection is that the mere resemblance of a few symbols in two different systems of writing does not make for a necessary connection between them. The attempt to establish a connection between a few Easter Island pictographs and symbols from the Indus valley on the basis of just such a resemblance has been criticized by one student of writing in the following terms:

The mere outward resemblance of the symbols, undeniable as it is . . ., is still no clue to the meanings or values, nor to the language and the

contents of the texts written with them. He who does not believe in
supernatural connections had better ascribe the outward similarity of
the two scripts to mere coincidence [Friedrich 1957:172].

Coincidence of this sort is bound to happen with the necessarily limited variety of simple symbols. Nor is there anything special about
impressing a picture or a symbol on clay or drawing it on some other
material. That happened thousands of times over thousands of years in
thousands of different places. Such activities go back to Stone-Age
cave paintings and to 30,000-year-old marks on bones that are claimed
to mark phases of the moon (Marshack 1964, 1972). They are amply
illustrated in comprehensive works on writing (Taylor 1899; Cohen
1958; Gelb 1963; Diringer 1968). The clay pebbles and the earliest
Uruk records were more numerous, more elaborate, and better preserved, but conceptually they differ little from other primitive symbolizations that at best are only partial writing.

Concentrating on the similarity among such symbols, which even if
used in both prehistoric and historic times would have constituted
merely another batch of dead-end symbols unless altered in function,
leads into the second and more important error in the approach noted
above. That is the failure to zero in on what marks the change in function that leads to the transition to potentially full writing. The element in question, of course, is the idea of using a pictograph as a
rebus, that is, not for its meaning but for its sound.

Such an idea either exists or does not exist and is brought into being
by a mental operation akin to activating a light switch—a sudden
physical (or mental) flick, and light (or phonetic writing) appears. It
makes no sense to view the idea as gestating over a period of five millennia, from 8000 B.C. to the time of the Sumerians. What actually
happened to those clay tokens in the intervening 5,000 years is the
same as what happened to most primitive notational systems in the
rest of the world—they died.

But something qualitatively different happened in Sumer—in Uruk
according to Powell (1981)—in Jemdet Nasr according to my analysis.
In my view someone in that city suddenly hit upon the completely
novel idea of using a pictographic symbol for its phonetic value. And
with this, the giant step was taken toward the development of the first
full system of writing.

Powell suggests Uruk as "the probable locus of invention" because
it "seems to have been not only the largest urban center in Mesopotamia but also the only one that could be called a city at all." He ascribes

the invention of Sumerian writing to an individual living in Uruk about 3000 B.C. whom he dubs *literatus Sumericus Urukeus.* But in referring to this individual as "the inventor of the pictorial writing system" of the Sumerians, Powell gives him too much credit for what, if it had simply continued along the same line, would have proven another cul-de-sac.

The real inventor of what became the full system of Sumerian writing appears to have been someone from Jemdet Nasr, who around the year 3000 B.C. first thought to use a pictograph as a phonetic symbol. Adam Falkenstein, the earliest Sumerologist to draw attention to this development, even thought that he had found, on several tablets unearthed in 1926–1928 at Jemdet Nasr (Langdon 1928), the very first example of a sign that was "consciously" employed to represent the sound of something with which it had no semantic or logical connection:

> The first recognizable example is provided by Jemdet Nasr tablets with the personal name *en-lil-ti* 'Enlil grant life!' The symbol for *ti* 'life' is the picture of an arrow; it derives from the Sumerian *ᵍⁱˢti* 'arrow' but is transferred to the homonym *ti(l)* 'life' which is difficult to write pictorially [Falkenstein 1936:33].

(Enlil is the name of the leading Sumerian deity. *Giš* is a "determinative" indicating that the *ti* occurring here refers to an item made of wood.)

A later scholar has challenged this specific application of the rebus principle. In the view of the Soviet Sumerologist A. A. Vaiman, the expression cited by Falkenstein should actually be read as É.EN.TI (É is apparently 'temple') with EN.TI possibly being another rendering of the place-name Ebeḫ (Vaiman 1974). Vaiman's work seems to have received the general approval of other Sumerologists (Edzard 1980; Thomsen 1984:20–21).

While rejecting Falkenstein's specific example, Vaiman accepts his procedure, concluding, "Nevertheless the methodology of ascertaining the Sumerian character of the language through proven Sumerian homonyms is in fact useful." Vaiman cites what he considers to be a more reliable example of the use of the rebus principle by presenting the tablet, also found at Jemdet Nasr, shown in figure 15. The sign in the top left corner of the tablet is interpreted as a pictograph representing the Sumerian word GI 'reed.' It is to be read here, however, as the homophonous word GI 'reimburse' (Vaiman 1974:17–18). This usage

Figure 15. Sumerian Full Writing: Jemdet Nasr Rebus Symbols
Inscription typical of the economic records of Sumerian temples. The sign in the upper left corner of the tablet is a pictograph representing the word GI 'reed' that is used here for the homophonous word GI 'reimburse.' From A. A. Vaiman, "Über die protosumerische Schrift." *Acta Antiqua Academiae Scientiarum Hungaricae* 22 (1974):18.

occurs on a tablet that is typical of the large number of economic records dealing with income and disbursements of Sumerian temples.

The preceding examples cited from Falkenstein and Vaiman give a small hint of the exceedingly complex problems involved in deciphering the signs used in the earliest stages of Sumerian writing. The interpretation of individual signs and of more extended inscriptions is much debated. There has been no thorough, overall study of the script. In particular, the use of the signs as phonetic symbols is often mentioned only in passing, along with many other aspects, instead of being given the primary attention that it deserves. The details of the language underlying the early inscriptions are widely debated, as indicated by the well-known joke among specialists that "there are as many Sumerian languages as there are Sumerologists" (Diakonoff 1975:99). The dating of the sites in which the inscriptions have been found is also a much-debated subject that is under constant review. Nevertheless, despite these and many other uncertainties and limitations, it seems possible to cite bits and pieces of evidence that throw some light on the evolution of the Sumerian system of writing.

It appears that from Jemdet Nasr, according to Falkenstein, originated also the sporadic use of semantic and phonetic indicators and the Sumerian plural sign (Falkenstein 1936:35–37). Driver, following Falkenstein, also notes the leading role played by Jemdet Nasr, where

a sign that had originally only a word-value acquired also a syllable-value which could be used to write any word which consisted of that syllable or of which that syllable was a component element. This practice was apparently initiated at Jemdet Nasr, where a phonetic *ME* was added to nouns to indicate the plural number, as in *AB-ME* 'elders' and *EN-ME* 'masters.' Soon other grammatical inflexions came to be so written [Driver 1976:57].[1]

The further extension of phonetic representation appears, from Driver's account, to be attested only for a somewhat later period, that of Shuruppak (ca. 2600–2500 B.C.):

The first phonetically written words were *MA.NA* 'maneh,' a very common measure of weight, and *TAM.KAR* 'merchant,' in texts from Shuruppak. Neither concept could easily or lucidly be represented in pictorial form, and both terms are probably foreign, namely Akkadian, loan-words, which would enhance the need of writing them out in phonetic form [Driver 1976:58].[2]

The scattered bits of information available, of which the chief items have been quoted above, leave much to be desired in enabling us to detail the chronological development of Sumerian writing. This important matter is even relegated to a footnote in another work which differs somewhat from Falkenstein and Driver's accounts and dates the archaeological sites several centuries earlier than the usual practice:

The whole process of development can be followed in the light of the tablets found on various sites. The lowest stratum at Erech, Uruk IV, produced tablets which consist entirely of pictured objects and numbers; these should be dated approximately 3500 BC. Texts from Jemdet Nasr (c. 3500 BC) are generaly similar but for the first time use signs with determinative values; the same is the case with tablets from Uruk III. Tablets from Ur dated about 3250 BC show a few signs sparingly used as syllables to indicate the case of nouns and verbal inflexions; this is the beginning of true writing. The process is carried on by tablets from Fara, where signs representing syllables are used not only for inflexions but also for the phonetic spelling of difficult words, a stage reached about 3200 BC, while in Uruk I, c. 2900 BC, signs are employed as syllables for the phonetic complement and for plural ending and the signs generally are strongly conventionalized [Hawkes and Woolley 1963:664].

It is also in the Jemdet Nasr period that we have the first use of the title *dub-sar* 'scribe.' The title is found in a single inscription on a tablet unearthed in that city. It occurs frequently in documents of the Shuruppak archives (Tyumenev 1969:73).

Despite the limited information provided in the foregoing accounts, and the discrepancies among them, the general outline of the evolution of Sumerian writing seems fairly clear. After what may have been a dead-end stage, Uruk IV, writing began in Jemdet Nasr, and in the relatively short time of a few hundred years evolved into a system that the Sumerians could use to write anything they wanted to express.

Not that they wanted to write much more at first. For some time they continued to limit their writing to simple accounting records marked by what the Soviet Sumerologist Diakonoff calls a "fortuitous word order, probably unrelated to the syntax of the spoken language." The same scholar cites other examples, some from post–Jemdet Nasr periods, in which "the still free sign order" prevails, "case relations are not registered," the dative and genitive and copula are missing. "Much of what must have existed in the spoken language is not registered in writing." But some items are registered: "the 'phonetic' (rebus type) inclusions" consisting of affixes and other elements. And, Diakonoff continues,

> With time, in order to convey the necessary information more precisely, more and more units of the spoken language came to be reflected by signs of writing through using various rebus devices, but the whole system was never meant to express all the phonetic or even the morphophonemic elements of the language. . . . Thus, when we try to find out the morphophonological structure of the Sumerian language, we must constantly bear in mind that we are not dealing with a language directly but are reconstructing it from a very imperfect mnemonic writing system which had not been basically aimed at the rendering of morphophonemics [Diakonoff 1975:106].

It apparently took quite some time for "the fortuitous word order" mentioned by Diakonoff to be replaced by a more fixed one. Another writer notes somewhat more specifically that in the inscriptions from one particular site "the signs were not written in that order in which they had to be read until ca. 2470" (Thomsen 1984:20).

Two other authorities make similar points and give further examples of the kind of writing just mentioned. They describe such writing as "nuclear." In accord with what they refer to as "the current American linguistic terminology," they suggest calling the writing "morphophonemic," in place of which, given the basically syllabic nature of the system, I have suggested the term *morphosyllabic*. To quote further:

> It is possible to summarize the evolution of the graphic system as follows: at first the writing was, so to say, *nuclear*. Only those elements indispensable for identifying the phrase are represented in the writing: all, or almost all, the roots and quite a limited number of affixes. . . .
>
> However, the use of this "nuclear" system cannot be considered evidence of "primitiveness." It is a matter of the free choice of the scribes, since they were able to write syllabically borrowed expressions (e.g., sa-hi-li[SAR] . . .) or names of persons. Obviously, they could have done the same for the other elements of the language. It was doubtless reasons of economy which determined their choice: a full syllabic system would have occupied an excessive amount of space on the clay tablets [Civil and Biggs 1966:12–14].

Perhaps another factor leading to this sort of "nuclear" writing was the limited content of much of early writing and the limited circle of scribes who dealt with it. They did not need to have everything spelled out for them. So it is that "Sumerian in its earlier stages goes further than any other known script in its omission of elements predictable only to the well-informed native reader" (Civil 1973:23).

It is also worth noting that the earliest writing consisted of accounting notes written by bookkeepers. Whether Sumerian or their modern counterparts, such scribes are hardly noted for a concern with the niceties of written expression that become possible only with more subtle graphic representation. When the Sumerians got around to it, they eventually did go in for belles lettres, and in the process they also expanded graphic representation of the phonetic component in their writing system.

Although it does not seem possible to sort out how much of Sumerian under-representation is due to ignorance of the problems involved, and how much is the result of deliberate omission of elements that skilled scribes could do without, the existence of a gap between spoken and written forms of Sumerian is not in the least to be wondered at. All writing systems exibit such a gap, including our own, as Pope notes in his mention of "the rudimentary attempts of our own script to express intonation even though intonation is one of the most important elements of meaning" (Pope 1966:22).

If the Sumerians had actually wanted to close the gap, and simplify the representation of their language, they could have explored alternatives that might have led to the discovery that their symbols could easily be simplified to make a close fit with the spoken language. The spoken language had a relatively simple system of sounds that, as can be demonstrated, were readily adaptable to syllabic representation.

It was earlier believed that the Sumerian language could be analyzed as having 6 vowels and 15 consonants (Kramer 1963:306–307). A later and apparently more generally accepted opinion presents an analysis with 16 consonants but only 4 vowels, namely *a, e, i,* and *u,* which were probably both long and short (Thomsen 1984:38–41). The consonants and vowels combine into syllables which, apart from the single vowels themselves, are generally believed to comprise three types: vowel + consonant (VC), consonant + vowel (CV), and consonant + vowel + consonant (CVC). The third class is the most numerous (Gadd 1924:15). If we accept the most recent analysis of the Sumerian sound system, the number of syllables that could be formed from all the theoretically possible combinations can be estimated as follows:

V	$4 \times 1 = 4$
VC (vowel + consonant)	$4 \times 16 = 64$
CV (consonant + vowel)	$16 \times 4 = 64$
CVC (consonant + vowel + consonant)	$16 \times 4 \times 16 = \underline{1024}$
Total	1156

The total figure of 1,156 distinct syllables is in sharp contrast with the 150,000 theoretically possible syllables estimated for English (Jespersen 1928:9). But English actually uses only 8,000 or so of the vast number of syllables available to it (Jespersen 1928), and it must be supposed that Sumerian also did not use all the combinations at its disposal.

I do not know how many syllables were actually used in Sumerian speech and hence needed to be represented in the writing system. Sumerologists do not appear to have estimated the number for us. However, we do know, according to one authority, that the Sumerians never used more than 1,200 signs—2,000 according to Gelb (1963:115)—and that was in the early Uruk and Jemdet Nasr stages when pictographs were still used extensively. Another authority goes on to state:

Later the character set was gradually reduced by various economizing principles, the pictorial content was gradually removed by various techniques of stylization, and the morphophonemic basis of the writing system was gradually transformed from chiefly logographic to chiefly syllabic [Green 1981:346].

As a result of these developments the writing system gradually became "a vehicle for approximating the spoken language in written form." The increased emphasis on representing actual speech is well summarized in the Sumerian proverb "a scribe whose hand matches the mouth, he is indeed a scribe" (Green 1981:351).

Apart from the relative paucity of spoken syllables and the concomitant need for relatively few symbols to represent them, one of the things that helped the syllabic script to function was the nature of its word roots and their expansion into longer expressions. In contrast to the English internal changes in *sing:sang:sung* and the expansion of the disyllabic root *settle* into *unsettle, settler, settling, settlement*, Sumerian word roots, according to Kramer, were mainly invariant monosyllables to which particles were attached that tended to retain their independent structure (Kramer 1963:306–307).[3] It was thus easier to represent each syllable with its own graphic symbol or syllobogram.

This does not mean that there was ever a one-to-one correspondence between spoken syllable and written symbol. Quite the contrary: some syllables were not represented at all (Gelb 1961:245). Others were represented by more than one syllabogram—23 in the case of *du* (Chiera 1938:63). The same symbol could have different pronunciations (Driver 1976:63). And syllables of the CVC type, the most numerous, were most often represented by a special technique which appeared in several variations in a number of other systems of writing.

This technique, which we might call the "syllable-telescoping" device, in its Sumerian variation involved the merger of two syllables CV and VC sharing a common vowel (Gelb 1963:70–71; Trager 1974: 388; Thomsen 1984:281). The procedure can be formalized and illustrated as follows:

$$C_1V_1 + V_1C_2 = C_1V_1C_2$$
$$da + am = dam$$

This technique could be extended to telescoping three syllables in order to indicate the distinction between syllables with short and long vowels, such as *kir:kîr.* The following examples (taken from Jensen

1969:95) illustrate the application of the technique to both kinds of syllables:

ki + ir = kir   ki + i + ir = kîr

There were, very exceptionally, a few single syllabograms for CVC syllables. Most were represented by combining CV and VC symbols. Apart from the CV, VC, and (rare) CVC signs, there were also syllabograms for the vowels *a, e, i,* and *u.* The inventory was not complete. There were no signs for many *C + e* syllables; these were expressed by the corresponding *C + i* symbols. The commonly used syllabic signs in early Sumerian texts numbered no more than 100 (Falkenstein 1936:34).

If the syllable-telescoping technique had been applied systematically to all the theoretically possible CVC syllables, by far the most abundant syllable-type, it would have been possible to express all of the Sumerian language in a relatively simple manner with only the 132 syllabograms needed to represent the 4 vowels and the theoretically possible 64 consonant + vowel syllables and 64 vowel + consonant syllables. In actual fact, Sumerian writing over time made use of some 150 syllable signs and 600 word signs, varying numbers of which were used by different writers at different times (Gelb 1963:108; Trager 1974:388). These figures tell us that they continued to make use of many nonphonetic symbols.

The features just mentioned occurred in different proportions at different times in the history of Sumerian writing. The same is true of the relative proportions of symbols used for their pictographic values and those used for their phonetic values. The roots of the language tended to be represented by the former, the grammatical elements by the latter. As one writer puts it, "Sumerian writing, as now known, is a combination of pictorial and phonetic writing of which it might be said that, for the most part, the former constitutes the skeleton of the speech, and the latter covers the flesh of grammatical coherence" (Gadd 1924:9).

To illustrate the foregoing points, the word for 'sheep' and some other common terms were usually represented by nonphonetic signs.

They were for the most part never spelled out, except in school texts and similar works. On the other hand, some symbols did double duty as pictures of objects and as purely phonetic symbols. Thus the sign for 'fish' also served as a phonetic symbol for the syllable *ḫa* (Driver 1976: 58). To give a specific example of the two kinds of usage, the word for 'sheep' was usually pictured, but the demonstrative 'that' was spelled out (Gadd 1924:12; Driver 1976:58). Sometimes the same symbol was used at one time for its meaning value, and at another for its sound value.

The Sumerians devised various means to cope with the ambiguity inherent in such diverse use of symbols. One device comprised what are called "determinatives." For example, as noted in the discussion of the previously cited quotation from Falkenstein regarding the symbol transcribed as *giš ti* 'arrow,' the raised prefix *giš* represents a symbol meaning 'wood' that determines the category to which this particular use of *ti* belongs. To give another example, a symbol that might be read either as APIN 'plow' or ENGAR 'plowman' had prefixed to it a sign for 'wood' in the first case and for 'person' in the second to show how the symbol was to be read. There were a dozen or so commonly used determinatives that signaled such categories of things as plants, people, cloth, and stars (Gadd 1924:13; Driver 1976:60).[4]

Another device was the use of "phonetic complements." This consists of attaching a phonetic symbol to an ambiguous sign to give some idea of the sign's pronunciation. As pointed out by a leading writer on techniques of decipherment, English can also be said to make use of such phonetic complements (Barber 1974:23). Thus the letters *nd* are added to the symbol *2* to distinguish between the words "second" and "two."

Phonetic complements were much more complicated and much more extensive in Sumerian. Thus the symbol that basically represented DU 'leg' represented also three related meanings, and three additional pronunciations, namely GUB, GIN, and TÚM, which were distinguished by adding other signs to DU to give a hint of the pronunciation intended, as follows (Falkenstein 1936:34; Driver 1976:61):

$$DU + ba = gub + a \text{ 'to stand'} \ (a \text{ is an affix})$$
$$DU + na = gin + a \text{ 'to go'} \qquad ''$$
$$DU + ma = túm + a \text{ 'to bring'} \qquad ''$$

To non-Sumerians like ourselves these phonetic hints may seem inadequate and impossibly clumsy. They suggest a guessing game at which one must learn to be adept: "Think of a word related to 'leg' that ends in the initial sound of BA." . . . "Why of course, that's GUB 'to stand'." To a learned native scribe, however, it may have been more a matter of memorizing that when the sign for 'leg' was followed by the sign for BA, then the sequence was to be read as GUB-A, and so on for the others.[5]

Since we shall encounter variations on the foregoing techniques in other systems, where they are given a variety of names, I should like at this point to introduce my own terminology for some of them in the interests of uniformity and simplicity. What the Sumerologists call a *determinative* I shall call a *semantic determinative*. What they label a *phonetic complement* I label a *phonetic determinative*. I lump both together as *determinatives*. Any symbol used for its phonetic value I call a *phonetic*. One used for its semantic value I call a *semantic*.

Just how these techniques were manipulated in Sumerian can be illustrated schematically as follows:

$$S \boxed{P?} \qquad P \boxed{S?}$$

The first case illustrates how the ambiguous phonetic symbol *P* (e.g., *ti*) is disambiguated by a semantic determinative (e.g., *giš* 'wood') placed before (or after) the symbol in question. The second illustrates how the ambiguous semantic symbol *S* (e.g., 'foot') is disambiguated by a phonetic determinative (e.g., *ba*) placed before (or after) the symbol in question. Variations on manipulations of phonetics and semantics figure prominently in other "meaning-plus-sound" writing systems, especially Chinese, and are discussed more extensively below.

In the case of Sumerian, the complexities of such mixed symbolization were somewhat eased over time as the result of a slow trend to reduce the number of symbols used for their meaning value and to increase those used for their sound value. There was also a gradual simplification of the syllabograms from their original pictographic forms to highly stylized cuneiform signs. This change, shown in figure 16, accompanied the shift from semantic to phonetic values for the signs.

A sampling of Sumerian texts shows that the syllabograms comprised between 36 and 54 percent of the total (Civil 1973:26). It was,

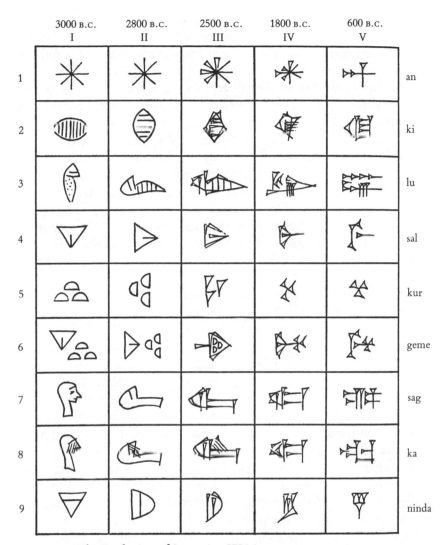

	3000 B.C. I	2800 B.C. II	2500 B.C. III	1800 B.C. IV	600 B.C. V	
1						an
2						ki
3						lu
4						sal
5						kur
6						geme
7						sag
8						ka
9						ninda

Figure 16. The Evolution of Sumerian Writing

The origin and development of nine representative cuneiform signs from about 3000 B.C. to about 600 B.C. The shift from pictographic to stylized forms was accompanied by a shift from semantic to phonetic values for the signs. The latter have been added on the right. The original meanings are as follows: (1) heaven, (2) earth, (3) man, (4) pudendum, (5) mountain, (6) slave girl, (7) head, (8) mouth, (9) food. Reprinted with permission from Samuel N. Kramer, *The Sumerians: Their History, Culture, and Character* (Chicago: University of Chicago Press, 1963), pp. 302–304.

of course, precisely this phonetic part of the writing which, even when it comprised only a lesser fraction of the total, was the indispensable element that enabled the script as a whole to function as a full system of writing.

Although Sumerian writing never evolved, as it might have, into a simple syllabic script of only one to two hundred signs, nevertheless it apparently worked very well as a medium of written communication for the elitist scribes who controlled it. It was used primarily for economic recordkeeping, as indicated by the fact that 95 percent of all Sumerian tablets that have been found were devoted to this purpose. But it was also used to produce a rich and varied literature that included myths, epics, hymns to gods and kings, prayers, incantations, satirical dialogues, debates, proverbs, and collections of letters (Kramer 1961:10–11; Thomsen 1984:30–31). And its influence lasted well beyond the overthrow of the Sumerian political entity by the Akkadians.

These Semitic successors of the Sumerians were by no means newcomers to the area. The two peoples had been in contact with each other even before the first appearance of writing. This is attested by the fact that Sumerian very early had some Semitic words embedded in the language, as for example *silim* 'well-being, peace' (cognate with modern Hebrew *šālôm* and Arabic *salâm* (Gordon 1982:155).

The Akkadians took over the Sumerian writing system and, to begin with, even the language. Mastery of Sumerian in both its spoken and written forms became a major preoccupation of Akkadian scribes (Kramer 1963; Vanstiphout 1979). In time emphasis on the spoken form declined, and the Sumerian language itself became extinct, no later, according to one authority, than the beginning of the second millennium B.C. (Wilhelm 1983:159). Another authority, stating that the Sumerian language probably died out in the last centuries of the third millennium B.C., adds that in the 900 years from ca. 2500 B.C. to ca. 1600 B.C., "Sumerian gradually changed from a spoken language to a literary language only." It was probably no longer spoken in the period from which by far the greatest number of Sumerian texts date (Thomsen 1984:13–15).

The influence of written Sumerian persisted long after the extinction of the spoken language. According to the authority just cited, the writing was still largely mnemonic in character, "since the Sumerian literary tradition was not only scribal, but also oral, and the texts were still a supplement to oral presentation (Thomsen 1984:22–23).

Eventually the cuneiform script was applied also to the Akkadian language. Scribes then had to learn to handle both Sumerian and Akkadian in written form. To meet this need, bilingual teaching aids were developed for use in the *edubba* 'school' where the scribes received their training. These instructional materials consisted chiefly of elaborate lists that included "syllabaries" or "vocabularies." One type of syllabary contained three columns with a symbol in the middle, its Sumerian reading on the left expressed in simple syllabic signs, and its Akkadian reading on the right. A somewhat more elaborate syllabary added the Akkadian translation, often several of these when a Sumerian sign had more than one meaning. This form was also adapted to teaching Sumerian grammar. Still other lists were topically arranged to provide the names of trees, wooden objects, garments, and many other classes of objects. The compilation of bilingual wordlists and the repeated copying of Sumerian and Akkadian texts resulted in the production of the many cuneiform tablets which have been such a boon to modern scholars in their decipherment of early writing systems (Oppenheim 1977:244–249).

Sumerian cuneiform was first applied to the Old Akkadian of the original conquerors. Later it was extended to the Assyrian spoken in the northern part of Mesopotamia and to the Babylonian of the south, as well as to other languages unrelated to Akkadian. As a result various names have been attached to what developed into an exceedingly complicated system of writing.

Although the sound system of Akkadian is somewhat more complicated than that of Sumerian, it is not so much more so as to constitute a major problem in fitting symbols to sounds. Akkadian has 8 vowels and between 20 and 30 consonants and a syllable structure no more complicated than the CV, VC, and CVC of Sumerian (Gelb 1961, 1982; Edzard, personal communication, 5/20/88). Nor does it appear that anything like all the theoretically possible syllables were ever actually used.

The main problem in the written representation of the Akkadian language is not the complexity of the sound system but the insistence of the Akkadian scribes on following slavishly in the footsteps of their Sumerian mentors. They took over both pictographic and syllabic symbols together with the techniques of telescoping CV and VC syllables and adding semantic and phonetic determinatives. Their only major innovation was one that simply made a bad situation even worse. This was adding to the symbols, already burdened with various

Sumerian meanings and their pronunciations, the further burden of the native pronunciations of the Akkadian words equivalent to the Sumerian originals. An example is the Sumerian word *an*, which means

> 1. '*An*, god of the sky,' and in addition 'god' in general; (2. 'to be high'); 3. 'sky.' The Semites used this word 1. as ideographic sign for their god of the sky *Anu*, taken over from the Sumerians, and likewise for 'god' in general, Semitic *ilu*; and also for the concept 'sky,' Semitic *šamû*; 2. as phonetic (syllabic) sign for the syllable *an* (from the Sumerian) and the syllable *il* (from the Semitic) [Jensen 1969:94].[6]

The use by the Akkadians of one and the same symbol to represent the Sumerian syllable *an* and the Akkadian words *Anu*, *ilu*, *šamû*, and *il* is paralleled in other writing systems which adapted alien scripts to their own use. The cuneiform script adapted by the Hittites from Sumero-Akkadian exhibits a similar complex mixture (Moorhouse 1953:65–67). The same is true of the hybrid system developed by the Japanese on the basis of Chinese. The complexity of these hybrid systems will be illustrated in further detail in connection with the discussion of Japanese below.

For all its fiendish complexity, the Akkadian adaptation of the Sumerian system was also able to function as a medium of full communication, since it too had the requisite phonetic base at its disposal. Scholars differ in their assessment of how much use was actually made of the phonetic component over time and from one literary genre to another (Cohen 1958:90; Oppenheim 1977:238–239; Civil 1973:26–27; Wilhelm 1983:159; Kramer 1986:119–120). Their comments on this matter are generally limited to rather summary statements which fall considerably short of what is needed for a clear picture—within a particular writing system and between different scripts—of the relative use of the phonetic and nonphonetic elements that my "Duality Principle" notes are inherent in all full systems of writing.

Some samplings of cuneiform writing suggest that the phonetic component was much higher in the Akkadian system than in that of the Sumerians: 70–96 percent in the former as against 36–54 in the latter (Civil 1973:26). Also it appears that the high figure of 1,200–2,000 signs of all kinds in early Sumerian writing was reduced to some 500–700 in that of the Akkadians, of which 300–350 were used to represent syllabic sounds (Cohen 1958:90; Jensen 1969:90; Driver 1976:67).

These figures, and the preceding discussion, give some suggestion of the flexibility inherent in the cuneiform system. The symbols could be and were adapted to a great variety of languages. In one form or another they served as the main vehicle of written communication in the Near East throughout their long history, which began about 3100 B.C. and ended in the first century A.D.

Chinese

In contrast to Sumerian writing, whose history can be traced to its very beginning, the origins of Chinese writing are obscure and much debated. The earliest form known to us dates from the Shang dynasty (1200–1045 B.C.). By that time the script was already a highly developed system based on principles which have continued to characterize the system to the present.

A major point of contention is, How did the idea of writing come into the minds of the Chinese? There are two opposing views of the matter based on different explanations for the emergence of civilized societies and the existence of specific elements of culture, including writing. One approach stresses "independent invention," the other "stimulus diffusion."

Chinese scholars tend to espouse the first approach. In support of this view a number of writers have attempted to push Chinese writing back before Sumerian by claiming a connection between some symbols of Shang date and those inscribed on pottery several millennia earlier (Chang 1983; Cheung 1983). However, as noted in the previous criticism of scholars who see a connection between Easter Island symbols and those of the Indus Valley, it is methodologically unacceptable to advance as evidence miscellaneous instances of similarity among the necessarily limited number of scratchings that can be made using only two or three lines. There is involved here is a sort of chauvinistic scholarship that seeks to prove an independent invention for Chinese writing by methodologically suspect means.

Exponents of the "stimulus diffusion" approach sometimes use the same dubious methodology to claim that some of the symbols found in China have been copied from earlier ones found in the Near East. Most diffusionists advance a broader and more general argument based on the amount and quality of correspondence between civilizations. They argue that while some simple aspects of culture, such as stone knives and drawings of familiar things, may have been independently invent-

ed by various peoples, more complicated ones like writing must have
had a single origin. In support of this thesis, diffusionists cite evidence
of borrowing of some other specific cultural items to prove the borrowing of the idea of writing. Thus the prominent Near Eastern
scholar Cyrus H. Gordon states that "China heard about casting
bronze from the West; and what impelled China to invent her own
system of writing was diffusion of the idea from the Near East" (Gordon 1971:16).

But here too the methodology is open to question. The borrowing
of one item—if it really is a case of borrowing—does not necessarily
prove the borrowing of another, though to be sure evidence of extensive borrowing is suggestive. Conversely, when instances of alleged
influence are shown to be based on dubious scholarship, this saps con-
fidence in the whole approach. Gordon's overall case for stimulus diffusion is hardly helped by his advancing the claim that "Chinese in
pigtails" (actually found only in the Manchu period, from 1644 to
1911) "are portrayed unmistakably in the art in pre-Columbian Middle America" (Gordon 1971:171).

My own view of the matter is that the arguments for both
approaches are seriously flawed and that at present there is simply not
enough evidence to provide convincing proof for either claim about
the origin of Shang writing. However, while keeping an open mind
on the matter, I feel that the burden of proof rests with the diffusionists. I therefore incline toward the belief that the Chinese independently invented writing, not because there is any proof for this, but
chiefly because I believe that human beings are sufficiently inventive to
have come up with the same idea more than just once.

Moreover, it seems to me that while some of the principles underlying Chinese writing are in fact similar to those underlying Sumerian
writing, in all probability the reason for this is not that one was influenced by the other. The distances in time and space, unlike the Sumerian–Egyptian and Phoenician–Greek situations (discussed in chapters 4
and 5, respectively), militate against such a hypothesis. A more reasonable explanation is that the two peoples independently thought up
somewhat similar solutions to somewhat similar problems. It is underlying principles, not the superficial outward form of symbols, that
should occupy most of our attention.

In approaching an analysis of the Chinese script we encounter quite
a different problem from that of Sumerian. In the case of Sumerian,
the language represented by the writing was completely unknown and

had to be reconstructed from scratch, in part with the help of information provided by peoples such as the Babylonians and Assyrians, who took over both the language and the writing system, applied the latter to their own language, and developed bilingual texts of various kinds. In the case of the Chinese, there is continuity, with gaps that can at least partially be filled in, between the earliest extant writing and that of the present day. And given the considerable amount of archaeological work going on in China and the exciting finds that have been made in recent years, there is hope of being able to fill in more gaps. Chief among these gaps is the huge void that must have contained an earlier stage of writing before the full-grown system emerged on the scene during the Shang dynasty.

Our knowledge of what is so far the earliest known Chinese writing is less than a hundred years old. Toward the end of the last century peasants working their fields in the district of Anyang, located in the northern part of Honan province a bit north of the Yellow River, turned up fragments of bone, some of which bore markings that Chinese scholars recognized as characters of an older form than any yet known. Owing to the turmoil attending the collapse of the imperial regime in 1911, it was several decades before scientific excavations could be conducted in the area. In the meantime large numbers of inscribed bone fragments found their way into the hands of scattered Chinese and foreign scholars. Scientific excavations began in 1928, were interrupted by the Sino-Japanese war of 1937–1945, and were resumed on a larger scale after the establishment of the People's Republic of China in 1949.

The result of all this activity has been the unearthing of over 100,000 inscriptions, many of them of a fragmentary nature, on pottery, stone, bronze, and, most important of all, bones and shells. The earliest date from about 1200 B.C. This was during the hitherto somewhat shadowy Shang dynasty that was overthrown in the middle of the eleventh century B.C. by conquerors who established the long-lived Zhou dynasty (1045–221 B.C.). The Zhou dynasty, in its middle course, produced the flourishing literate culture of which Confucius is an outstanding exemplar.

The extension of our knowledge of Chinese civilization back from Zhou to Shang owes much to the inscriptions found on bones and shells. Inscriptions on other materials tell us little, since they are in general restricted to a few characters. Thus the second most important group, those on bronze vessels, consist in part of so-called "clan-name" inscriptions. These are pictographs often encased in a sort of rectangular cartouche that is reminiscent of those found in Egyptian hieroglyphic inscriptions containing the names of royal personages. Some bronze vessels have slightly more extended inscriptions specifying who made the vessel and for whom it was made (Boltz 1986).

In contrast, the inscriptions on bones and shells are much more informative. This is due only in part to their somewhat greater length, for most of the texts are less than 15 characters in length, and very few exceed 50 characters (Mickel 1986:256). The nature of the inscriptions and how they came to be written provide most of the information.

The Shang people wrote on bones and shells for purposes of divination. Through their priests, who were scribes and had the power to communicate with their ancestors and their gods, they sought oracular advice on all sorts of matters, from the most serious affairs of state to lesser problems such as what to do about toothaches and how to interpret dreams. In this the Shang were like people today who run their lives by consulting astrologers, ouija boards, or other sources of spiritualistic "guidance." The Shang divination texts are known as "oracle bone inscriptions" (OBI).

The texts were written on the large shoulder bones of cattle and the shells of turtles. These were much prized. Some nondivination texts record the receipt of these valuable items. However, unlike the extensive accountancy of the Sumerian temple scribes, there are only a few Shang inscriptions of this sort.

The bones and shells, especially the latter, were prepared by being smoothed to a high polish and were stored until brought out for the divination ceremony. The diviner asked a question, such as "Shall an army of five thousand men be raised?" or "Will it rain?" Then heat was applied to the back of the bone or shell, causing cracks to appear on the face. The cracks were interpreted by the diviner, or perhaps even by the king himself. Finally a record of the whole matter, including the follow-up on the final outcome, was incised, or sometimes written with a brush, on the bone or shell.

It is of interest to note that at this early stage the characters were not yet standardized as to shape and size. It was only later that they came to occupy the uniform square space that has earned them the Chinese name of *fāngkuàizì* 'square block characters,' which one Western scholar has rendered as 'tetragraphs' (Mair 1988). Moroever, in the early inscriptions there was no fixed direction of writing. The sequence of characters varied from left to right, right to left, top to bottom, and various mixtures of direction within the same inscription and even within the same sentence (Serruys 1974:16). When we add to this the fragmentary nature of many of the bones and shells, it goes without saying that the interpretation of the inscriptions is a highly complicated and controversial matter.

A full inscription consists of four parts: (1) a preface stating that on such-and-such a day a bone or shell was cracked and that So-and-so divined; (2) a "charge" asking a question; (3) the prognostication; and (4) the verification, telling what actually happened. Few inscriptions contain all four parts. The dating of the inscriptions is also generally limited to the specification of a day within a chronological system containing a cycle of sixty days. From this information, the naming of the diviner, and other clues, it is sometimes possible to achieve a more precise dating, as in the case of some solar-eclipse inscriptions during the reign of King Wu Ding (1200–1181 B.C.) (Keightley 1978:174).

A full oracle bone inscription dating from the same period is of particular interest because it reveals the existence, as early as the second millennium B.C., of concerns that are still very much in evidence in Chinese society. The inscription deals with the pregnancy of King Wu Ding's consort, Wife Hao. The preface states that on day 21 a shell was cracked and a certain Ge divined. The charge notes that Wife Hao was to give birth and asks: "Will it be a happy event?" The prognostication was undertaken by the king himself. Reading the cracks, he said that if the birth occurred on one of certain specified days, it would be a happy event; if it happened on any of some other specified days, it would be "hugely auspicious"; but if it occurred on another specified day, it would not be good. Three weeks and one day later came the verification telling what had actually happened: "The birthing was not a happy event. It was a girl" (Keightley 1978:41; Mickel 1986:255).

Shang divination practices of the sort just described are attested for a period of only about a century and a half, that is until the overthrow of the dynasty in 1045 B.C. The Zhou successors did not take over the Shang practice of divining by the use of bones and shells, but they did continue the practice of inscribing on bronze. The earliest identifiable Zhou text is on a bronze vessel with an inscription stating that it was commissioned only eight days after the Zhou victory over the Shang. It is typical of a large number of vessels cast during the early Zhou period that contained texts stating the date, discussing the meritorious deed which led to the casting of the vessel, noting the generosity of the ruler as represented by the gift of metal, and expressing the desire that future generations take note and use the vessel. Some of the inscriptions are quite long. One that can be precisely dated as incised in the reign of a Zhou king who ruled from 946 to 935 B.C. contains 284 characters. The practice of incising inscriptions on bronze vessels continued for close to a thousand years, until the early Han period (206 B.C.–9 A.D.) (Mickel 1986:295).

Important as these inscriptions were, they were overshadowed by Zhou texts written with a brush on bamboo, wood, and silk, and carved on stone and other hard substances. These materials were the basis of the extensive literary remains that survive from before the invention of paper in the second century A.D. Following that there was a considerable increase in output, particularly after the invention first of block-printing about 600 A.D. and then, well before Gutenberg, of printing from movable type. This resulted in a veritable explosion of publications. The total Chinese output prior to the nineteenth century may have exceeded that of the rest of the world combined.

These developments occurred over a long period, more than three thousand years, and in a huge area populated by people who commanded various forms of speech that have conventionally been grouped together as "Chinese." This term is an umbrella designation for at least eight present-day varieties of what are usually called "dialects" but, since they are mutually unintelligible, might better be considered parallel to the various languages that make up the Romance group of languages. The main varieties are Mandarin (750 million speakers), Wu or Shanghainese (85 million speakers), and Cantonese (50 million speakers). Even these terms are imprecise, as emphasized in a study entitled *The Four Languages of "Mandarin"* which notes that "Mandarin" is itself an umbrella term for "Idealized Mandarin" (*Putonghua* 'Common Speech' or *Guoyu* 'National Language'), "Imperial Mandarin" (the largely uncodified language spoken by the scholar-official class in imperial China), "Geographical Mandarin" (the invention of twentieth-century linguists, created in an effort to delineate the language of a particular area sharing certain common phonological traits), and "Local Mandarin" (every locale, because of its unique linguistic composition, treated as an independent speech community) (Sanders 1987).

In earlier times most literature was produced in a style loosely called "classical Chinese" that was written by people who spoke some form of language ancestral to the varieties of current "Chinese" noted above. Such literature was also produced by many people who were not even native speakers of Chinese, but who adopted the system for want of a script of their own.

The classical Chinese literature written by people with such diverse linguistic backgrounds had about the same status as Latin in the Romance situation. In modern times the primary emphasis in writing has been on a style based more or less on speech, chiefly Mandarin but to some extent also other varieties, notably Shanghainese and Cantonese. Just as these varieties of speech are mutually unintelligible, so are the varieties of written language based on them. It is a widespread myth that Chinese characters cut across boundaries of speech. This is no more true than the claim of universality for the Latin alphabet. It is necessary to learn the concrete application of the symbols to each specific form of speech. Since the version of Mandarin that is officially called Putonghua or Common Speech is the standard language in China, the writing system based on it is also the written standard. But it takes more effort for a Cantonese to learn to read and write in the national standard than it does for a Spaniard to learn to read and write French (DeFrancis 1984a).

The realities of speech and writing in China that are obscured by the myth of the universality of Chinese characters and by the ambiguity of the umbrella term "Chinese" should be kept in mind in considering the evolution of Chinese writing. There has been continuity as well as change in this long period. Characters have been created by speakers of many different varieties of Chinese and often reflect the peculiarities of their speech. There have been historical changes in word order, and the characters have been shuffled around to adapt to these changes. Characters have died out as the words that they represented have become obsolete. New characters and new combinations of characters have been created to express new words that have entered into the vocabulary. In common with all writing systems with a long history, the pronunciation of the symbols has changed greatly over time, as is readily apparent in a recently published dictionary of Early Zhou Chinese (Schuessler 1987).

The forms or shapes of the characters have also undergone change. On the oracle bones many characters are clear pictographs. Their modern descendants have been so stylized, abbreviated, distorted, and otherwise modified that it is often difficult to see the relationship with the ancestral character, as can be illustrated by the following example (from DeFrancis 1984a:83) showing the loss of iconicity in the evolution of the character for *mǎ* 'horse':

Shang	Great Seal	Small Seal	Scribal	Regular	Simplified

The styles illustrated are those of the Shang oracle bones, the Great Seal style of the Zhou dynasty, the Small Seal style of the short-lived Qin dynasty (221–206 B.C.), and the Scribal and Regular styles of the Han dynasty (206 B.C.–220 A.D.), the last being the most commonly used script until the official simplification of characters in the PRC in the 1950s. Figure 17 compares the OBI and modern forms of a number of characters.

As the examples presented in the illustration suggest, the task of deciphering Shang characters, of which some 1,000 out of a total of 4,500 have been identified to date, is facilitated by the fact that in many cases it is possible to trace the evolution of a character from its Shang to its contemporary form. There are many instances, however, of "descendantless" graphs. These constitute a problem in decipherment. Some descendantless characters appear to be completely unrelated to any modern symbols. Others are complex characters whose component elements have modern counterparts but are not now combined in the same way as in the Shang graphs.

This mention of the component elements in Chinese characters and how they are combined raises the crucial question of the principles behind the Chinese system of writing. To obtain a clear understanding of this system it is essential that we recognize what the principles are and—a much neglected aspect—how they were applied in different proportions over time.

It has been the traditional practice to classify Chinese characters into several groups. The first group, about which there is general agreement, consists of pictographs. As we have already seen, many of the earliest characters, as represented on the OBIs, are clearly pictographic in nature.

What might be called the "simple indicative principle" identifies a second group of characters which represent words not exactly pictorially but in some other representational manner. For example, the words for "one," "two," and "three" are respectively represented by one, two, and three horizontal lines:

	OBI graph	modern character	modern reading	meaning
1.		象	xiàng	'elephant'
2.		求	qiú	'pelt' (mod. 裘)
3.		口	kǒu	'opening, orifice, mouth'
4.		目	mù	'eye'
5.		月	yuè	'moon, month'
6.		田	tián	'(cultivated) field'
7.		女	nǚ	'(kneeling) woman'
8.		其	qí	'(winnowing) basket' (mod. 箕)
9.		天	tiān	'overhead' > 'sky, heaven'
10.		羊	yáng	'sheep, ram'
11.		馬	mǎ	'horse'
12.		龜	quī	'turtle'
13.		魚	yú	'fish'
14.		鼎	dǐng	'tripod, cauldron'

Figure 17. Chinese Writing: A 1% Pictographic Script
The evolution of fourteen Chinese characters representative of the mere one percent that go back to pictographs, chiefly those found on oracle bone inscriptions (OBI) of around 1200–1045 B.C. All but two—12 and 14, the most complicated—have been used as phonetic symbols in the formation of multielement characters. Adapted with permission from William G. Boltz, "Early Chinese Writing." *World Archaeology* 17 (3) (1986):427.

	1	2	3
Shang	一	二	三
Modern	一	二	三

The words for "above" and "below" are represented by a horizontal line with another graphic element placed above or below it:

above   below

Shang   二   二

Modern   上   下

What might be called the "compound indicative principle" involves a somewhat more elaborate version of the preceding. It is frequently illustrated by the combination of the characters for "sun" and "moon" to represent the word *míng* 'bright,' as follows:

sun   moon   bright

日   月   明

The fourth principle is the familiar rebus device which we first encountered in Sumerian with the use of *gi* 'reed' borrowed to represent the homophonous word *gi* 'reimburse.' A Chinese example is the borrowing of a character representing *xiàng* 'elephant' to represent the homophonous word *xiàng* 'image.'

The final principle is one which combines a rebus-like symbol with another symbol giving, generally, a semantic clue to the meaning. One example is the addition (on the left) of the symbol for 'person' to that (on the right) for *xiàng* 'elephant' to produce an unambiguous character *xiàng* 'image':

亻 + 象 = 像

Another example is the previously cited character for *mā* 'mother' formed by combining the character for *mǎ* 'horse' (on the right) with another for 'female' (on the left):

女 + 馬 = 媽

I call this the SP principle, since it involves joining a semantic element S—such as the symbols for 'person' and 'female' in the previous examples—to a phonetic element P—such as the symbols for *xiàng* 'elephant' and *mǎ* 'horse.' I also designate as SP characters those, to be discussed below, that are formed by joining a phonetic element P to a semantic element S. We can think of both of these types as MS (meaning-plus-sound) characters.

The proportions in which the foregoing principles have been applied in the formation of Chinese characters have varied over time. This can be seen in the following table (adapted from DeFrancis 1984a:84) summarizing the structural classification of 977 Shang characters, 9,353 characters of a second-century dictionary by Xu Shen, and 48,641 characters of the great imperial Kang Xi dictionary of the eighteenth century:

Structural Classification of Characters

Principle	Shang Dynasty	2nd century	18th century
Pictographic	227 (23%)	364 (4%)	
Simple indicative	20 (2%)	125 (1%)	± 1,500 (3%)
Compound indicative	396 (41%)	1,167 (13%)	
Semantic-phonetic	334 (34%)	7,697 (82%)	47,141 (97%)
Total	977	9,353	48,641

The traditional view of Chinese characters summarized above has been challenged in some important respects by Peter A. Boodberg, a leading student of early Chinese writing whose views are receiving more and more acceptance since they were propounded several decades ago (Boodberg 1937, 1940, 1957). His criticisms center on two main points. The first is the failure of many people, sinologists included, to realize the importance of SP characters because of neglecting or minimizing the phonetic contribution of the P element and exaggerating the semantic contribution of the the S element. The second extends Boodberg's criticism of underestimating the significance of the phonetic element by dealing especially with those characters traditionally classified under the "compound indicative principle."

The majority of these characters, Boodberg contends, are in reality SP characters. Indeed, he goes so far as to claim that apart from "a few exceptional cases" there is simply no such thing as a class of characters constructed on semantic principles (1937:345–347). This view has recently been reiterated by another scholar, William G. Boltz, who has also done significant work on early Chinese writing. He asserts:

"Characters were not invented by just putting together two or more elements based on their semantic values alone. At least of one of the components must have had a phonetic function" (Boltz 1986:428).

Boodberg's "few exceptional cases" include chiefly single characters of clearly pictographic origin. There are at most only a few hundred of these, and the number has not increased for some two millennia. These simple characters of pictographic origin, examples of which appear in figure 17, comprise only about one percent of the total number of Chinese characters. The remaining 99 percent, examples of which are presented in figure 18, are compound characters whose main component is a phonetic element.

As an example of the need to rethink characters allegedly based on semantic principles, Boodberg cites the case of the previously mentioned character for *míng* 'bright.' He rejects the traditional approach which begins with a disembodied concept supposedly represented by a character formed by combining the symbols for "sun" and "moon." Instead he starts by assuming definite spoken words related to the meaning "bright." This leads him to note the existence of an earlier form of the character for *míng* 'bright' (Morohashi 1955–1960, 5:14, 366) that I present below in juxtaposition with the later version:

朙　明

In both cases the element 'moon' on the right-hand side of the characters is a semantic determinative. The element on the left-hand side of the first character is originally a picture of a window, with a pronunciation related to *míng*. In short, the present character representing *míng* 'bright' is simply a later variant with what is usually taken as a semantic "sun"—which has caused us to overlook an earlier version with a phonetic *míng* element that more closely relates the character to a spoken word (Boodberg 1937:344–345; 1940:270–274).

Boodberg also cites the case of the following two characters:

目　見

In modern transcription, the first character is *mù* 'eye,' the second *jiàn* 'see.' But the first was also used to write the related word 'see.' Hence it represented two related meanings and had two quite different pronunciations, which have become modern *mù* 'eye' and *jiàn* 'see.' In order to distinguish the two meanings, the 'eye' character was supplemented with a phonetic determinative, the bottom part of the second character, whose earlier pronunciation *ńźiĕn* provided a better phonetic clue than the modern pronunciation *rén* (Boodberg 1937:343).

In presenting these and other cases Boodberg stresses an aspect of Chinese writing that we have already encountered in Sumerian. That is the fact that many sounds are represented by more than one symbol (recall the 23 for Sumerian *du*) and that the same symbol may represent several different words (recall the different words represented by the pronunciations *gub, gin, tŭm* for the same symbol with the basic meaning 'leg'). Chinese words are also often written with different characters, and the same character may be read in several different ways. It is a major challenge to modern scholarship to unravel the interconnections that have grown up among Chinese characters in the several millennia that they have been handled and mishandled by millions of scholars with widely different backgrounds in the many varieties of spoken and written Chinese.

Because of his emphasis on relating writing to speech, Boodberg presents a clearer analysis of the evolution of Chinese writing than that suggested by the conventional listing of its underlying principles. It is summarized in even simpler terms by Boltz as a three-stage development: (1) a pictographic stage, which in its pure form could write only the limited part of the language that was clearly picturable; (2) a multivalent stage, which included the use of the rebus principle whereby the same symbol might stand for unrelated homophonous words, and the use of the same character to represent words semantically related but with different pronunciations; and (3) a stage in which the ambiguity that grew up with the multivalent use of characters was resolved by resort to semantic and phonetic determinatives, as in the case of Near Eastern writing (Boltz 1986). The following examples illustrate these stages:

Stage	A xiàng 'elephant'	A xiàng 'image'	B mù 'eye'	B jiàn 'see'
Pictographic	𢓃/象	(none)	⬭/目	(none)
Rebus	象	象	目	目
Determinative (A. Semantic) (B. Phonetic)	象	像	目	見

Syllabary	75 皇 huáng	158 辟 pì	255 馬 mǎ	391 堯 yáo
Derivatives	喤 huáng	僻 pì	瑪 mǎ	嶢 yáo
	徨 huáng	譬 pì	碼 mǎ	顤 yǎo
	惶 huáng	鬪 pì	螞 mǎ	僥 jiāo
	湟 huáng	擘 pì	鎷 mǎ	澆 jiāo
	煌 huáng	避 pì	媽 mǎ	翹 qiáo
	鰉 huáng	壁 pì	犕 mà	磽 qiáo
	蝗 huáng	璧 pì	禡 mà	嶢 qiāo
	鍠 huáng	劈 pì	罵 mà	嘵 xiāo
	隍 huáng	癖 pǐ	獁 mà	驍 xiāo
	遑 huáng	臂 pèi	嗎 ma	曉 xiāo
	篁 huáng	擘 pò		燒 shāo
	凰 huáng	孽 niè		譊 náo
	堭 huáng			橈 náo
	艎 huáng			鐃 náo
				撓 nǎo
				髟堯 nào
				嬈 ráo
				蕘 ráo
				蟯 ráo
				饒 ráo
				繞 rào
				遶 rào

Figure 18. Chinese Writing: A 100% Syllabic Script

Examples of Chinese characters, which always represent syllables, showing their derivation (except for the 1% noted in Figure 17) from two elements—a primary pho-

453 莫 mò	511 利 lì	635 門 mén	784 中 zhōng	822 黃 huáng
漠 mò	俐 lì	鍆 mén	鍾 zhōng	潢 huáng
膜 mò	唎 lì	捫 mēn	仲 zhòng	璜 huáng
寞 mò	涮 lì	悶 mèn	妊 zhōng	磺 huáng
摹 mò	痢 lì	們 men	忠 zhōng	蟥 huáng
鄚 mò	箌 lì	閩 mín	盅 zhōng	簧 huáng
嫫 mò	莉 lì	閔 wén	衷 zhōng	黐 huáng
鏌 mò	鵹 lì	聞 wén	神 zhǒng	黀 huáng
煤 mò	鶆 lì	問 wèn	夌 zhòng	廣 huáng
瘼 mò	悧 lì	閃 shǎn	蚛 zhòng	廣 kuǎng
驀 mò	梨 lí	閑 xián	鴫 zhòng	橫 héng
貘 mò	鬎 lì	閂 shuān	沖 chōng	
鬃 mò	蜊 lí	關 guān	忡 chōng	
摸 mō	犁 lí		沖 chōng	
謨 mó	猁 lí		宔 chōng	
模 mó	莉 lǐ		笰 chōng	
糢 mó	砅 lé		翀 chōng	
暮 mú	剺 lé		苩 chōng	
墓 mù	颲 lè		种 chóng	
慕 mù	詈 lián		屾 nōng	
募 mù	剳 qián		馽 zhí	
幕 mù				
蟆 má				

netic element (i.e., one of the 895 syllabic elements in the "Soothill Syllabary"), and an added semantic element (i.e., one of the 214 elements traditionally called radicals or keys).

Note that in column A a semantic determinative, a variant of the symbol for 'person,' is added to the phonetic base *xiàng* to distinguish the meaning 'image.' In column B a phonetic determinative, another variant of the symbol for 'person,' is added to the semantic base *mù* 'eye' to distinguish the meaning 'see.' Both types are SP characters. Note also that the three stages should not be viewed as chronologically distinct. They define the stage of an individual character as determined by its function.

It is useful now to take a closer look at the preponderant category of characters of the determinative stage. Particularly illuminating is a comparison of Chinese and Sumerian in their approaches to an essentially similar problem of coping with the ambiguity inherent in writing systems in which one word might be written many different ways and one graph might be read many different ways. We can schematize the Sumerian and Chinese approaches as follows:

Sumerian　　S $\boxed{\text{P?}}$　　　P $\boxed{\text{S?}}$

Chinese　　　　$\boxed{\text{SP?}}$　　　　$\boxed{\text{PS?}}$

The Sumerian examples have already been discussed in the preceding section. It was explained there that an ambiguous phonetic symbol (P?) is disambiguated by adding a semantic determinative (S), and an ambiguous semantic symbol (S?) is disambiguated by adding a phonetic determinative (P). Chinese does exactly the same thing, but it developed a variation that has had a profound influence on how the characters have been viewed. That variation is to weld the determinative, whether semantic or phonetic, with the ambiguous element to form a tightly knit symbol that is rigidly confined within its own square space of exactly the same size as that for every other character, regardless of simplicity or complexity.

With his usual perspicuity, Boodberg notes this important difference between Chinese and Sumerian (and Egyptian also) in the following passage:

> Egyptian and cuneiform, where the use of semantic determinatives remained optional and the determinatives themselves detachable from the graphs they determined, moved on apace toward phonetization. In Chinese, the determinatives, semantic or phonetic, were welded securely to their graphs so as to form one single graphic body; diagram-

matic structure became thus the dominant type of character building. This may have been caused by a more pronounced homophony of the Chinese vocabulary, but it must have also been influenced by an aesthetic imperative in the Chinese which prompted them, apparently quite early in the development of the script, to enforce the principle of EQUIDIMENSIONALISM. . . . of the graphs [Boodberg 1957:115].

With respect to the two kinds of SP characters, namely those formed by adding an S to a P or a P to an S, which kind is more important? On this there has been considerable disagreement among specialists in Chinese. Earlier scholars, and a few still today, consider that the complex characters of this category were formed chiefly by adding a phonetic determinative to a semantic base. The popular names given to the semantic element reflect this view. It is frequently referred to as a "radical," sometimes as a "key," the latter being used especially in connection with its function as the unit (comparable to our *abc . . . xyz*) for filing characters in a dictionary. The semantic element is considerably less often called a "signific" or "determinative."

Noel Barnard, who has done some of the most important research on this aspect of Chinese, is firmly of the opinion that the phonetic element is the real core of compound characters. For the most part semantic elements were added to phonetic elements, not the other way around (Barnard 1978). This is the prevailing view among most specialists today. I hold strongly to this opinion also.

Leaving aside the matter of priority, it should be noted that the result of adding an S to a P is essentially the same as that of adding a P to an S. That is to say, PS = SP. The order in which the two elements merged is now largely of only historical interest. And the location within a character (e.g., left side versus right side) is also of secondary importance.

If almost all characters are of the SP variety, and if most of these were formed by adding a semantic to a phonetic, then we need to take a closer look at just how the combination was effected. Part of the task is easy. It has been the tradition, as illustrated in the Kang Xi Dictionary, to identify exactly 214 key semantic elements. Until the PRC simplification of the 1950s, all characters were analyzed, sometimes quite arbitrarily, as having one of these 214 keys, and they were listed in dictionaries under the appropriate key. However, there is a good deal of artificiality and arbitrariness in all this, as is indicated by the fact that the first Chinese dictionary, of the second century B.C., listed characters under 540 keys, while the most recent PRC dictionaries have variously classified them under 186, 191, 225, 226, and 250 keys.

What of the phonetic elements? The Chinese have in general paid much less attention to this aspect, though some philologists have compiled rhyming dictionaries based on the sounds of the characters. Some scholars, including some foreign pathbreakers like Bernhard Karlgren, have made good use of the phonetic elements in reconstructing the pronunciation of earlier stages of Chinese. A few have also attempted to use the phonetic elements in teaching. Two well known examples of pedagogical use are works by Wieger (1965) and Soothill (1942) that classify characters under 850–900 phonetics based on Mandarin pronunciations.

An extremely useful, if somewhat flawed, study was published in 1814 by the missionary-scholar Joshua Marshman, who analyzed the characters in the eighteenth-century Kang Xi dictionary. He excluded from consideration more than a third of the characters on various grounds, such as their being mere stylistic variants or lacking explanations. This left him with about 25,000 characters that can more or less be viewed as the total unabridged lexicon of Chinese over the past two millennia. Removing from each character what he called its "Element," that is, the semantic element or key under which the character was classified, he arrived at a figure of 3,867 residual components, which he called "Primitives." He concluded that all characters, apart from the few hundred consisting only of a single component, are formed by combining one of the 214 elements with one of the 3,867 primitives. He referred to the combinations thus formed as "Derivatives."

By his use of the term *primitives* we can conclude that Marshman correctly assigned the primary role to this category of components that enter into the composition of Chinese characters. At the same time, however, he was so firmly convinced that the primitives "convey a general idea" that he failed to appreciate the significance of the fact (which he himself pointed out) that, for example, 11 of the 16 derivatives (actually there are more) formed with a primitive *lì* had exactly the same pronunciation, and all but one had the same initial. Despite his myopia regarding the precise function of the primitives, which was of course chiefly phonetic, his work remains valuable, for it shows that Chinese characters are not all idiosyncratic entities like, as is frequently alleged, our numerals 1, 2, 3.

All Chinese characters, or at least all the characters one is likely to encounter in reading a text written within the past two millennia or so, and excluding a few of direct pictographic origin, are actually combinations of some 200 semantics and 4,000 phonetics. These numbers are large, but they are not open-ended, and above all they are finite enough to make the Chinese system manageable. It works because the phonetic elements are syllabograms that comprise a sort of syllabary. It is, to be sure, an outsized, haphazard, inefficient, and only partially reliable syllabary. Nevertheless it works, as is apparent from the examples given in figure 18.

Perhaps it will help to visualize the structure of Chinese characters if we imagine a huge "Semantic-plus-Phonetic Matrix" composed by listing the 214 semantics on the left and the 3,867 phonetics across the top. Of course not all semantics combine with all phonetics, so that of the over 800,000 cells contained in our matrix, only some 25,000 would be occupied by the derivatives that Marshman selected for study from the Kang Xi dictionary. We can also imagine a smaller matrix based on Soothill's classification of 4,300 of the more frequently used characters (approximately the number needed for full literacy) under 895 phonetics, combined of course with the usual 214 semantics. We extract from the imagined overarching matrix a few examples (from DeFrancis 1984a:106) of cells filled by derivatives that are actually formed by combining one of the 3,867 phonetics with one of the 214 semantics. The numbering system follows that of what might be called the "Soothill Syllabary" of 895 phonetics that is contained within the "Marshman Syllabary" of 3,867 phonetics.

Semantic-plus-Phonetic Matrix

semantic	Phonetic 264 敖 (*áo*)	Phonetic 282 參 (*cān*)	Phonetic 391 堯 (*yáo*)	Phonetic 597 甫 (*fŭ*)
9 亻 'person'	傲 (*ào:* 'proud')	傪 (*cān:* 'good')	僥 (*jiǎo:* 'lucky')	俌 (*fŭ:* 'help')
64 扌 'hand'	㩧 (*ào:* 'shake')	摻 (*shán:* 'seize')	撓 (*náo:* 'scratch')	捕 (*bŭ:* 'catch')
75 木 'wood'	檄 (*áo:* 'barge')	槮 (*shēn:* 'beam')	橈 (*náo:* 'oar')	楠 (*fú:* 'trellis')
85 氵 'water'	潀 (*ào:* 'stream')	渗 (*shèn:* 'leak')	澆 (*jiāo:* 'sprinkle')	浦 (*pŭ:* 'creek')

As can be seen by reading across the rows, in many but not all cases the semantic element on the left provides a sort of thesaurus-like clue to the meaning of the items on the right. All those to the right of no. 85, for example, have something to do with water. The phonetics noted at the top of the chart appear to give some clues to the pronunciation of the characters of which they form a part. Although the clues vary in the degree to which they suggest the pronunciation of the full characters, overall they are far more specific than the semantic clues.

Some phonetics are more productive of derivatives than others—from as few as two or three to as many as almost two dozen. In figure 18 the *lì* phonetic (no. 511) and the *zhōng* phonetic (no. 784) both occur as a component in 20 characters. *Yāo* (no. 391) and *mò* (no. 453) each has 22 derivatives. The phonetics are more likely to be evident in less frequently used characters, as attested by the fact that they enter into an average of 6.5 characters in the Kang Xi list of 25,000 characters but only about 5.0 in the Soothill selection of 4,300. The lower ratio in the latter shows the effect of attrition in more frequently used characters, where the original structure of the graphs has often become so distorted as not to be readily recognizable.

Some semantics also occur more frequently than others in compound characters. The "vegetation" semantic occurs in hundreds of characters. The "step forward" semantic occurs in 17 derivatives, all but two or three of which are quite rare.

The illustration in the matrix of the way semantics and phonetics combine to form new characters in Chinese can be used to expand on the important difference between Sumerian and Chinese mentioned earlier. If Chinese combined the two elements along the same lines as Sumerian, the two characters for *ào* 'proud' and *ào* 'stream' might appear as on the left below instead of as they actually do on the right:

亻敖   傲   *ào* 'proud'

vs.

氵敖   潋   *ào* 'stream'

The detachability of the semantic elements for 'person' and 'water' in the characters to the left would incline us to view these characters rather differently from those on the right. We would surely pay as much if not more attention to the phonetic elements like *ào* than to the determinatives and would view them all as separate entities. In counting symbols we would therefore most likely say that the virtually unabridged historical lexicon based on the Kang Xi dictionary has

3867 + 214 = 4081 different symbols instead of the astronomical 25,000 that we see in the more closely-knit derived characters. Similarly, the abridged modern selection presented by Soothill might be said to comprise 895 + 214 = 1109 different symbols instead of the 4,300 obtained by combining semantics and phonetics.

Another point we have to consider is this: Just how useful are these semantic and phonetic elements? The former, it is clear, can at best suggest only a general semantic area. Thus we know that characters containing semantic no. 85 most likely have something to do with water, and those containing semantic no. 140 with vegetation. In fact the so-called semantic in many characters does not provide even this limited amount of information. They often offer no real semantic information at all and merely serve to differentiate one character from another, as do our spelling distinctions in *hair* and *hare*.

There is a wide range in the usefulness of the phonetic elements. We can distinguish four degrees of correspondence between a phonetic and the derivative of which it forms part:

1. In some cases the phonetic tells us with 100 percent accuracy the pronunciation, even as to tone, of the full character of which it forms part. So phonetic no. 74, *huáng* (see figure 18), indicates exactly the pronunciation of the 14 derivatives of which it forms part. An example is one in which it combines with the semantic key no. 142, 'insect,' to form the first part of the two-syllable word *huángchóng* 'locust':

key	phonetic	derivative
虫	皇	蝗
insect	*huáng*	*huáng*

2. Some phonetics indicate the pronunciation of the derivative character except possibly for tone. Phonetic no. 255, *mǎ*, is such a phonetic in 10 derivatives. One example is the character for the word *mā* 'mother,' in which, as already noted, it represents the pronunciation with complete accuracy except for tone:

key	phonetic	derivative
女	馬	媽
female	*mǎ*	*mā*

3. Some phonetics indicate only part of the sounds which comprise the syllable represented by the derivative. Usually it is the final, the major component of a syllable, that is represented. Thus phonetic no. 391, *yāo*, enters into 22 derivatives variously read as *yáo, yǎo, jiǎo, jiāo, qiāo, qiáo, xiǎo, xiāo, náo, nǎo, nào, ráo, rào, shāo*. One example is the character for *jiāo* 'to sprinkle' composed of this phonetic and the 'water' determinative as its key:

key	phonetic	derivative
氵	堯	澆
water	*yāo*	*jiāo*

4. Some so-called phonetics provide no useful phonetic clue. This is sometimes due to the mistaken analysis and classification of characters by dictionary makers, including Soothill, but perhaps even more, as Ramsey reminds us (personal communication, 5/26/88), to the extensive phonological changes that have taken place during the long stretch of time over which the series was built. Sound changes of various kinds have obscured some of the homophony or near-homophony that once existed.

An example of a useless phonetic appears in the character *xià* 'below.' Its actual etymology, as mentioned earlier, goes back to a simple indicative graph consisting of a dot or dash below a horizontal line. The modern character is mechanically analyzed by Soothill, whose popular and convenient work I largely follow despite some points of disagreement, as a derivative made up by combining key no. 1 'one,' under which it is customarily classified, and phonetic no. 119 *bǔ* 'to divine':

key	phonetic	derivative
一	卜	下
one	*bǔ*	*xià*

Clearly *bǔ* is completely useless as a phonetic for *xià*.

A somewhat different group of characters in this category consists of those which some specialists in Chinese, though not ordinary readers, might be able to identify as having useful phonetics. A case in point is the last character, *guān* 'gate,' which Soothill places under phonetic no. 635 *mén* (see figure 18). Specialists like Karlgren (1940: 187) may be able to correct Soothill's misplacement of this character under the phonetic *mén* by noting that it is a derivative made up by combining elements which include key no. 169 'door' and a rare phonetic (the bottom part of the character) which had the early pronunciation *kwan:*

	key	phonetic	derivative
Soothill	門		
	門	*mén*	鬧
Karlgren	屮		
	door	*kwan*	*guān*

The potential utility of phonetics in this last group of characters is not reflected in figure 18, which is mainly limited to examples of the first three groups of characters.

There is ample evidence that while what we might call the "spelling" of derived characters indicated by the phonetic element is not a completely reliable guide to pronunciation, any more than is the case with English spelling, nevertheless it is by no means useless or unused. Readers of Chinese frequently guess at the pronunciation of unknown characters by referring to the phonetic component. Writers frequently make mistakes by writing wrong characters that have the same or similar sounds as the intended graphs.

It is pertinent, therefore, to look a bit more closely at the issue of phoneticity that was mentioned earlier in citing Y. R. Chao's estimate that Chinese writing is 25 percent phonetic as against 75 percent for English. Research done on this issue indicates that if one has memorized the pronunciation of the 895 phonetic elements singled out by Soothill, it is possible in 66 percent of the cases to guess the pronunciation of any given character one is likely to encounter in reading a modern text.

If we apply only those phonetics like the aforementioned *huáng*, which reflect pronunciation with complete accuracy, we have a 25 percent chance of guessing the pronunciation of the characters in a given text. It is probably not coincidental that this figure is identical with Chao's estimate. His definition of phoneticity may well have been based only on such cases, where a phonetic precisely matches the pronunciation of a character of which it forms part, even including the tone.

But symbols which represent accurately the phonemes of a syllable other than the tones are also generally useful. This is attested by the fact that much has been published in a variety of Chinese scripts which do not indicate tones. One such is the Latinxua or Latinization scheme in use before World War II (DeFrancis 1950). Since the early 1950s newspapers, poetry, fiction, and works on linguistics, history, and politics have been published in a Cyrillic transcription of Dungan, a dialect of Northwestern Mandarin. This dialect is spoken by some 36,000 people in Soviet Central Asia descended from Muslim Chinese refugees who fled persecution at the hands of the Manchus in the nineteenth century (Isayev 1977:186–187; Rimsky-Korsakoff 1967:356, 410–413; Rimsky-Korsakoff Dyer 1987:235). If we add the 17 percent of phonetics of this type, represented by the phonetic *mǎ*, phoneticity increases to 42 percent.

Even phonetic elements of the *yāo* type are useful since they give hints about the pronunciation of part of a syllable, usually the final part, which is the most distinctive part of the syllable. Hence they generally permit a good guess at the pronunciation of a character in context. If we add the 24 percent of phonetics of this type, phoneticity increases to the figure of 66 percent mentioned above (DeFrancis 1984a:105–110).[7]

The 66 percent figure represents a conservative estimate of the phoneticity of Chinese characters. Scholars with specialized knowledge of Chinese historical phonology can often derive additional phonetic information from the previously mentioned fourth category, which I have dismissed as providing no useful phonetic clues. This rejection is based on my estimate of utility for the average, linguistically unsophisticated reader of Chinese texts. More knowledgeable readers such as the specialized scholars Bernhard Karlgren and William S.-Y. Wang are able to discern corespondence between phonetic elements and full characters that is not apparent to ordinary readers. They arrive at a somewhat different classification of characters, primarily those in my fourth category. Those of the *xià* 'below' type they consider as not belonging to the SP catergory at all. Some others, such as *guān* 'gate,' are reclassified into my third category on the basis of a more refined phonological analysis that is made possible by a more sophisticated understanding of the history of a character and the sounds attached to it. The net result of all this is that their estimate of phoneticity (as defined by my first three categories) rises to as high as 90 percent (Karlgren 1923:4; Wang 1981:232).[8]

Apart from the multielement (SP) graphs which contain phonetics of the varying degrees of utility described, there are also single-element graphs which themselves comprise phonetics. (Some also function as keys.) Here are a few examples of characters we have already encountered:

馬 *mǎ* 'horse'

門 *mén* 'door'

目 *mù* 'eye'

人 *rén* 'person'

象 *xiàng* 'elephant'

The overall distribution of the various kinds of characters can be roughly summarized as follows:

Kind of Character		Example	Percent
A. single-element characters	馬	*mǎ* 'horse'	1
B. multielement (SP) characters			
1. completely useful phonetic (represents all the phonemes of the derivative)	蝗	*huáng* 'locust'	25
2. generally useful phonetic (represents all the segmental phonemes, but perhaps not the tone)	媽	*mā* 'mother'	17
3. contextually useful phonetic (represents most of segmental phonemes)	澆	*jiāo* 'sprinkle'	24
4. useless phonetic (represents no significant phonemes)	下	*xià* 'below'	33
Total			100

The utility of the first three categories of phonetic elements becomes even more apparent if we look at the phonetics not merely in isolated graphs but also in characters as we normally encounter them, which is, of course, in context. Even the minimal environment provided by two-character expressions illustrates this point, as in the following examples consisting of several pairs of phonetics and their derivatives:

	phonetics		derivatives	meanings
分 方	*fēnfāng*	芬 芳	*fēnfāng*	fragrant
免 属	*miǎnlì*	勉 勵	*miǎnlì*	encourage
山 夭	*shānyāo*	訕 笑	*shānxiào*	ridicule
士 原	*shìyuán*	志 愿	*zhìyuàn*	aspiration
亡 生	*wángshēng*	忘 性	*wàngxing*	forgetfulness

The wider contexts in which these words are normally encountered will enable readers to handle the disparity in pronunciation between phonetics and derivatives, just as readers of this book will no doubt, either consciously or unconsciously, carrect the preceding misspelled word.

Chinese spelling as represented by its phonetic elements is erratic, inefficient, and difficult to master. But the same has been said about English spelling. Chinese writing deserves these opprobrious labels even more than does English, but this should not obscure the fact that phoneticity, deficient though it has become, far surpasses iconicity, which actually approaches zero.

Yet this fact is indeed commonly overlooked by people who mistakenly call Chinese "pictographic" or "ideographic." These labels are popularly attached to Chinese characters by Western writers. The Chinese themselves are also almost universally convinced that theirs is a unique system that they call *biǎoyì* 'semantic' or 'ideographic' writing. The writing system does contain some symbols that might, very loosely, be so labeled, but a few, or even a few hundred, such symbols do not make a system of writing. In actual fact, there never has been, and never can be, a full system of writing based on the pictographic or ideographic principle.

What then of the frequent designation, especially in academic circles, of Chinese as a logographic or morphemic system of writing? Other writing systems, such as Sumerian, are also described by these terms, but Chinese is usually taken as the example par excellence of this category of scripts. I think this too is a serious error, and the error is compounded by sinologists because they have been unduly influenced by the previously mentioned difference between Chinese and

Sumerian in the way they handle semantic and phonetic determinatives. In contrast to Sumerian writing, in which the determinatives are detachable from the graphs they determine, Chinese writing welds these elements so tightly together that the characters, surrounded as they are by white space in their little square cubicles, are usually viewed as unitary symbols, or at least as the basic unit in the writing system.

The error here will become clearer if we invoke the concepts of grapheme and frame (or lexeme) that were discussed in the section "The Forest of Family Trees" in chapter 2. The grapheme, as we recall, is the indispensable meaningless unit that corresponds to the smallest segment of speech represented in the writing system. The frame is the dispensable meaningful unit that corresponds to the smallest segment of writing conventionally receiving special status, such as being surrounded by white space and listed in dictionaries.

In English, the grapheme is a letter or combination of letters corresponding to one of the approximately forty smallest units of speech, the phonemes, that are represented in the writing system. The frame is a word, the smallest unit of writing that is conventionally surrounded by white space and listed in dictionaries.

It is my contention that in Chinese the syllabic element P, such as that in the overwhelmingly preponderant SP characters, must be viewed as the grapheme, the indispensable phonetic unit without which the system would not work. Whole characters are frames or lexemes, secondary units that in a reformed system of writing could be dispensed with entirely, along with the semantic element S. The Chinese frame is a derivative, as is true also of the English frame. Chinese writing, consisting as it does of derived characters, can be called logographic (or morphemic) only if English writing is also called logographic because it too consists of derived frames, in this case called words. But by this standard most, if not all, systems of writing must be called logographic, which then becomes a vacuous term utterly lacking in any power to differentiate systems of writing.

The Chinese system must be classified as a syllabic system of writing. More specifically, it belongs to the subcategory that I have labeled meaning-plus-sound syllabic systems or morphosyllabic systems.

I use the term *morphosyllabic* in two senses. The first applies to the Chinese characters taken as individual units. Individual characters are morphosyllabic in the sense that they represent at once a single syllable and a single morpheme (except for the 11 percent or so of meaningless characters that represent sound only). In this usage the term is intended to replace the more widely used expressions *logographic, word-syllabic,* and *morphemic,* all of which are applied to individual characters taken as a unit. The second sense of the term refers to the structure of Chinese characters and is intended to draw attention to the fact that, in most cases, a character is composed of two elements, a phonetic grapheme which suggests the syllabic pronunciation of the full character, and a semantic element which hints at its meaning.

The aspect of the Chinese system of writing covered by this second sense of the term often receives little if any attention. This applies particularly to the phonetic grapheme. Its neglect leads to widespread errors in viewing characters as either (1) unitary symbols with no representation of sound, or (2) compound symbols made up by combining semantic elements with no representation of sound, or (3) compound symbols with phonetic elements of so little importance that they can be disregarded.

Whereas English graphemes represent phonemes, Chinese graphemes represent syllables, or better still, accepting Boodberg's felicitous label, "syllabic phonemes" (Boodberg 1937:331). There are in current Chinese some 1,277 syllabic phonemes counting tones, about 400 not counting tones. For purposes of comparison, let us say that, in round figures, there are 40 phonemes in English and 400 toneless and 1,300 tonal syllabic phonemes in Chinese.[9]

A sampling of the characters in a dictionary with about 4,800 entries indicates that 44 percent represent free words, 45 percent are bound morphemes, like *-er* in English *teacher,* and 11 percent are meaningless symbols that represent only sounds, like the *cor* and *al* of English *coral* (DeFrancis 1984a:184–187). On the basis of these figures Chinese characters are at best 44 percent logographic and 89 percent morphemic. But the Chinese *writing system* is 100 percent syllabic since all characters (except that for the suffix *r*) represent syllables, either as single-element graphs which themselves comprise phonetics or as multielement graphs which include phonetics of the varying degrees of utility noted earlier. It is a mistake to take Chinese frames, or lexemes, as the basis for defining a writing system, just as it would be a mistake to call English logographic because its frames are words. Yet the superficial approach of equating Chinese characters with the Chinese writing system is often adopted. People fail to look below the surface of the characters to what makes the characters work and allows new ones to be generated as needed.

It would be quite impossible to write Chinese exclusively with logographic or morphemic frames not further divisible into components that minimally include a phonetic grapheme. The number of words, in the order of hundred of thousands if not more than a million, is much too large.

The number of morphemes is harder to estimate. If we accept the conventional view that Chinese characters represent morphemes, which as noted above is approximately 89 percent true, then there are at least 25,000 morphemes in the Kang Xi dictionary. An incomplete study based on only 4,200 characters estimates the number of morphemes at 5,000 in modern Mandarin. The author notes that this figure includes only "frequently used morphemes" and should be increased to 7,000 or 8,000, which even so excludes polysyllabic morphemes, foreign loanwords, and personal and place names (Yin Bin-yong 1984 and personal communication, 1/8/87). Regardless of the precise figure, it is obviously very great, much too large for a purely morphemic script.

On the other hand, it would be a relatively simple matter to write Mandarin Chinese with a standardized syllabary of only 1,277 signs, which could be reduced to 398 if tones were separately indicated. Figure 19 presents such a standardized syllabary based largely on the Soothill Syllabary (DeFrancis 1984a). The pronunciation of the characters is indicated by the Pinyin transcription that was adopted in 1958 as the official way of transcribing the characters.

But instead of a relatively small number of syllabic graphemes, Chinese has, according to the Marshman study cited earlier, something like 4,000 such basic signs. It is partially coincidental, but not completely unrelated, that the figure approximates the picture of maximum syllabic complexity attributed to a sixth-century dictionary which divides all the sounds of the language into 3,877 groups (Kennedy 1964:113–114). Actually this figure is suspect, and it is unlikely that Chinese ever had this many syllables. Boodberg makes the startling suggestion that the number of different syllables in the still earlier phase of Chinese, which some scholars consider to have been phonologically the most complex, was more limited than in modern Mandarin (Boodberg 1937:360).

Regardless of the precise number of syllables in Chinese in the various periods of its evolution, it is clear that there have always been many symbols for the same sound. Chinese writing never underwent the reduction in number of symbols that characterized the evolution of

	a	o	e	-i	er	ai	ei	ao	ou	an	en	ang	eng	ong	i	ia	iao	ie	iu	ian	in	iang	ing	iong	u	ua	uo	uai	ui	uan	un	uang	ueng	ü	üe	üan	ün
b	八	帛				白	北	保		半	本	邦	崩		必		表	别		扁	賓		丙		不												
p	怕	坡				𠂢	培	泡	剖	判	盆	旁	朋		皮		票	丿		片	品		平		菐												
m	馬	末				買	每	毛	某	曼	門	忙	孟		米		苗	蔑	謬	免	民		明		木												
f	乏	佛					非		缶	凡	分	方	風												夫												
d	大		惪			代	得	刀	斗	旦		當	登	東	弟		弔	爹	丟	典			丁		度		多		兑	段	盾						
t	𦐇		特			台		匋	亠	覃		唐	疼	同	梯		挑	帖		天			亭		土		妥		推	彖	屯						
n	那		呢			乃	內	𡿺	耨	南	嫩	囊	能	農	尼		鳥	圼	牛	念	您	娘	寧		奴		諾			暖				女	虐		
l	拉		勒			賴	累	老	婁	闌		郎	冷	龍	力	倆	尞	列	留	連	林	良	另		彔		羅			𤔔	侖			呂	掠		
z	雜		則	子		在	賊	早	走	贊	怎	臧	曾	宗											足		左		最	鑽	夋						
c	擦		册	此		才		曹	湊	參	岑	倉	層	從											粗		錯		崔	篡	寸						
s	薩		色	死		塞		掃	叟	散	森	桑	僧	松											肅		𧴪		隋	算	巽						
zh	乍		折	之		宅	這	召	州	占	貞	章	正	中											主	爪	卓	曳	隹	專	准	庄					
ch	叉		車	赤		差		巢	丑	詹	臣	昌	成	虫											出		綽	揣	垂	川	春	床					
sh	殺		舌	尸		篩	誰	少	手	山	申	尚	生												叔	耍	朔	帥	水	閂	隼	雙					
r			惹	日				擾	肉	然	人	攘	扔	容											入		若		瑞	軟	閏						
j															及	甲	交	皆	久	見	今	將	京	冂										句	欮	卷	君
q															七	掐	丂	切	求	欠	親	羌	青	睘										去	缺	全	裙
x															西	夏	小	血	休	先	心	向	星	兄										虛	穴	玄	旬
g	生		戈			改	給	高	冓	甘	根	岡	更	工											古	卦	果	乖	貴	官	丨	光					
k	卡		可			開		考	口	看	肯	康	坑	孔											苦	夸	括	快	盔	款	困	狂					
h	哈		禾			害	黑	好	后	含	很	行	亨	厷											胡	化	火	褱	灰	奐	昏	皇					
ø	阿		咢		兒	㝵		敖	歐	安	恩	卬			一	亞	夭	也	又	炎	因	羊	䧹	用	五	哇	我	外	韋	丸	文	王	翁	于	月	元	云

Figure 19. Chinese Writing: A Simple Syllabary and a Simpler Alphabet
A standardized syllabary of 398 signs which with four additional marks for tones would enable Chinese to be written with full accuracy and relative ease in a way comparable to the Japanese use of kana symbols. The Pinyin transcription of the 398 basic syllabic signs combines an initial consonant (shown in the left-hand column) with a final (shown in the top row) made up of one or more vowels and an occasional ending in *n* or *ng*. Reprinted with permission from John DeFrancis, *The Chinese Language: Fact and Fantasy.* (Honolulu: University of Hawaii Press, 1984), p. 27.

the cuneiform scripts. Indeed, the Chinese seem to have almost a penchant for avoiding simplification and standardization. This is seen also in the failure to make efficient use of a syllable-telescoping technique that has some similarity with that devised by the Sumerians.

The Chinese variation of this technique, which they call *fǎnqiè* 'reverse-cutting,' indicates the syllabic pronunciation of an unknown character C through the intermediary of two presumably known characters A and B by cutting off the final part of the syllable from A and removing the initial in B. This is as if in English we indicated the spelling of *cat* by telescoping *cup* and *rat* as follows: *c(up r)at.*

With a stock of only about 40 A's and about 200 B's this could have have been made into a fairly simple standardized system capable of expressing all the syllables. But the Chinese never standardized the system, and indeed selected characters, some of them quite obscure, at random, as if we spelled *cat* indiscriminantly as *cup-rat, cow-fat, coal-hat, cap-mat,* and so on. This failure resulted in the haphazard use of about 500 A's and 1,200 B's. And sometimes the "reverse-cutting" was circular, with C being explained by reverse-cutting A and B, and A by reverse-cutting C and B (Kennedy 1953:8, 146–147).

But the shortcomings of the Chinese "reverse-cutting" device, which not surprisingly confused Gelb (Gelb 1963:87–88; DeFrancis 1950:40–47), are not particularly relevant, since little use was made of it. Unlike the Sumerian technique, which played an important role in that writing system, the Chinese variation did not form part of the writing system itself but was confined to lexicographic use. Modern dictionaries have now abandoned this inefficient way of indicating the pronunciation of characters in favor of newer techniques closer to the alphabetic principle.

Traditional Chinese writing never attained even the limited degree of simplification that marked the evolution of cuneiform writing. Throughout its history the actual sound-to-symbol relationship in Chinese has approximated on the syllabic level the much-maligned situation in English on the phonemic level. In contrast to the one-to-one relationship, where there is close correspondence between sound and symbol, both writing systems are characterized by a highly complex many-to-many relationship. Thus English spells the same sound *o* in at least ten different ways: *so, sow, sew, oh, owe, dough, doe, beau, soak, soul.* It uses the same letter *o* to represent at least 8 different sounds in *so, to, on, honey, horse, woman, borough* (DeFrancis 1984a:112). The situation is the same, on the syllabic level, in Chinese. Here some syllables are represented by many different symbols, which may be either whole characters or the phonetic components in more complex characters of the SP type. And some symbols have several different pronunciations.

The poor fit between sound and symbol in both English and Chinese should not obscure the key fact that both are based on phonetic principles, with the 40 phonemes of English being represented by various alphabetic spellings, and the syllables of Mandarin Chinese being represented by various syllabic spellings. The number of different spellings for the 40 English phonemes has been variously estimated at 600 (Zachrisson 1931:4), 1,120–1,768 (Nyikos 1988; see 298 below), and 2,000 (Alisjahbana 1965:530; Daniels 1985:34). The ratio between syllabic spellings and syllabic phonemes in Chinese is much smaller, but the greater complexity of its graphic symbols makes for a system the cumbersomeness of which considerably surpasses that of English and perhaps of all other systems ever created.

It hasn't needed to be so. As noted earlier, it would be possible to write Mandarin Chinese quite simply and accurately with only 1,300 different signs. It would be possible to manage with only 400 symbols if tones are separately indicated, or not indicated at all. But writing with a simple phonetic script, whether syllabic or alphabetic, would be impossible without the adoption of a further feature that has characterized Chinese written in an alphabetic script. This is a literary style that is more closely based on actual speech.

Over the past hundred years there has been a long-running debate regarding the Chinese literary style and the Chinese character system of writing. Proponents of reform are urging a more colloquial style of writing and the extended use of the simple romanization system called Pinyin, not as a replacement for the characters, but as part of a policy of digraphia, that is, the use of two more or less equal systems of writing, each to be used in the areas for which it is best suited, such as Pinyin for computers, characters for historical research (DeFrancis 1984a, 1984b). The promulgation in July 1988 of rules for Pinyin orthography, that is, rules for such things as punctuation and use of blank space, hyphens, and closed juncture between syllables, is expected by Chinese reformers to help create digraphic literates who would extend the use of Pinyin from a mere tool for annotating characters to an auxiliary system for writing the language.

However, reformers seeking to speed China's modernization by modernizing the writing system through a policy of digraphia have to contend not only with the natural attachment of Chinese to their familiar script but also with chauvinistic and mindless claims for its superiority. For years the official *People's Daily* has promoted a cabal of conservative dabblers in the area of writing, headed by a wealthy returned expatriate, as part of a campaign attacking the reformers and extolling the traditional characters. The intellectual level of the campaign is indicated by an item, carried in *China Daily* (11/15/1984) under the headline "Characters 'easier than ABC to read'," which retailed the preposterous claim of an establishment psycholinguist that "children aged 2 to 4 can easily learn 3,000 characters." China's writing reformers and forward-looking educators, in their uphill battle against such drivel, are beleaguered in an atmosphere of intimidation and quackery reminiscent of the intellectual climate in the Stalinist period that earned Soviet linguistics and genetics, long dominated respectively by N. Y. Marr and T. D. Lysenko, the contempt of scholars throughout the world. In contrast to countries like Turkey (Heyd 1954; Bazin 1983), North Korea (Blank 1981), and Viet Nam (DeFrancis 1977), where writing systems and writing styles were reformed in a matter of a few years or a few decades, it appears that controversy over basic problems of writing is likely to drag on indefinitely in China.

Mayan

The origin of Mayan writing is the subject of the same disagreement between original inventionists and diffusionists as Chinese. The diffusionist Cyrus H. Gordon and the Mayanist David H. Kelley have seen a connection between the "Phoenician-Hebrew alphabet" and Mesoamerican lists of signs for days of the month, and they consider that "the origin and the transmission of both the alphabet and the lists are the achievement of intercontinental mariners" (Gordon 1970:193; also Gordon 1971 and Moran and Kelley 1969). It appears, however, that most Mayanists strongly reject the notion of contact with the Old World (Lyle Campbell, personal communication, 5/13/87). The generally accepted view is that Mayan writing is an indigenous creation—the third in the history of syllabic writing—and that in the development of their system the Maya were influenced by antecedents in the form of pictographic or hieroglyphic symbols that were executed by various neighboring peoples. However, the precise nature of these symbols and their relationship to those developed by the Maya has yet to be fully established (Justeson et al. 1985).

Despite this general agreement regarding the origin of Mayan writing, there has been sharp disagreement among Mayanists on other matters that have occupied most of their attention. Chief among these areas of disagreement is the basic nature of the symbols that make up the Mayan system of writing.

Mayan writing consists of distinctive symbols, called glyphs, which are often recognizable pictures such as those of animals and human beings. Inscriptions containing these symbols have been found in most of the Mayan-inhabited region, namely a nearly continuous territory in southern Mexico, Guatemala, and northern Belize (formerly British Honduras). However, documentation is most extensive in two areas:

1. The southern lowlands. Several thousand inscriptions, chiefly on stone but sometimes on wood, shells, stucco, and pots; these were made in the period 300–900 A.D. and deal with local historical-genealogical matters.

2. The northern part of the Yucatan peninsula. Several illustrated manuscripts, called codices by Mayanists, that contain calendrical, astrological, and augural content and were executed some time between 1200 and the Spanish conquest after 1540 (Prem and Riese 1983:177; Kelley 1962, 1976).

An additional source of information about Mayan writing that has to be used with great caution is a sixteenth-century work by Bishop Diego de Landa which was written shortly after the Spanish conquests that destroyed Mayan power and much of its civilization, including its writing. His long-ignored *Account of the Things of Yucatan,* which was not published until 1864, became the basis for attempts at deciphering the script that centered on the three extant codices, now known as the Dresden, Paris, and Madrid codices after the places where they came to be deposited (Kelley 1976).

Landa believed that Mayan writing was alphabetic. The first would-be decipherers accepted this premise, expressed in the "Landa alphabet" that appeared in his book. As a result, much of the early effort centered on attempts to find alphabetic readings for the symbols in the three codices and to relate them to the Mayan language. This alphabetic orientation was followed so assiduously and so uncritically by some students of the script that they committed excesses which gave the whole subject of phoneticism a bad name. These initial attempts at decipherment collapsed in 1904 when a leading exponent of phoneticism repudiated his previous attempts at phonetic readings.

In the next period little attention was paid to the earlier work as scholars concentrated their attention on the increasing number of inscriptions which were becoming available for study. Reflecting the main content of the inscriptions, calendrical and astronomical studies dominated the field. For the most part researchers treated the glyphs as ideographic symbols and largely ignored the Maya language. It was some time before interest in phoneticism was revived.

When Mayanists finally did get around to this approach again, they began to treat Mayan as a family of languages and to search for modern offshoots leading back to the earlier forms in the inscriptions. The elaborate family tree presents thirty-one modern Mayan languages that go back to Proto-Mayan, around 2100 B.C. One Mayanist speaks of "the rather recent accurate identification of the language of the glyphs" and identifies the language of most of the monumental glyphs as Cholan, which branched off from Proto-Mayan (Campbell 1984a, 1984b).

The research done on Mayan languages indicates that they are characterized by a preponderance of monosyllabic roots which combine with equally monosyllabic prefixes and postfixes to form noun phrases and verb phrases. The syllable structure is quite simple: only consonant + vowel (CV) and consonant + vowel + consonant (CVC) syllables occur. Most word roots are of the CVC type. Proto-Mayan has been reconstructed by T. S. Kaufman as having 38 consonants and 6 vowels (cited in Kelley 1976:167). The total number of theoretically possible CV and CVC syllables is rather large: 228 of the CV type and 8,864 of the CVC type. It is unclear how many of these actually occurred.

The idea that it was the syllables of early Mayan that were represented by the glyphic writing was slow to receive acceptance by students of the script. One of the first to propound the idea was Benjamin Lee Whorf, who in a succession of papers (1933, 1935, 1942) argued that

> The Maya writing system was a complex but very natural way . . . of using small picturelike signs to represent the sounds of fractions of utterances (usually a syllable or less in extent), combining these signs so that the combined fractions of utterances outlined the total utterance of a word or a sentence [Whorf 1942:482–483].

However, Whorf's specific decipherments did not receive general acceptance, so that he appears to have exercised little influence on the direction of Mayan studies.

Through a series of works published between 1952 and 1967, a Soviet scholar, Yurij Knorozov, is credited with the "breakthrough" that has convinced many Mayanists of the basically syllabic nature of Mayan writing (Kelley 1976:305). Part of the breakthrough was the recognition that some of the glyphs might be employed solely for their phonetic value, as in the case of the symbol for a "pocket gopher," which in Cholan had a pronunciation that has been reconstructed as *b'ah* and was used also for the sound *b'a*. Another aspect of the breakthrough was the discovery by Knorozov (1958:290) that "the typically CVC Mayan roots could be spelled with two signs of CV value, where the vowel of the second was silent, but was chosen to match the vowel of the root, e.g., /kuȼ/ 'turkey' was spelled (ku-ȼu) [ȼ = ts]" (Campbell 1984a:622). The procedure can be formalized and further illustrated as follows:

$$C_1V_1 + C_2V_1 = C_1V_1C_2$$
$$\text{ma} + \text{ca} = \text{mac}$$

This technique, whereby a CVC syllable could be written phonetically by two CV glyphs, neither of which had any semantic relation to the CVC root, has been characterized by one writer as "not merely rebus writing, but a true phonetic script" (Kelley 1976:8). The Mayan syllable-telescoping technique, which differs only in detail from the parallel Sumerian and Chinese techniques, obviously made possible a great economy in the number of signs needed, since it appears that the ancestral Mayan language could have had no more than 228 syllables of the CV type.

Apart from the practices just mentioned, other techniques have been noted which also parallel those in both Sumerian and Chinese writing. Thus Mayanists also speak of "phonetic complements" and "determinatives" or "determiners." However, the determiners appear to have a broader usage, not being confined to providing semantic clues such as "person" or "wood," for one Mayanist has defined a determinative as "a glyph accompanying or infixed in another glyph in order to help read it correctly, either to choose between homonyms with different meanings or to choose between phonetically different synonyms" (Kelley 1976:295).

Just when and where these techniques first appeared and how they were developed are being more intensively studied as Mayanists focus attention on the phonetic aspects of the writing (Justeson and Camp-

bell 1984; Justeson et al. 1985). The overall evolution of the system
has been summarized by various scholars as follows:

> The earliest inscriptions lack phonetic or syllabic values and deter-
> miners; these develop gradually until they are in some abundance in
> later texts [Lyle Campbell, personal communication, 5/13/87].

> The Maya must have developed their own writing system into a full-
> fledged script in the incredibly short time-span of 400 years. It repre-
> sented language exactly and completely and thus did not develop fur-
> ther once this stage was reached at about 400 A.D. [Prem and Riese
> 1983:177–178].

Although the Maya were capable of representing their spoken language "exactly and completely" in relatively simple fashion by the use
of syllabic signs, they clearly did not choose to do so. Throughout its
history their writing remained a mixed script—morphosyllabic according to my classification, "partly phonetic, partly pictographic, and
partly ideographic," according to Marcus (1976:57). How much of
each is represented is a subject of considerable debate. "Most of the
recent epigraphic controversy," adds Marcus, "has centered around
the question: How phonetic or syllabic is it?—a question which cannot as yet be answered." It is nevertheless clear that as far as its superficial visual aspect is concerned, Mayan writing retained much more of
the purely pictographic component than did either Sumerian or Chinese. Moreover, the Maya went considerably further than either the
Sumerians or the Chinese in fusing various components into seemingly
integral wholes. In the case of determinatives, for example, we have
already noted that in Sumerian writing these were optional and
detachable, thus leading more easily to phonetization, whereas in Chinese the determinatives and the graphs were firmly welded together.
In Mayan writing the component elements were even more tightly
fused together, so much so that they are not easily identified as separate entities.

Apparently aesthetic considerations also loomed very large in the
Mayan approach to writing. This is indicated in part by the general
appearance of the script. It is also indicated by the fact that "position-
ing of a sign is often governed more by aesthetics than by rules of reading order, and moreover, to such an extent that a sign can be doubled
just for symmetrical purposes without affecting the reading" (Prem
and Riese 1983:182).

Despite the fact that Mayan writing has retained such a large amount of purely pictographic representation, and despite the inability to answer the quantitative question as to just how phonetic the script is, there can be no doubt that those Mayanists are correct who have stressed the qualitative significance of the phonetic aspect. It took a long time to reach agreement on this point. One writer records that

> In the spring of 1979, a group of Mayan linguists and epigraphers met at SUNY Albany to discuss phoneticism in Mayan hieroglyphic writing. That conference marked a turning point in the history of Mayan epigraphy, for it was the first time that the phonetic basis of the script was taken for granted. Not a single paper in the volume that has resulted from that meeting mentions the acrimonious debate between J. Eric S. Thompson and Yurij Knorozov over the nature of Mayan writing—a dispute that had retarded progress in decipherment for several decades. It seems that, by the end of the 1970's, Mayan epigraphers had reached a consensus rejecting much of Thompson's position, and were eager to get on with the task of assigning phonetic values to individual signs [Bricker 1986:694–695].

Although Thompson's antiphonetic views have now been rejected, his work in collecting and annotating Mayan glyphs constitutes a major contribution to Mayan studies.

Given the still incomplete status of decipherment, there is considerable question as to how many glyphs there are. Soviet scholars have advanced the figure of about 5,300 differentiable hieroglyphs (Marek 1966:418). Thompson provides an annotated list of some 862 glyphs in his *Catalogue of Maya Hieroglyphs* (1962). In view of the difficulty of reproducing the complex symbols that make up the script, the numbering system he introduced in this important work is the standard means by which Mayanists refer to specific glyphs.

Thompson's numbering scheme appears in the example of Mayan writing that is presented in figure 20. It deals with the name of a ruler who reigned in Palenque (in present southeastern Mexico) from 615 to 682 A.D. According to one interpretation, glyphs 74 and 184 spell out the sounds for *makina,* a title applying to lineage heads that is rendered as 'lord.' The other signs give the ruler's name in two forms. Sign 624a represents the name by the pictograph of a shield, for which there were two words, namely *chimal* and *pacal.* Signs 602–25–178 indicate the reading to be selected by representing the name by three syllabic signs pronounced respectively as *pa–ca–l(a),* the vowel in the last syllable being understood as not pronounced (Prem and Riese 1983).

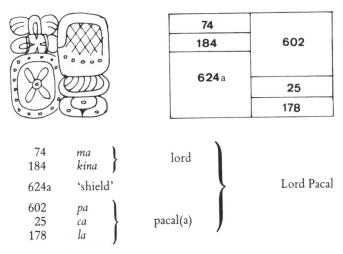

74	602
184	
624a	
	25
	178

74	*ma*	} lord	}
184	*kina*		
624a	'shield'		} Lord Pacal
602	*pa*	} pacal(a)	
25	*ca*		
178	*la*		

Figure 20. Mayan Syllabic Writing
Symbols numbered 74–184 and 602–25–178 illustrate the phonetic use of Mayan glyphs. Sign 624a is a picture of a shield. Glyphs 602–25–178 spell out the word *pacal* 'shield.' All the symbols combine to give the full title *Makina Pacal* 'Lord Pacal' or 'Lord Shield.' Illustration reprinted with permission from Hanns J. Prem and Berthold Riese, "Autochthonous American Writing Systems: The Aztec and Maya Examples." In Florian Coulmas and Konrad Ehlich, eds., *Writing in Focus* (Berlin: Mouton, 1983), p. 178.

Another interpretation, while accepting the logographic and phonetic renditions of the name, contends that the *chimal* reading is wrong and that there were not two synonyms for shield (Lyle Campbell, personal communication, 3/13/87, and Justeson et al. 1985).

The same sound, such as *pa* here represented by the symbol 602, can also be represented by other symbols. Some symbols have more than one sound. And some syllables are not represented at all. These phenomena, which parallel those in Sumerian and Chinese writing, are also apparent in a tentative syllabary that was drawn up following the SUNY conference in Albany referred to earlier. At that conference suggestions were advanced that related 108 symbols to 55 syllables. The phonetic values suggested were purely tentative and did not imply a consensus among the participants that the values are necessarily correct (Mathews 1984:311–314). The fragmentary and tentative nature of the syllabary seems to be an accurate reflection of where the decipherment of the Mayan system of writing stood at the time of the 1979 conference. However, one prominent Mayanist reports that work on decipherment has been advancing at a fast pace since then.

Among other things, several additional syllables have been identified (Lyle Campbell, personal communication, 5/13/87).

Although the Albany conference and other recent work by Mayanists suggest the distance yet to be covered in the decipherment of the script, nevertheless they also indicate the considerable progress that has been made in the past decade or two. And they give promise of further success now that the phonetic aspect of Mayan writing has received its due recognition.

"Pure" Syllabic Systems

From the preceding account of the three separate inventions of writing, it is clear that all three started on the road to full writing by using pictographic symbols in their dual capacity as semantic and phonetic—more precisely, syllabic—signs. The relative proportions in which the two aspects in these meaning-plus-sound scripts were utilized appear to have varied over time, with the semantic aspect ascendant in the early stage and the phonetic gradually increasing in importance. For Chinese this is clearly attested by the change from the minority status of phonetic elements in the Shang writing of the second millennium B.C. to its overwhelming preponderance in the writing of later years. The same pattern appears in the two stages represented by the Sumerian invention of writing and its subsequent takeover by the Akkadians. Phonetic elements in Sumerian reached a high of 54 percent, but in Akkadian as much as 96 percent of a text was phonetic.

The last-cited figure indicates that Akkadian was on the verge of becoming a pure syllabic system, purged of nonphonetic elements. But the Akkadians never pushed matters to the point of writing exclusively in the limited number of syllabic signs available to them. Neither did any of the three inventors of morphosyllabic writing.

Actually the situation is not entirely clear with respect to the Akkadians and their Sumerian mentors. One historian of writing asserts that in the case of the Akkadians "the possibility existed, and it was used in certain circumstances, to write everything phonetically" (Cohen 1958:90). He does not, however, spell out what the "certain circumstances" were, nor do other specialists expand on this matter.

Another historian of writing in his discussion of Sumerian states that writing was done "entirely with syllable-signs" in Emesal, and only in Emesal, which he characterizes as "a special dialect, or at least stylized variety of the usual Sumerian" (Jensen 1969:93). However, the highly regarded Soviet Sumerologist I. M. Diakonoff, who describes Emesal as "a woman's language" used to represent the speech of women and goddesses in religious and literary contexts, says that "no Emesal text is ever written entirely in 'pure' Emesal, that is, completely phonetically" (Diakonoff 1975:112–116). More or less along the same line is Gelb's comment that Emesal was written "to a great extent with syllabic signs, while the few word signs which were used were confined to some of the most common expressions of the language" (Gelb 1963:120).

Gelb has made the interesting assertion that the "sacred traditions" of writing prevented creators of scripts from making changes in them, and it was only foreigners who, because they did not fear to break from these traditions, were able to introduce reforms (Gelb 1963:196). But even the early borrowers of scripts, though they went further than the original creators in eliminating nonphonetic elements, were rarely able to make a complete break with tradition.

Apart from the example already cited of Akkadian writing, the script of their contemporaries the Elamites, who also borrowed from the Sumerians, can be cited as typical of the failure to chart a completely new course. The Elamite cuneiform system consisted of 131 syllabic signs, 25 word-signs, and 7 determinatives. The last two appear to have been largely ornamental, since the syllabic signs were overwhelmingly preponderant in actual texts (Gelb 1963:121).

There are actually very few well attested cases of pure syllabic writing, unless of course one accepts Gelb's contention that what I have classified as consonantal scripts should be counted as syllabic. Leaving aside a number of little-used systems that have received only cursory attention in the literature devoted to writing systems, there are only two syllabic scripts, Japanese and Yi, which deserve close examination, and two others of perhaps lesser importance, used by the Cherokee and by the Vai of Liberia, which will be briefly noted here. These last two were developed in the last century as a result of contact between their creators and people who already possessed writing.

In 1821 a Cherokee Indian by the name of Sequoya created a set of 85 signs based largely on assigning syllabic values to individual letters of the Latin alphabet. The letters were used either in their original form or were slightly modified and augmented by additional symbols. Thus capital *H* represents the sound *mi*, and capital *W* represents *l* or *la*. The system, which is usually referred to as the "Cherokee Sylla-

bary," has been much praised for its excellence in representing the
Cherokee language (Feeling 1975; Holmes and Smith 1977).

While the system does seem to have worked quite well, a closer
examination reveals that it is far from perfect. The 85 symbols are used
to represent 6 vowels, 22 consonants, and some 200 phoneme clusters
(e.g., *hl, ts*) and syllables (e.g., *hu, wa, hwa*), almost all of which end in
a vowel. The same symbol can represent anywhere from one to seven
of these sounds, and the same sound is sometimes represented by different symbols (four in the case of *k*). It is thus quite a mixed system—
primarily syllabic, but also including both individual phonemes and
phoneme clusters. It underdifferentiates many sounds but tends to
group only related sounds under the same symbol. The vagaries of the
system apparently cause little difficulty for native speakers.

The syllabary was learned by many Cherokees, first in North Caro-
lina, where the system originated, and later in Oklahoma, to which
many of the Cherokees emigrated after 1830. It was used to publish
newspapers, official documents of the Cherokee nation, and other
materials, using type that had been created for the symbols in Boston
in 1827. Its wide diffusion among the Cherokees is indicated by the
estimate that they were 90 percent literate in their native language in
the 1830s (Walker n.d.:3, cited in Halle 1972:152). The system later
fell into disuse and was confined largely to correspondence between
individuals and to religious and medical practices. Recent attempts
have been made to revitalize the system and to extend literacy in the
syllabary (Trager 1974:470–471).

In recent years there has been a flurry of renewed interest in the
writing of the Vai people of Liberia. First reported in the late 1840s,
the script was apparently created a decade or so earlier, though its precise origins are uncertain. The Vai language for which the system was
created is a tonal language with a simple syllabic structure, chiefly consonant + vowel (CV) syllables. There are 226 symbols to represent
vowels or CV syllables. In addition there are separate signs for tones,
but these are seldom employed in practice (Diringer 1968, 1:130–131,
2:133; Klingenheben 1933).

The system is widely learned in the home and other nonschool situations. This unusual acquisition of literacy in a noninstitutional setting
accounts for the recent attention devoted to Vai writing by psychologists and other scholars interested in diverse aspects of literacy (Scribner and Cole 1981).

In contrast to the somewhat uncertain fate of the Cherokee and Vai scripts, the Japanese and Yi systems are both alive and flourishing. They are also both of special interest as distinctive examples of the category of pure syllabic scripts.

Japanese

The development of writing in Japan is a good illustration of the partial truth of Gelb's dictum that foreigners have been able to introduce variations in scripts whose inventors remained stuck in their old ways. It is an even better illustration of the fuller truth that even foreign innovators have seldom been able to make a complete break with the past. Akkadian and other disciples of the Sumerians only partially liberated themselves from the mixed phonetic and semantic symbols taken over from their mentors. The Japanese disciples of the Chinese were likewise only partially able to free themselves from the overwhelming influence of their preceptors.

When the Japanese first encountered the idea of writing, about 400 A.D., the Chinese had already been exercising this arcane art for close to two millennia. About a century and a half after their initial exposure to Chinese writing, the Japanese began to learn about Buddhism. The tenets of this new and appealing religion, which spread rapidly after its introduction in the middle of the sixth century, were presented in a huge body of material, written in Chinese, that was later brought to Japan. Buddhism provided an added spur to the Japanese acquisition of book-learning.

In this endeavor the Japanese were aided by the Koreans. Because their closer proximity to China had earlier exposed them to Chinese writing, the Koreans were able to serve as intermediaries in introducing books and Buddhism and as tutors to their island neighbors.

The Japanese developed a positive passion for all aspects of Chinese writing. They borrowed indiscriminately over long periods of time and from different areas of China. From the fifth to the seventh centuries they borrowed chiefly from the Shanghai area, and from the seventh to the tenth, and again in the thirteenth, chiefly from the capital area in northwest China. In these later periods, if not earlier, it is likely that the speech of these two areas was, as it is now, as far apart as French and Spanish, perhaps even further. Given this fact, plus the inevitable changes that take place in pronunciation of all languages over time, the Japanese ended up borrowing various Chinese pronunciations which they tried to adapt to their own speech habits.

Because Japanese has always had many fewer different syllables than Chinese, never more than about a hundred (Martin 1972:87; Miller 1967:194), many distinctions are lost in the borrowing. Thus seven characters that are now transcribed in Chinese as *shao, xiao, shang, zheng, sheng, xiang, song* are all pronounced *shō* in modern Japanese. Such approximations to the original sounds of Chinese are called *Sino-Japanese pronunciations.*

Since Chinese words, and the characters which represented them, were pronounced differently in different parts of China, in the course of the transition to Japanese they often acquired more than one Sino-Japanese pronunciation. Thus a character representing the Chinese word for 'bright' was read as *nyō* in imitation of the Shanghai pronunciation and as *mei* after that of northwest China.

Noting that a word in their native language might have a meaning similar to a word in Chinese, the Japanese sometimes associated still another reading, that of the native word, with the character that had already been borrowed with a Sino-Japanese reading. Thus the Chinese character for *shān* 'mountain' was read as *san* in Sino-Japanese and as *yama* in rendering the native word for 'mountain.'

Initially the Japanese took over not only the Chinese characters but the whole of the writing system—that is, what is now known as classical Chinese. The oldest extant Japanese book, the *Kojiki* or *Record of Ancient Matters,* which was completed in 712, is partially written in this classical literary style, or in as close an approximation of the style as the still uncertain Japanese scribes could get.

In reading classical Chinese texts (*kanbun,* from Chinese *hanwen* 'Chinese writing'), the Japanese sometimes approached a text approximately as the Chinese themselves would, that is, following the Chinese grammatical order and perhaps pronouncing the characters in the Sino-Japanese fashion. But they also devised techniques in which they read a classical text as if it were Japanese. This included mentally changing the word order (e.g., Chinese subject-verb-object) to Japanese subject-object-verb and applying conventional native readings to the characters. This procedure is similar to our use of a literal translation to render a Latin text, as in the following example:

Gallia	est	omnis	divisa	in	partes	tres
2	3	1	4	5	7	6
Gaul	is	all	divided	into	parts	three

A better analogy would be the reverse situation—Caesar rendering an English text in his native language and adding Latin case endings.

In the course of writing about things Japanese, the scribes faced the perennial problem faced by borrowers of foreign scripts, namely how to apply these alien symbols to the representation of indigenous sounds. The Japanese learned, especially from their reading of Buddhist literature written by Chinese, that the Chinese had encountered a similar problem in rendering religious terms expressed in Sanskrit and related languages. The Chinese had solved the problem by applying the phonetic values of Chinese characters to represent the sounds of the foreign terms. They approximated the Sanskrit word *bhikshu* 'monk' with two characters which are now transcribed as *biqiu* in Mandarin Chinese but had an earlier pronunciation something like *pji-kiəŭ* (Sansom 1928:10–12; Karlgren 1940:566, 994).

The *Kojiki* exhibits the dual use of characters in their phonetic and semantic values. In part of the text the characters appear as meaningful units arranged like classical Chinese but with occasional lapses into Japanese grammatical usages. Embedded in this rather awkward more or less classical Chinese text are Japanese personal names such as Susa and Suga that are rendered by characters used as purely phonetic symbols. The phonetic use of characters was also applied to the writing of whole songs and direct quotation of speeches (Kōno 1969:118–122; Miller 1967:32).

The Japanese referred to Chinese characters as *kanji,* their approximation of the pronunciation of the Chinese term *hanzi* 'Chinese characters.' When they used the characters to represent the sounds of their own language, they referred to the symbols as *kana.* This term is usually explained as meaning 'borrowed names,' meaning by this that the characters were borrowed to perform a phonetic function (Sansom 1928:23). This explanation is questioned in a recent article which traces the etymology of the term to a thirteenth-century word meaning 'unit' and referring to "a name for Chinese graphs which had been reduced to their smallest recognizable shapes" (Unger 1980). The use of Chinese characters as kana became more and more common as the Japanese increasingly attempted to write not only occasional names or words but whole texts in their own language. The first great anthology of Japanese verse, the *Man'yōshu* or *Collection of a Myriad Leaves,* which was compiled about half a century after the *Kojiki,* is written in large part in Chinese characters used as kana (Sansom 1928:23).

The Japanese probably learned about the phonetic use of Chinese characters from the Koreans who, having been in contact earlier with the Chinese, where the first to become acquainted with the Chinese practice of using characters for their phonetic value in rendering Buddhist terms. The Koreans had also attempted to apply the same principle to their own language. There was thus considerable precedent available to the Japanese as they sought to use Chinese characters to represent their own sounds.

One of the practices common to both the Japanese and Korean writing systems was that of writing characters in smaller size when used to show particles and inflectional endings. This marked the beginning of the practice, which was more fully developed later, of distinguishing the "functional" elements from the more "conceptual" words which were written in a larger size (Yamagiwa 1969:242).

In the initial stages of using Chinese characters for their phonetic value, there was no uniformity about which symbols represented which sounds. This chaotic situation slowly gave way before tendencies toward standardization, that is, always representing a particular sound with the same symbol, and toward simplification, reducing the complexity of the individual characters.

The result of these tendencies was the development in the ninth century of two simple syllabaries that later came to be called *hiragana* 'Easy Kana' and *katakana* 'Side Kana.' (*Kana* sometimes becomes *-gana* in compound words.)[10] Each syllabary consisted of close to four dozen symbols, which we can conveniently refer to as syllabograms, to represent the syllabic sounds that the early Japanese considered to be the basic sounds of their language.

Originally the main distinction between the two syllabaries was the use of hiragana for informal writing and of katakana for more formal works such as official documents, histories, and lexical works (Miller 1967:124). Today hiragana is the more commonly used syllabary, and katakana serves roughly the same functions as our italic type. It is used especially often in writing terms borrowed from foreign languages (Sansom 1928:41–46).

The hiragana symbols are derived from the cursive form of Chinese characters, that is, from forms that are written hastily and summarily, with about as much deviation from the ideal as one sees in some prescriptions dashed off by our doctors. The katakana symbols are derived from a part, usually a side, of a character in its usual printed form. A few examples of each are given here:

Chinese character	Hiragana	Katakana	Transcription
仁	に	ニ	ni
保	ほ	ホ	ho
加	か	カ	ka

It took a long time for the kana syllabaries to evolve into their present standardized form. Originally there were several hiragana and katakana symbols for each syllable. There were, for example, some 300 hiragana symbols to represent 47 syllables (Sansom 1928:42). Some syllables appear not to have been distinguished initially. In the eleventh century a diacritic was created to represent what the Japanese, following Chinese usage, called "impure" sounds. These consisted of voiced sounds, which are represented by two slanted dittolike lines placed to the top right of a syllabic sign. In the twelfth century a symbol was created to represent a final *n* sound, which counts as a separate syllable in Japanese. In the sixteenth century what the Japanese called "half-impure" sounds, a group of five *p*-initial syllables, were represented by a small circle[11] placed in the same position as the diacritic for voicing (Kokugogakkai 1966:622, 750–751, 758). The function of the two diacritics can be illustrated as follows:[12]

ho bo po
ほ ぼ ぽ

A major standardization of the kana symbols occurred in the nineteenth century when standard forms were carefully and deliberately selected by reformers. They now number 46.

Japanese as spoken today is considered to have 105 or 113 syllables, depending on the dialect taken as standard. If we accept the smaller figure, there are still more than twice as many syllables as there are syllabic signs. While it would have been a very simple matter for the Japanese to develop syllabaries with a one-to-one correspondence between sound and symbol, they instead reduced the number of symbols needed by various techniques, of which only the two principal ones are noted here.

One of these, already mentioned above, is the use of the "impure" and "half-impure" diacritics, which together did away with the need for almost two dozen signs. The other, more important, device, which saves almost three dozen signs, is a variation of what I have called the "syllable-telescoping technique" in discussing Sumerian, Chinese, and Mayan. The variation developed by the Japanese, who may have gotten the basic idea from the Chinese *fănqiè* technique discussed earlier, is more restrictive; most of the occurrences can be summarized and illustrated as follows:

$$C(i) + yV = CyV$$
$$ki + yo = kyo$$

The first syllable in the formula is limited to the 11 syllables that consist of a consonant followed by the vowel *i*. The second syllable is limited to those consisting of the semivowel *y* followed by either *a, o,* or *u.* The telescoping of the syllables is now normally indicated by writing the second symbol in smaller than usual size, as indicated in the following comparison:

ki + yo = kiyo   ki + yo = kyo

A further adaptation of this technique resulted in the telescoping of the two syllables *ku + wa* to *kwa.*

The actual number of syllabic symbols used by the Japanese has varied historically depending on exactly what sounds are represented and whether or not different symbols are used for the same sound performing a special function, such as representing a case ending. In the past, many graphic variants were used to represent the same syllable. Today 46 signs are in common use, though there is a certain amount of individual variation. The hiragana and katakana forms of the signs are shown in figure 21.

These signs are transcribed in various ways. The two main systems of *rōmaji* (romanization) are the "New Official System," adopted by the Japanese government, and the "Hepburn System," the system best known to foreigners, named after an American missionary doctor.

In creating the syllabaries the Japanese were clearly influenced by the Chinese idea of syllabic writing and by the specific forms of the symbols used in that writing. But they were also influenced by the phonological structure of their own language. The simple structure of the syllables, and the extensive concatenation of syllables to form polysyl-

a	ka	sa	ta	na	ha	ma	ya	ra	wa
あ	か	さ	た	な	は	ま	や	ら	わ
ア	カ	サ	タ	ナ	ハ	マ	ヤ	ラ	ワ

i	ki	shi	chi	ni	hi	mi		ri	
い	き	し	ち	に	ひ	み		り	
イ	キ	シ	チ	ニ	ヒ	ミ		リ	

u	ku	su	tsu	nu	fu	mu	yu	ru	
う	く	す	つ	ぬ	ふ	む	ゆ	る	
ウ	ク	ス	ツ	ヌ	フ	ム	ユ	ル	

e	ke	se	te	ne	he	me		re	
え	け	せ	て	ね	へ	め		れ	
エ	ケ	セ	テ	ネ	ヘ	メ		レ	

o	ko	so	to	no	ho	mo	yo	ro	(w)o	n
お	こ	そ	と	の	ほ	も	よ	ろ	を	ん
オ	コ	ソ	ト	ノ	ホ	モ	ヨ	ロ	ヲ	ン

Figure 21. Japanese Kana Syllabaries

The 46 syllabic kana symbols (hiragana above, katakana below) which, augmented by two special diacritics and by a technique of combining two symbols to represent one syllable, comprise a relatively simple way of writing the 105 or 113 syllables of standard Japanese. The symbols are transcribed in the *rōmaji* or romanization system best known to non-Japanese, Hepburn romanization.

labic words, favored representing the language with a simple set of syllabic signs. It has been argued that an orthography based on an alphabetic system would not necessarily be superior to one based exclusively on kana (Cheng 1975).

It is an ironic fact, however, that while the Japanese developed a system of sound representation that was almost perfectly suited to their language, they ended up with one of the worst overall systems of writing ever created. This came about because of the Japanese inability, or refusal, to make a clean break with the characters that had been the source of their inspiration in the first place. Instead they combined Chinese characters with Japanese syllabograms, that is kana and kanji, in a way that closely parallels the equally clumsy Akkadian adaptation of the Sumerian symbols. Indeed the parallels are so close that we can say that Japanese is to Chinese as Akkadian is to Sumerian.

In the modern mixed script developed by the Japanese the main words, very roughly speaking, tend to be written in kanji, and the secondary items, such as case endings, in kana. The vast number of words taken over from Chinese, which now constitute more than half of the total vocabulary, are almost always written in kanji and are always read in some version of the Sino-Japanese pronunciations mentioned earlier. Some characters are also given a reading, as noted earlier in the case of *yama* 'mountain,' corresponding to the native word with a meaning similar to that of the Chinese original. Some thousand or so characters, out of an earlier total of about 7,000 in general use, had such native readings. Chinese characters are further used to represent the roots of Japanese verbs, in which, as will be noted below, they often do not even correspond to morphemes.

In contrast to Chinese, whose root words are invariable, the Japanese language, in common with other "agglutinative" languages like Korean and Manchu and related languages of northeast Asia, tacks on a succession of affixes to the basic root. In the writing system these additions are represented by kana symbols added to the kanji root.

Some of the complexities resulting from the potpourri of Chinese and Japanese sounds and symbols can be illustrated by the changes rung on the relatively simple character with the original meaning in Chinese of 'to eat; food' and an early pronunciation something like *dź'iək* (Karlgren 1940:921). The character has been taken over into Japanese in its original meanings and with the Sino-Japanese pronunciations SHOKU, JIKI, and SHI. It is also used in the representation of different words, including the indigenous word for 'to eat,' namely *taberu.* (I am following the conventional practice of indicating Sino-Japanese pronunciations with capitals and native pronunciations with lowercase letters.) Let us first note the following pair of nominal expressions:

食 道 *SHOKUDŌ* 'esophagus' (literally *SHOKU* 'eat' + *DŌ* 'road')

食 過 *tabesugi* 'overeating' (literally *tabe* 'eat' + *sugi* 'exceeding')

The first term is borrowed from Chinese. The second term is a purely indigenous expression. There is nothing in the appearance of the characters to distinguish native from foreign or to indicate how the terms are to be pronounced.

In its generalized use in the meaning 'to eat' the main kanji we are discussing occurs in combination with kana symbols to indicate the various inflections. These are extensive. Here are a few examples:

食 べ	*tabe* '(will) eat [and. . .]'
食 べ る	*taberu* 'eats'
食 べ た	*tabeta* 'ate'
食 べ ま す	*tabemasu* 'eats/will eat'
食 べ ら れ る	*taberareru* 'will be/get(s) eaten'
食 べ な い	*tabenai* 'doesn't/won't eat'
食 べ た い	*tabetai* 'wants to eat'
食 べ さ せ る	*tabesaseru* 'makes eat/feeds'
食 べ よ う	*tabeyō* 'let's eat'

The essence of the mixed system of writing will perhaps become clearer if we adapt the procedure to English, using the Chinese character for the basic word 'eat' and our ordinary letters for amplifications of the word, as follows:

to 食

食 ing

食 er

食 en

食 s

食 ible

Note that in the preceding Japanese examples involving the verb 'to eat,' the Chinese character represents only the indigenous sound *ta*, which is not even a morpheme, whereas in the nominal expressions presented earlier it had either the native pronunciation *tabe* or the Sino-Japanese pronunciation *SHOKU*.

The examples that have been cited here are among the simpler illustrations of the mixed use of kanji and kana. There are many more complexities that we need not go into here, since it is already apparent that a particularly troublesome problem in Japanese mixed writing is how a particular Chinese character is pronounced in a given context. Even the erudite encounter difficulties in this area. For the public at large the problem is so great that a special tactic has been resorted to in popular publications such as newspapers and magazines. These have adopted the practice of attaching to every kanji small kana symbols (*furigana*) to represent the sound. The symbols are placed to the right of the character in vertical writing and above a character in horizontal writing, as illustrated in the following renderings of the surname Kindaichi:

金 kin   kin   da   ichi

田 da

一 ichi   金   田   一

The need to resort to such an expedient has led one of the foremost authorities on Japanese to the following assessment of the writing system: "One hesitates for an epithet to describe a writing system which is so complex that it needs the aid of another system to explain it. There is no doubt that it provides for some a fascinating field of study, but as a practical instrument it is surely without inferiors" (Sansom 1928:44).

It is precisely this inferior system which has dominated Japanese writing despite the existence of a simpler system of syllabic signs. The literate elite which from the beginning has set the intellectual tone for Japanese society is notorious for its addiction to preciosity in this as in many other areas. A writing system that was complicated enough to begin with even became the subject of word games and deliberate obscurity of style.

There was, to be sure, some writing in the simpler kana script, but in general it was considered of secondary importance. The early (eleventh century) masterpiece of Japanese literature *The Tale of Genji* was written almost entirely in kana. It is significant that the author was a woman, as such much less inhibited by macho constraints that ranged from the one extreme—disdain for book-learning—to the other—sinological pedantry and obscurantism.

The complicated hybrid system of Japanese writing served well enough when it was required only to meet the limited needs of the feudal society that characterized Japan up until recent times. But in the nineteenth century, as Japan attempted to cope with the modern world that was pressing against it, thoughts turned to doing something about the system of writing.

Considerable attention was paid initially to the possibility of abandoning Chinese characters completely and writing only either in kana or in some form of romanized writing. Debate in this area focused particularly on the social and cultural aspects of such a drastic change. There was also widespread discussion regarding the technical feasibility of writing in a purely phonetic script. Advocates of such a move demonstrated that the characters were not indispensable by extensive publication which dispensed with them completely. Publication in rōmaji included treatises in the field of mechanics and aeronautics, novels by the popular writer Natsume Sōseki, translations of the Bible and books by H. G. Wells and Robert Louis Stevenson, and many other works. There was an equally impressive group of publications in kana (Hall 1949:377).

Demands for "language reform" that were based on practical considerations were voiced by people who spanned the political spectrum. Broader considerations were advanced by advocates of greater democracy and social reform, especially in the decades preceding World War II, evoking strong opposition from reactionary elements. In the twenties and thirties scores were arrested for belonging to linguistic societies advocating reform of the writing system. Saito Hidekatsu, the editor of two journals devoted to the subject, was arrested in 1938 and died in prison the following year (Hall 1949:19).

In the spring of 1946 a United States Education Mission that included some of the most distinguished American educators was sent to advise General Douglas MacArthur on educational policy. One of its major recommendations was replacing characters with rōmaji. In advancing this recommendation the mission stressed the social and political as well as linguistic aspects of the reform. There appears to have been considerable public support for such a move, but the entrenched bureaucracy, heartened by the failure of MacArthur to support the recommendation, rejected such a drastic change (Hall 1949; DeFrancis 1947).

Instead a limited change, for which planning had been going on since the 1920s, was instituted. It placed primary emphasis on reduction in the number of Chinese characters to be used in general publication, together with simplification and regularization of kana spellings. Before the war newspapers maintained a font of some 7,500 kanji, actually almost double that number if we count pieces of type which combined kanji with furigana. The government recommended a limitation to 1,850 kanji, later increased to 1,945, the abandoned kanji being replaced by kana. The regulations that have been adopted apply mainly to official documents, mass publications such as newspapers, and textbooks. They do not apply to private communication (e.g., correspondence), nor to the areas of science and technology, literature, and book publishing in general. There is no limit to the number of characters that can be used in these areas (Neustupný 1984:57). However, in actual practice, many characters have been dropped, and many antiquated usages have been abandoned.

At the same time the practice of indicating the pronunciation of kanji by writing furigana alongside the characters has been considerably reduced. Much depends on the preference of individual publishers. Although largely discontinued in newspapers, the supplementary symbols are used in varying degrees in some books for children, in many literary works aimed at a mass audience, and in all sorts of publication if a particular kanji presents a special problem. In the last case it is also a common practice to indicate the reading of the character with parenthetical kana placed after the ambiguous kanji.

The current situation is one in which the kanji-cum-kana mixed system appears to dominate the writing scene to the complete exclusion of any possibility of the exclusive use of either kana or rōmaji. The appearance may be deceptive, however. It is true that what is officially promoted by the government, and what seems to be exclusively used by those who set the intellectual tone of society, is the mixed script. Moreover, it is unquestionable that kanji, in comparison to the generally denigrated kana and rōmaji scripts, have a prestige value in that their mastery defines an individual's level of *kyōyō,* a concept combining the ideas of education, cultivation, and refinement (Brown 1987). Despite all this, one observant student of the Japanese linguistic scene has noted the existence of small but persistent groups which continue to advocate a move toward rōmaji, further limitations on kanji, and other measures aimed at the simplification of the writing system (Unger, personal communication, 6/23/87).

And even though the mixed script continues to dominate publications that most strike the eye, rōmaji and kana play a not inconsiderable role in several areas. Most telex messages are conveyed in rōmaji, the rest in kana. Telegrams are sent exclusively in katakana. All reading matter prepared for the blind is in Braille-dot equivalents for the kana symbols, which means, incidentally, that reading is easier for the blind than for the sighted (Unger 1984:103–104, 201). Bank statements and gas and electricity bills are all in kana. Both of the simple scripts are widely used in signs, shop names, and other areas. Katakana is also used in connection with the massive borrowings from other languages (especially English as *the* language of prestige), resulting in an influx that may alter the whole balance of the Japanese language.

The advent of computers and word processors is also playing a role. Although these can output kanji as well as kana, the preferred inputting of kanji is via kana or rōmaji. That is, the Japanese typically type the kana or rōmaji equivalent of the kanji expression they wish to print out, see on the screen the various kanji that share the transcription, and then press a key to select the desired kanji. This means that the Japanese are getting less and less practice in writing characters.

And less writing means weakened command of kanji. Control over this difficult script was never very firmly established among the population as a whole, and in the postwar period has become even more problematic (Unger 1987, 1988). In 1980 Sato Hideo, head of a research unit in the Ministry of Education, estimated that while most Japanese probably retain recognition knowledge of the 1,945 kanji in general use, on the average they remember how to write only about five hundred (Sato, personal communication, 1980).

All this raises the possibility of a future with a continued emphasis on kanji-cum-kana as the writing of prestige, but with actual reliance on kana and rōmaji on an increased scale that may eventually, in a few generations, result in the demise of the traditional system of writing.

Yi

The little-known Yi syllabary shown in figure 22 deserves special attention as the best example of a "pure" syllabic system because of its one-to-one correspondence between syllabic sound and syllabic representation.

The system is the creation of the Yi people, a minority nationality in southwest China who in 1978 were estimated to number over 4,800,000 people. Of these, 3,000,000 were said to be scattered throughout the province of Yunnan and another 400,000 in Guizhou. The largest single concentration, about 1,100,000, was located in the Liangshan (Cool Mountain) Yi Autonomous Prefecture in Sichuan (ZSM 1981:296). The 1982 census showed an overall increase in population to five and a half million. Most of these Yi people live in areas demarcated as autonomous regions: 3 autonomous prefectures and a dozen autonomous counties (Hu Qingjun 1986).

The Yi were originally known to the Chinese, and to the foreigners who first came in contact with them, by the pejorative name *Lolo*. One explanation for the name is that it derives from the Chinese pronunciation of the Yi word for "spirit box," an object of considerable importance in the people's shamanistic religion (Dreyer 1976:292). Another explanation is that the name meant something like "vagabond" or "bandit" (Eberhard 1982:76, 103). The Chinese characters used to render the name were originally composed with the "dog" determinative. After the Chinese Communists encountered this minority group in the course of their Long March, they forbade the use of the term Lolo as part of a conciliatory policy that included replacing the "dog" determinative with that for "human being" in names for minority peoples (Dreyer 1976:118, 292).

After coming to power in 1949, the Communists proceeded cautiously in their efforts to transform Yi society. The society presented special difficulties because it was based on a slave system in which almost half the people were enslaved by a powerful noble class comprising 5 percent of the population and by a commoner class making up the rest. In 1956, after carefully laying the groundwork, the Chinese gradually began to introduce measures which ended slavery and altered the class structure of Yi society (Winnington 1959).

In the same year, as part of an overall policy of aiding minority peoples to improve their writing systems or to create new ones if these did not already exist, a number of teams was formed, and 700 people,

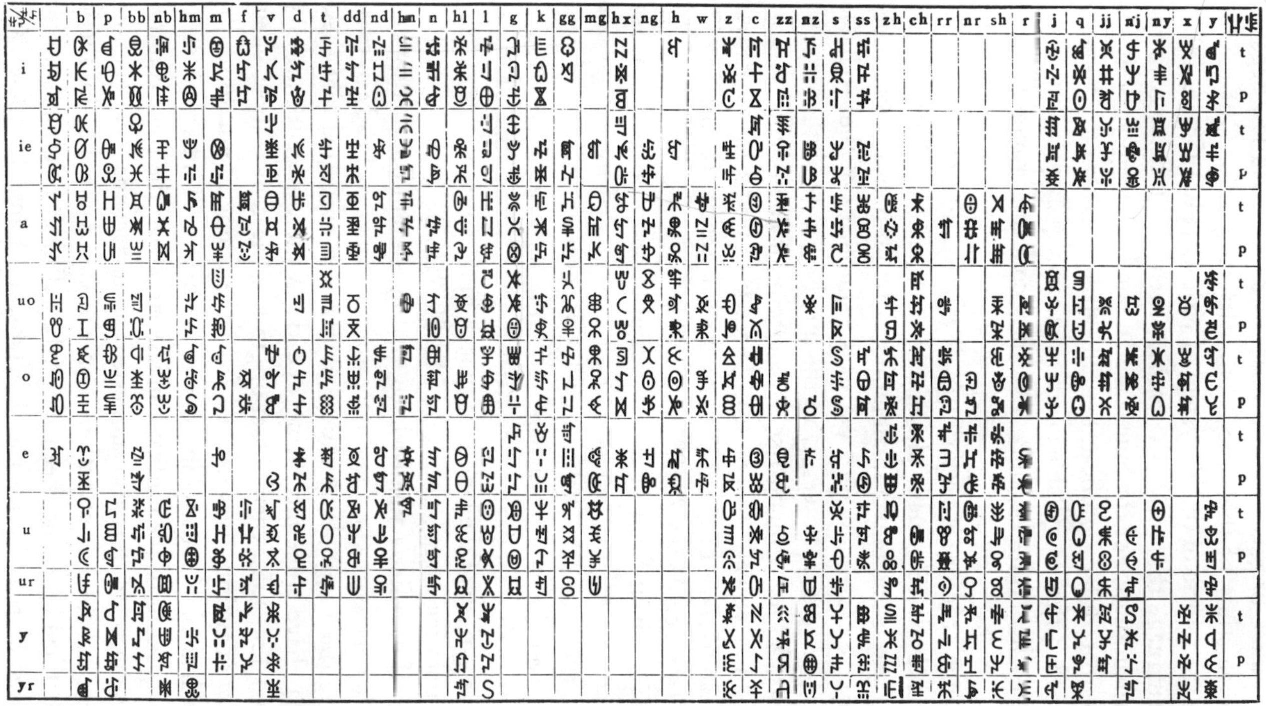

Figure 22. Yi Syllabic Writing

A syllabary of 819 signs standardized in 1975 from the thousands of centuries-old symbols used by the Yi people of southwest China. It is the basis of Yi writing in schools, publications, and other areas. Reprinted with permission from John DeFrancis, *The Chinese Language: Fact and Fantasy* (Honolulu: University of Hawaii Press, 1984), p. 28.

including Chinese linguists and members of 20 nationalities, began a comprehensive study of the various minority languages. Out of this effort came the reform of the Yi system of writing (PR 1958:16–17).

The Yi language that forms the basis of the writing belongs to the Tibeto-Burman branch of the Sino-Tibetan family of languages. It has six dialects that differ significantly. One dialect has been estimated as having 813 different syllables counting tones (Chen Shilin 1979: 243) and another 700—or only 180, not counting tones (Février 1948:83).

The syllable structure is very simple. Typically, all syllables consist of at most a single consonant plus a vowel and a tone. There are no consonant clusters and only a small number of diphthongs. Tone aside, Yi and Japanese are almost on a par in the simplicity of their syllable structures. They differ, however, in the number of items that can fill the CV slots. Yi has a much richer repertoire of consonants (almost four dozen) and vowels (ten or so). These are in addition to tones, which appear to vary in number from four to seven (Ramsey 1987: 254–255; DeFrancis 1984a:28, 291).

In deciding which form of the language to adopt as the basis for reforming the script, the working team was guided by the general principle of selecting "the dialect used by the greatest number of people, spoken over the largest area, and reflecting the general direction of development of the language" (Ma Xueliang 1962:25). This led to the selection of a variety of the language spoken in the northern part of the Cool Mountain region in Sichuan (Li Min 1979:305).

The task of devising a standardized writing system for this spoken norm had to cope with the conglomeration of symbols already in existence among the Yi people. Although it has been suggested that these symbols may have come into being as early as the thirteenth century (Pelliot 1904:154–155), their actual origin is unclear. It is most likely that the *idea* of writing was derived from the Chinese, whose southward push had placed them in contact with the Yi-inhabited areas since the beginning of the unified Chinese empire in the third century B.C. Chinese inspiration is also suggested by the fact that the Yi chose to develop a syllabic script rather than one based on the alphabetic principle that had long since been adopted by all their neighbors except the Vietnamese, that is, by the Tibetans, Laotians, Burmese, and Thai. This, however, is the full extent of the influence that may have been exercised by Chinese writing, for the Yi symbols bear no resemblance to those of the Chinese.

The earliest extant examples are some genealogical stone inscriptions that date from the sixteenth century (d'Ollone 1912; Ma Xueliang 1981). Later manuscript materials that have survived include songs, legends, and accounts of various social practices. In the main, however, they are concerned with religious matters—divination, prayers, and sacrifices. Most of this material was composed and jealously guarded by a group of hereditary shamans called *pimo* (Young 1935–1936). In recent years efforts have been made to sift through and translate some of the more than one thousand manuscript items that have been found to date (Hu Qingjun 1986:501).

The script used by the *pimo* comprised syllabic signs that a Qing dynasty source has likened to tadpoles (Li Min 1979:304). Many of the symbols were idiosyncratic, created deliberately as a kind of secret writing. While any one individual probably used only a limited number of symbols, the total number has been variously estimated as exceeding 8,000 and even 10,000 (Li Min 1979:305; Ma Xueliang 1981:14).

In attempting to reduce this chaotic mass to a serviceable script, the language workers, basing themselves on the spoken norm mentioned above, were guided by the further principle that "one symbol should have only one sound, and one sound should have only one symbol." This procedure led to the creation and official adoption in 1975 of the "Yi Writing Standard Scheme" consisting of 819 symbols—756 to represent the Yi language itself, and another 63 to transcribe loanwords, mainly from Chinese (Li Min 1979:305; Hu Tan, personal communication, 1983).

The system was formally introduced into the school system starting in 1978. It has also come to be widely used in the publication of books, newspapers, and other materials (Chen Shilin 1979). Apart from works printed in the Cool Mountain area itself, there are also publications from the Sichuan Nationalities Press, including such miscellaneous items as bilingual (Yi and Chinese) conversation texts, bilingual studies of Yi grammar, and assortments of artistic forms of the Yi symbols.

A transcription system based on the Latin alphabet has also been created for the Yi language by the Chinese linguist Chen Shilin. Of the four tones, the first is represented by final *t,* the second is unmarked, the third is represented by a special ligature, and the fourth is represented by final *p.* This system, which has undergone repeated changes, is used only to transcribe the system of syllabic signs.

The number of symbols comprising the syllabic script makes it the largest standardized syllabary ever created. Its great size contradicts a thesis propounded by Gelb regarding the application of what he calls "grammatology," that is, the study of writing systems, to the field of decipherment. In a given system of writing, he says, it is easy to count the number of different graphemes, or signs with distinctive features. From this he concludes:

> The teachings of grammatology tell us that a writing consisting of about sixty graphemes should represent a syllabary. Similarly, if the number of counted graphemes reaches several hundred, it is safe to assume in the light of grammatology that the underlying writing represents a logo-syllabic system [Gelb 1974:302–303].

The number of counted graphemes in the Yi syllabary reaches the uniquely large figure of over eight hundred, but for all that the system is unquestionably syllabic, not what Gelb calls "logo-syllabic," since the symbols are purely phonetic.

The notion that a syllabary must have only a limited number of symbols is shared by most students of writing, including Sampson, who contends that only "a few dozen" are to be found in phonemic and syllabic scripts (1985:145). Perhaps the existence of the Yi syllabary of 819 signs will help shake the dogmatic belief that Chinese cannot possibly be a syllabic system of writing because of its even more numerous and far less reliable phonetic symbols.

The Yi system of writing also contradicts another idea of Gelb's which he emphasizes with italics: *"All syllabic writings are either identical with, or simplified from, the respective syllabaries of the word-syllabic writings from which they are derived"* (1963:162). In the first place, the assumption that all syllabic systems are derived from "word-syllabic" systems is untrue. Gelb classifies Chinese as a "word-syllabic" system, and while it is true that the Japanese syllabaries were derived from Chinese symbols, the Yi syllabary was influenced only by the Chinese idea of syllabic writing, and not by the form of the graphs. Gelb's thesis is all the more surprising since he is quite aware that Sequoya developed his syllabary on the basis of the letters of the English alphabet (1963: 206–207).

Apart from the extraordinary number of Yi symbols, another distinctive feature of the system is the incorporation of the tone within the syllabic sign. That is to say, unlike the Vai syllabary, which marks tones—when they are indicated at all—by separate external symbols (Scribner and Cole 1981), the Yi system has distinctly different symbols for syllables with different tones. If the practice had been adopted of using separate diacritics to represent tones, in the fashion of the Vai system and of various transcription systems of Chinese (as in *mā, má, mǎ, mà*), the number of basic syllabic signs could have been reduced to around 300. But such a simplification was rejected in favor of what was apparently the well-established practice of using a single sign to represent all the elements, including tone, that enter into the makeup of Yi syllables.

This handling of tone representation, together with the size of the syllabary and the close correspondence between sound and symbol, combine to make the Yi system of writing the most outstanding example of the category of "pure" syllabic scripts.

4.

Consonantal Systems

There is a great deal of disagreement among scholars as to how to label the writing systems that are classified here as consonantal scripts. I. J. Gelb, whose primary expertise is in Sumerian and Akkadian, insists on labeling all of them as "syllabic" in his *Study of Writing*—in both the first edition (1952) and the second (1963). Gelb's main argument in support of his classification is his contention that writing must develop "from a logographic to a syllabic" writing and cannot skip the syllabic stage by going directly to consonantal writing (1963:78–79).

In a quick reaction to Gelb's first edition, William F. Edgerton, a leading Egyptologist, reflects the general opinion of his field by taking issue with his "friend and colleague," asserting that "Gelb's characterization of normal Egyptian phonetic writing as 'syllabic' is contradicted by facts which are as certain as anything whatever in the pre-Greek history of writing" (Edgerton 1952:290). These remarks are a brief restatement of a more elaborate presentation in which Edgerton, who regards the script as consonantal, had opposed some other proponents of the syllabic thesis (Edgerton 1940).

The Semitist Joseph Naveh follows Gelb in referring to the Egyptian phonetic symbols as "syllabic." However, he disagrees with Gelb on Phoenician, Hebrew, and Arabic, all of which he insists should be considered alphabetic (Naveh 1982). Another opponent of Gelb's view contends that "It is more economical and sensible to regard a Semitic consonant writing as an alphabetic writing in which vowels are not marked" (Barr 1976:75).

Although the last viewpoint has much to commend it, after reviewing the arguments presented by these and other scholars, I have decided to classify all four writing systems as consonantal, and this for two reasons. The first is that the facts and arguments presented by Edgerton seem to me to be more persuasive than those advanced by his opponents. The second is that since, as most of the rival claimants seem to agree, the scripts in question differ to some extent from both syllabic Sumero-Akkadian and alphabetic Greek and Latin, setting up an intermediate group of consonantal scripts seems a reasonable compromise.

"Meaning-plus-Sound" Consonantal System

Egyptian

Up until two hundred years ago the prevailing view about Egyptian was that it simply was not a phonetic system of any kind. This was the opinion of a Greek historian, Diodorus Siculus, who visited Egypt in the first century B.C., a time when the traditional script was still in use. He was the first to describe the writing. Obviously impressed chiefly by its appearance, and not understanding how the script really worked, he said that the Egyptians called their peculiar symbols "hieroglyphs" and that "their script does not work by putting syllables together to render an underlying sense, but by drawing objects whose metaphorical meaning is impressed on the memory" (Pope 1975:17). For two thousand years decipherment of the script was held back by the tenaciously held belief that the signs were symbolic and not phonetic.

The signs certainly do give the impression of being mere pictographics. Many, strikingly iconic, depict recognizable objects—a hand, an eye, an owl, a snake, a giraffe, and many others. Some symbols are more stylized, but they, too, often suggest things or actions.

The belief that these symbols conveyed thought without regard to sound was reinforced when Westerners came in contact with the Chinese system of writing. Here was another system that was believed to be symbolic and nonphonetic, a property credited with giving to Chinese characters a timelessness and universality unmatched by scripts that were acknowledged to be tied to particular forms of speech. The discovery of another system with such marvelous communicative power helped spark an interest, shared by Leibniz and other leading thinkers, in developing a universal writing system.

The converging strands of interest in Egyptian, Chinese, and universal writing systems led Leibniz in 1714 to suggest a new theoretical approach to decipherment that grew out of the problem of rendering proper names in writing systems which might otherwise have no relation to spoken language. His novel suggestion was, in the case of bilingual texts, to use the notation for the sounds of proper names in a known language and a known script to decipher the equivalent notation in an unknown script (Pope 1975:95).

In a work published in 1797 another scholar, Georg Zoëga, a Dane, pushed this idea further by suggesting that the symbols enclosed in the cartouches or oblong frames that appeared in some Egyptian inscriptions probably contained personal names or religious formulas. He also counted the different symbols on inscriptions available in Europe and concluded that the total, 958, was too small for anyone to claim that the symbols expressed words, since any language would have far more words than this. He therefore argued that some of the hieroglyphs must represent what he called *notae phoneticae* 'phonetic signs'—the first appearance, according to one student of the subject, of the word *phonetic* in modern European usage (Pope 1975:57–58).

These ideas were taken up by several scholars who concentrated their efforts on inscriptions incised on an obelisk and on the famous Rosetta Stone that had been found during Napoleon's invasion of Egypt in 1798. The Rosetta Stone seemed particularly promising because of its bilingual inscription in Greek and two versions of Egyptian script, one hieroglyphic and the other a more abstract form called demotic. The inscriptions date from the first century B.C., a time of Greco-Roman domination.

Although others made important contributions, the person primarily credited with the decipherment of Egyptian is a young French scholar by the name of Jean-François Champollion. Extending the work of other scholars who had partially deciphered some names appearing in cartouches, Champollion positively identified a number of names, including those for Caesar, Alexander, and Cleopatra.

The last name is presented below, first as it appeared in a cartouche, and then with the serial arrangement of the individual symbols and their transcription:

The last two symbols indicate that the name is feminine (Gordon 1982:28–35).

In his brief initial report, made in 1822, Champollion described the Egyptian symbols as "ideograms" and the writing as "ideographic," new terms coined by him, but said that the same signs might be used as phonetic symbols to write proper names and words foreign to the Egyptian language, as he had ascertained by comparing the renditions of the names of Ptolemy and Cleopatra in the Greek text of the Rosetta Stone with those in the Egyptian texts occurring there and elsewhere (Champollion 1822).

In a longer work published two years later, Champollion showed that "the alphabet of the phonetic hieroglyphs" actually had a much wider application than he had thought originally. Using his knowledge of the Coptic language, a late form of Egyptian which was on the verge of dying out, he showed that the symbols were also used phonetically to write ordinary words and grammatical inflections, as in the case of the symbols derived from a picture of a horned viper that were used to denote the sound *f* for the third person pronoun in Coptic and earlier Egyptian (Pope 1975:79). With procedures like these, Champollion showed the way to the decipherment of Egyptian writing and to the reconstruction of the ancient spoken language on which it was based.

The earliest Egyptian writing is either contemporaneous with or slightly later than Sumerian, depending in part on the chronology adopted in dating the two civilizations. Most scholars, even some Egyptologists, give priority to the emergence of the Sumerian script. This raises the question of a possible connection between the two.

The Egyptologist William F. Edgerton seems to exclude consideration of a possible Sumerian influence on Egyptian writing, for he states: "Presumably it was invented by a person or group living in a particular part of Egypt and speaking a particular dialect of the Egyptian language." Dating the earliest hieroglyphic inscriptions known to us at approximately the founding of the First Dynasty (about 3100 B.C.), he adds: "We have no proof that the invention of writing, in any form, was old at that time" (Edgerton 1940:474).

It appears, however, that most scholars who express themselves on the subject think it likely that the Egyptians took the idea of writing from Mesopotamia (Pope 1966:21–23; Hawkes and Woolley 1963: 642, 645; Hodge 1975; Ray 1986:309). Why, then, is there such a difference in appearance between the symbols used in Sumerian and Egyptian writing?

In a recent study which specifically addresses this point, the Egyptologist John D. Ray reiterates the generally held view that it was only the *idea* of writing that was taken over. The Egyptians, he says, had their own forms of pictographic representation, but he rejects the suggestion that it was these forms which led them to the idea of writing. They were, however, receptive to the idea:

> The more likely conclusion seems to be at the moment that, throughout the predynastic period, characteristically Egyptian ways of portraying the natural world were slowly developed, and it was from this 'reserve', or artistic repertoire, that the first hieroglyphs were chosen. . . .
> What then did the Egyptians adapt from Mesopotamia? The simplest answer is probably the best: they took the idea of writing. . . .
> Can we talk about an invention of writing in Egypt at all? Since . . . the only element necessary to set off a chain reaction within protodynastic Egypt was the knowledge that ways to do things the Egyptians wished to do existed elsewhere, the realization that in Sumer pictures of material objects were being used in a punning way to express ideas, or other objects which were impossible to draw explicitly, was the only catalyst required; and this was in fact the only element which was borrowed [Ray 1986: 309–310].

There were other factors that doubtless exercised an influence on the different forms of the symbols used in the two writing systems. The Sumerians wrote chiefly on clay, a medium which did not lend itself very readily to calligraphic artistry. The Egyptians wrote on papyrus and carved on stone, even adding color to their representational symbols (Budge 1963:4). The Sumerian and Egyptian temple accountants used their unadorned writing for utilitarian economic purposes, but the Egyptians made more extensive use of artistic symbols in their religious writings and referred to their script as "divine words." Modern students of the scripts refer to the Sumerian symbols by the prosaic term *cuneiform* 'wedge-shaped.' They refer to the Egyptian symbols as *hieroglyphs* 'sacred carvings.'

Throughout the history of Egyptian writing, from around 3000 B.C. to the fourth century A.D., artists painstakingly continued to draw and carve hieroglyphs whose iconic appearance and delicate execution make the symbols striking to the eye. Such writing was particularly employed for religious and state purposes.

The miniature pictures that comprised hieroglyphic inscriptions were arranged in vertical columns or horizontal lines. The preferred writing order was from right to left, but less often, for special purposes, the left-to-right order was adopted. The direction is generally evident from the fact that reading begins from the direction faced by signs representing persons, animals, and other items with front and back (Gardiner 1927:25).

The need for more rapid transmission of government orders and letters led scribes to abbreviate and modify the picture signs, creating a secondary cursive system known as *hieratic*. This came into being not long after the beginning of hieroglyphic, which itself evolved in a matter of three or four generations, a rapidity which some writers take as further evidence that the principle of writing "was borrowed ready-made from abroad" (Hawkes and Woolley 1963:648). Much later a still more rapid form of writing, called *demotic* 'popular,' was developed, at first chiefly for business and social purposes, later for literary composition as well. Although hieroglyphic writing has received the bulk of scholarly attention, the vast majority of everyday writing was not in that medium but in the two cursive scripts, which students learned first before the hieroglyphs (Meltzer 1980:60–61).

In both of the rapid forms of writing the resemblance to the hieroglyphic forms was largely lost, as can be seen from figure 23. Nevertheless, in neither of the cursive scripts was there any basic modification of the underlying principles (Budge 1963:7–10; Hawkes and Woolley 1963:648). These principles were largely determined by the character of the Egyptian spoken language on which the writing was based.

The ancient Egyptian language, which developed into what was later called Coptic, belongs in part to the Afro-Asiatic family of languages, a rather diffuse collection that includes such Semitic languages as Akkadian, Phoenician, Hebrew, and Arabic. Egyptian shares some features with these languages, but it is not a Semitic language (Callender 1984:57; Hodge 1984:240).

One of the unusual features of Egyptian is its sentence structure. In verbal sentences, that is those having a verb form comparable to a simple verb in English like 'loves,' the verb comes at the beginning of the sentence. In such sentences the normal word order is verb-subject-object-adverb or adverbial phrase, that is a preposition with a noun (Gardiner 1927:34).

As regards the sound structure of the language, early Egyptian apparently had 24 consonants and the vowels *a, i,* and *u,* each of which could be both long and short. Owing to a number of sound changes,

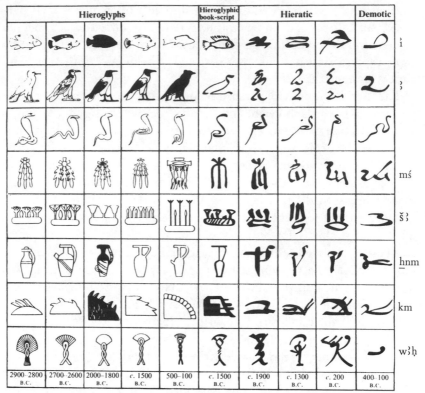

	Hieroglyphs				Hieroglyphic book-script	Hieratic			Demotic	
2900–2800 B.C.	2700–2600 B.C.	2000–1800 B.C.	*c.* 1500 B.C.	500–100 B.C.	*c.* 1500 B.C.	*c.* 1900 B.C.	*c.* 1300 B.C.	*c.* 200 B.C.	400–100 B.C.	

Figure 23. The Evolution of Egyptian Writing

The origin and development of eight representative hieroglyphic symbols from about 2900 B.C. to 100 B.C. The loss in iconicity in the shift from pictographic to stylized forms resulted from a shift from semantic to phonetic values for the signs. The phonetic values have been added on the right in the transcription favored by Egyptologists. The original meanings of the symbols are as follows: (1) fish, (2) vulture, (3) nonphonetic determinative for goddesses, (4) three foxskins tied together, (5) pool with lotus flowers, (6) stone jug with handle, (7) piece of crocodile skin with spines, (8) swab made with hank of fiber. Illustration reprinted with permission from Hans Jensen, *Sign, Symbol and Script* (New York: G. P. Putnam & Sons, 1969), p. 72.

two additional vowels, *o* and *e,* developed about 1500 B.C. Syllables appear to have been limited to consonant + vowel (CV) and consonant + vowel + consonant (CVC), since every syllable begins with a consonant, and no syllable can begin or end with two consonants (Gardiner 1927:27, 423; Callender 1984:57).

The most distinctive feature of the Egyptian sound system is the fact that syllables underwent vowel changes of the type represented by

English *sing:sang:sung*. Roots, inflectional elements, and affixes were all subject to such changes. According to one authority,

> It has been established beyond doubt that the characteristic root idea of every Old Egyptian verb was carried by its consonantal skeleton (as is the case, for instance, in Arabic) while internal vocalic changes, partly accompanied and partly unaccompanied by external prefixes and affixes, served the purpose of inflection.
>
> Corresponding evidence regarding the inflection of the Old Egyptian noun may be said to tend in the same direction [Edgerton 1940:476].

In English, vocalic changes of the type represented by *sing:sang:sung* and *man:men* indicate changes in grammatical function, as in the singular-plural contrast in *one man:two men*. If these words were written without vowels—*one mn:two mn*—native speakers of English would have no trouble inserting the proper vowel.

In Egyptian, even more than in English, the main burden of conveying meaning is carried by consonants. This fact underlies one of the most distinctive features of the Egyptian system of writing, namely the omission of indication of vowels. Although this aspect of the writing system has been much discussed and debated (Gelb 1963; Bowman 1960; Edgerton 1940, 1952), nevertheless one thing is quite clear. Owing to the special nature of the Egyptian language, a writing system that represented only consonants was sufficient to write the basic structure of the language. For native speakers of the language, particularly for learned Egyptian scribes, such reduced phonetic representation did not significantly interfere with its ability to function as a workable system of writing.

It is quite otherwise for nonnative students of Egyptian writing. There is no way that scholars like Gardiner, on whose work (1927) figure 24 is based, can now reconstruct the specific vowels that were omitted in a particular passage. It was only late in the history of Egyptian writing, when Greek and Roman influence became dominant (and eventually eliminated the script), that representation of vowels, especially in transcriptions of foreign names like Cleopatra, was included in such inscriptions as those made famous by the Rosetta Stone (Jensen 1969:68).

The consonant sounds of Egyptian are represented by inventories of generally iconic symbols. The basic inventory comprises 24 hieroglyphs representing as many single consonants. These are called

SIGN	TRANS-LITERATION	OBJECT DEPICTED	APPROXIMATE SOUND-VALUE	REMARKS
	ꜣ	Egyptian vulture	the glottal stop heard at the commencement of German words beginning with a vowel, ex. *der Adler*.	corresponds to Hebrew א *'āleph* and to Arabic *'elif hamzatum*.
	i	flowering reed	usually consonantal *y*; at the beginning of words sometimes identical with ꜣ.	corresponds to Hebrew ' *yōdh*, Arabic ی *yā*.
(1) (2) \\	y	(1) two reed-flowers (2) oblique strokes	*y*	used under specific conditions in the last syllable of words, see § 20.
	ꜥ	forearm	a guttural sound unknown to English	corresponds to Hebrew ע *ʿayin*, Arabic ع *ʿain*.
	w	quail chick	*w*	
	b	foot (position of foot)	*b*	
	p	stool	*p*	
	f	horned viper	*f*	
	m	eagle owl	*m*	
	n	water	*n*	corresponds to Hebrew נ *nūn*, but also to Hebrew ל *lāmedh*.
	r	mouth	*r*	corresponds to Hebrew ר *rōsh*, more rarely to Hebrew ל *lāmedh*.
	ḥ	courtyard	*ḥ* as in English	corresponds to Hebrew ח *ḥē*, Arabic ح *ḥā*.

	ḥ	twisted hank of flax	emphatic h	corresponds to Arabic ح ḥā.
	ḫ	placenta (?)	like ch in Scotch loch	corresponds to Arabic خ ḫā.
	ẖ	animal's belly with teats	perhaps like ch in German ich	{ interchanging early with ⊐ š, later with ● ḫ, in certain words.
	s	{(1) bolt {(2) folded cloth	s	{ originally two separate sounds: (1) z, much like our z; (2) ś, emphatic s, early hardly different from ● ḥ.
	š	pool	sh	
	ḳ	hill-slope	backward k; rather like our q in queen	{ corresponds to Hebrew ק qōph, Arabic ق ḳāf.
	k	basket with handle	k	{ corresponds to Hebrew כ kaph, Arabic ك kāf.
	g	stand for jar	hard g	
	t	loaf	t	
	ṯ	tethering rope	originally tsh (č)	{ during Middle Kingdom persists in some words, in others is replaced by ◠ t.
	d	hand	d	
	ḏ	snake	originally dj and also a dull emphatic s (Hebrew ṣ)	{ during Middle Kingdom persists in some words, in others is replaced by ◠ d.

Figure 24. The Egyptian "Alphabet"
Symbols representing twenty-four single consonants that some Egyptologists refer to as an alphabet. Reprinted with permission of the Griffith Institute, Oxford, from Alan Gardiner, *Egyptian Grammar*. First edition. (Oxford: Clarendon Press, 1927), p. 27.

"uniconsonantal" or "uniliteral" signs. Many scholars also refer to them as "the alphabet," although Edgerton (1940:482) considers this to be a misnomer. In addition there are some 80 "biconsonantal" or "biliteral" signs, i.e., single signs representing two consonants, as well as "triconsonantal" or "triliteral" signs—single signs representing three consonants. The uniconsonantals or uniliterals are the most important, occurring most frequently (Gardiner 1927; Edgerton 1940).

These consonantal signs derive from an extremely simple application of the rebus principle that appears to have made use, at least in part, of what is known as the acrophonic principle, that is using the name of a symbol for its initial sound only. This is the *"a* as in *apple"* principle that is similar to the American "military phonetic alphabet" used to overcome interference from noise in oral communication by calling out (in the latest revised version) "Alpha" for *a,* "Bravo" for *b,* . . . "Zulu" for *z.*

Thus in Egyptian the hieroglyph depicting a "horned viper" *(ft)* is used for *f* and the wavy line representing "water" *(nt)* is used for *n* (Edgerton 1940:479). The acrophonic principle has also been invoked to explain, through Coptic and other indirect means, several uniconsonantal signs, such as a "horned owl" for *m* and a "door" for *p* (Budge 1963:30–31).[1] In all these cases the Egyptian words are presumed to have begun with the consonants indicated, though the full pronunciation cannot now be reconstructed. Gelb, however, rejects the idea that this principle was used to any significant extent, stating that some marginal examples can be found in the system "only in the late period of degeneration" (1963:111).

The symbols are referred to by some modern scholars by the name of the object which they depict. Thus the uniconsonantal symbol representing *m* is referred to as "the owl" since it is a drawing of that bird. Similarly the biconsonantal symbol for *wr* is referred to as "the swallow." In speaking of the sounds represented by the symbols, the convention is to insert a vowel *e* in most cases in order to create a pronounceable syllable. This leads to the pronunciation of *mn* as *men* for the biconsonantal hieroglyph depicting the silhouette of a game board.

As to the transliteration of the symbols, in scholarly studies only the consonants are written, but in popular works vowels are inserted, as in *neferet* for *nfrt.* However, it must be remembered that the actual pronunciation may have involved other vowels before, after, or between the consonants recorded (Gardiner 1927).

The Egyptian approach to phonetic representation that has just been described marks it as different from both Sumerian writing and full alphabetic notation. In Sumerian, the vowels are represented within the syllabic signs: the symbols that stand for the sounds *sib* and *sub* would be integral symbols that represent the whole syllable, not its separate phonemes. On the other hand, in an alphabetic system such as English each of the phonemes in a word like *sub* is of course separately represented.

There are, however, some important points of similarity between Egyptian and Sumerian. As in the case of Sumerian, the use by the Egyptians of certain hieroglyphs for their phonetic value did not preclude their continued use for their purely pictographic value. And also as in the case of Sumerian, the Egyptians resorted to techniques involving the use of determinatives and phonetic complements to help disambiguate the confusion that frequently resulted from the diverse use of the same symbol.

In Egyptian the disambiguating devices are much more elaborate. There are, for example, both specific and general determinatives, as in the case of the symbols for dog and for animals in general. The same word can often be written with a specific or a general determinative. Only the most common words lack determinatives. Some take more than one determinative. As to the phonetic complements or phonograms—the various consonantal symbols noted above—these also are used in various complicated ways (Meltzer 1980:43–34; Gardiner 1927; Huang 1939). And according to one authority,

> The name 'determinative' is in many cases historically inaccurate, the ideogram having been the original sign with which the word was first written, and the phonograms having been prefixed to it subsequently for the sake of clearness. In such cases it might more truly be said that the phonograms determine the *sound* of the ideogram, than that the ideogram determines the *sense* of the phonograms [Gardiner 1927:312].

Determinatives and phonetic complements were often piled onto basic elements. They also were often used even when they were not needed. As has been pointed out, "The habitual employment of absolutely useless signs is a conspicuous characteristic of Egyptian orthography" (Edgerton 1940:485).

The following example (taken from Budge 1963:38) illustrates the use of a semantic determinative in the writing of the word *hememu* meaning "humanity, humankind":

$$ḥ \quad m \quad m \quad u$$

Here the determinative is made up of figures for a seated man and a seated woman followed by three vertical lines to convey the idea of plurality.

The following example (taken from Gardiner 1927:518, 558) illustrates the use of determinatives to disambiguate the multiple meanings of the word *eseš*:

1. _____ *sš* scribe's outfit: reed-holder, water-bowl, palette
2. _____ *sš* to write
3. _____ *sš* writing, papyrus, book
4. _____ *sš* scribe

Here the addition of the "scroll" determinative in 2 and 3 fixes the meaning of *sš* as either 'to write' or 'writing, papyrus, book,' and the addition in 4 of the "person" determinative fixes it as 'scribe.'

The following example (taken from Budge 1963:38) nicely illustrates the point of unnecessary redundancy:

$$ḥ \quad a \quad i$$

Here the first symbol is a biconsonantal approximating the sound *ha*. (The *a* actually stands for a sort of coughed consonantal sound called a glottal stop.) The second symbol is a uniconsonantal representing the same sound *a* and functioning as a phonetic complement reinforcing the sound *a* in the preceding symbol. The third symbol represents a sound somewhat like the *y* of English *hay*, conventionally written as *i*. The fourth is a semantic determinative referring to rain. All four taken together represent the word *ḥai* 'rain.'

In his comprehensive study of writing Gelb has enunciated what he describes as "the principle of economy aiming at the expression of linguistic forms by the smallest possible number of signs" (1963:69). The examples just cited suggest that Egyptian hardly supports this view. "Actually," according to one source, "it was an extremely clumsy and difficult medium. So far from its being simplified as time went on, the need to clarify expression and to avoid ambiguities led to an even greater complication, more and more signs being inserted as determinatives and phonetic complements" (Hawkes and Woolley 1963: 658). The total number of signs has been estimated at 2,150. (Ray 1986:314).

Instead of the economy principle, another scholar advances what he calls "the mnemonic principle" as a basic factor in the Egyptian system of writing. In his view the principle involves "not the complete and accurate representation of the utterances of language, but a representation which provides enough information to bring an item unambiguously to mind" (Meltzer 1980:53). Information might be provided by pictographic symbols used for their semantic value, by the same symbols used for their phonetic value, by special symbols used only to represent sounds, and by various devices to suggest meaning or sound in specific utterances. What strikes the eye most is the pictographic element in the writing, but "it should be noted that a number of words of primarily grammatical function (prepositions, particles, demonstratives) are written purely with phonograms (in a number of uses alphabetic signs)" (Meltzer 1980:55).

It is clear that the aptly named mnemonic principle is an approach that consists of nudging the reader to a particular understanding of a cluster of symbols by giving various hints as to how they should be interpreted. The generally more easily depicted content words are as much as possible represented by iconic hieroglyphs. The less easily depicted function words, those all-important grammatical units that determine the structure of a passage, are written phonetically with symbols that may look the same as those for the content words but perform a completely different function. Thus the symbol called "the owl" serves as a content word referring to that bird but also represents the sound *m* of a preposition meaning 'in; by means of, with (of instrument); from, out of' (Gardiner 1927:29).

To drive home precisely how this key aspect of Egyptian writing worked, we can imagine a parallel in English written with pictographic symbols instead of alphabetic letters. We could make dual use, say, of a picture of a colonial inn, one of those that advertises itself with "George Washington slept here." The picture could represent the sound of both the noun *inn* and the preposition *in,* with the added bonus that we would not have to memorize a difference in spelling.

The vital phonetic component without which the system would not have worked at all was available in Egyptian as a means of writing the whole of the language with comparative ease, much more easily than would be possible if we extended the example of syllabic English just cited—especially if vowels were also indicated. As early as the second half of the second millennium B.C., the Egyptians had actually begun to indicate vowels by means of signs originally intended to represent consonants (Driver 1976:266), but they did not choose to make full use of this simple technique. Only a few scribes produced texts using an entirely phonetic writing based on a few simple symbols. These included some late demotic texts and a few hieroglyphic inscriptions written out entirely in alphabetic signs, for example, an experimental text of about 600 B.C. and a stone inscription dating from the fourth century B.C. (Meltzer 1980:62–63).

But that was only in the terminal stage of a writing system which, thanks to its three and a half millennia of existence, appears to have had the longest history of continued use. The latest datable hieroglyphic inscriptions were carved in 394 A.D. (Davies 1987:10). Egyptian writing gave way first to Coptic written in the Greek alphabet, with the addition of symbols from demotic for sounds not in the Greek alphabet, and later to Arabic written in its own script.

"Pure" Consonantal Systems

In the third millennium B.C. writing was limited, if we exclude undeciphered scripts, to three systems—one developed by the Sumerians, another by the Akkadians, who took both the idea and the form of writing from the Sumerians, and still another by the Egyptians, who appear to have obtained the idea but not the form from the first inventors of writing.

The second millennium B.C. witnessed a proliferation of schemes throughout the Near East and the eastern Mediterranean areas. Although there is some support for the idea of independent invention, it seems to be more generally agreed that these diverse writing systems came about through borrowing. There is less agreement, however, as to who borrowed from whom.

One writer avoids a specific commitment by attributing the origin of several partly pictographic, partly syllabic Aegean scripts to "the process of stimulus diffusion" in a world acquainted with various systems of writing that included Sumero-Akkadian cuneiform and hieroglyphic Egyptian (Gordon 1982:121). Gelb tentatively traces these scripts to Egyptian influence (Gelb 1963:x–xi). Pope argues that the scripts were created under the influence of a partly hieroglyphic, partly syllabic system that he attributes to the Hittites, an Indo-European people who were a power in the area of what is now Turkey and northern Syria. In his opinion this Hittite script in turn was influenced by Sumerian writing in its Jemdet Nasr stage (Pope 1966). All these early Aegean scripts, which were basically syllabic in structure, died out without having any apparent affect on subsequent systems of writing.

The situation is otherwise with the scripts that were developed for a number of languages belonging to the northwestern and southwestern branches of the great Semitic family. The eastern branch of this family, comprising Akkadian, Babylonian, and Assyrian, had earlier devised scripts that were based on Sumerian cuneiform. They borrowed from Sumerian not only the cuneiform symbols but the technique of syllabic representation that included vowels as well as consonants.

The northwestern and southwestern branches, located respectively in the Syria-Palestine area and the Arabian peninsula, adopted a different approach that has emerged as the most distinctive feature of Semitic writing. This is the representation of consonants only, an approach which is generally traced to Egyptian influence, though a Mediterranean origin has also been claimed (Powell 1981:434).

The ability to dispense with representation of vowels is due to a special characteristic that is found to some extent in various linguistic systems but is most highly developed in the Semitic family of languages. It is a well-known characteristic of these languages that their word roots consist only of consonants, usually three in number, and that their vowels express grammatical categories through a richly developed system of internal inflections. An example of a three-consonant root is the word *qrn* 'horn' that is common to Akkadian, Hebrew, and Arabic. The way in which vowels express inflection has already been illustrated, in the previous discussion of Egyptian, with the English examples *sing:sang:sung* and *man:men*.

Two kinds of scripts that represented consonants but not vowels were developed by various Semitic peoples. One consisted of linear symbols whose form was largely determined by the materials used in writing—a pointed instrument applied mainly to stone or metal, and pen and ink applied to parchment, potsherds, and papyrus. Another consisted of cuneiform symbols written on clay tablets (Naveh 1982:2–8).

The Ugaritic script of about thirty cuneiform signs was apparently developed in the fourteenth and thirteenth centuries B.C. in the Semitic area of Syria near the Mediterranean. Gelb insists that these symbols were not borrowed but were "the result of free individual creation" (1963:133). Unlike the Sumero-Akkadian cuneiform symbols, they were applied only to the representation of consonants. Even earlier the same approach to restricted phonetic representation had been adopted in other Semitic scripts that made use of linear symbols. Chief among these is Phoenician.

Phoenician

It appears that the Phoenicians called themselves, in their own language, *Kenan'ni* 'Canaanites.' In Hebrew this word has the secondary meaning 'merchant' (EBMIC 1988b:392).

The predilection of the Phoenicians for commercial activities has been cited to explain their central role in the dissemination of writing. As merchants they needed to keep records. As traveling salespeople they came in contact with Egypt and Mesopotamia, from which they could learn about writing, and with the Mediterranean area, to which they might disseminate their acquired knowledge (Hawkes and Woolley 1963:653–658).

The script devised by the Phoenicians is an outgrowth of early consonantal writing, much of it pictographic in form, called Proto-Canaanite or Old Canaanite. Many of the inscriptions in this early writing are fragmentary in nature and have not been completely deciphered. Nevertheless it appears that the evolution from the early symbols to the later Phoenician script can be summarized as follows:

1. The Proto-Canaanite script was devised about 1700 B.C. by Canaanites who had some knowledge of Egyptian writing.

2. The number of letters representing the consonantal system was initially 27. By the thirteenth century B.C. it had been reduced to 22.

3. The signs were originally pictographs, and most had acrophonic values. These evolved into linear signs.

4. Writing originally went in various directions but was stabilized at right to left about 1100 B.C.

5. When in the middle of the eleventh century the script was stabilized at 22 linear letters written only from right to left, it is no longer called Proto-Canaanite but Phoenician. (Based on Naveh 1982:42).

Most of the preceding points have received general acceptance, but there is some difference of opinion regarding the pictographic origin of the symbols and the use of the acrophonic principle. The great variation in the Proto-Canaanite symbols, and their changes over time, make it difficult to trace specific letters back to specific pictographic symbols. One example that has been advanced is that of the triangle-shaped symbol that stands for the letter *D*. Its origin has been explained by the fact that "*daleth* means 'door,' and the character may very well represent a three-cornered tent-door" (Pedersen 1931:182).

Another frequently cited example is one that shows the involved process by which Egyptian writing influenced the Phoenician script. Among the Egyptian uniconsonantal symbols is a wavy line that stands for the word *nt* 'water' (here the final *t* marks the feminine gender) and was used to represent the sound *n*. The Phoenicians took over the symbol but applied to it their own word for water, which was something like *muw,* and so came to use it, slightly modified, as a letter standing for the sound *m* (Driver 1976:162).

If various forms of Proto-Canaanite writing, rather than just a late stage of Phoenician, are taken into consideration, it may be that "the names of the letters . . . agree fairly with the objects which the forms of fourteen out of twenty-two letters of the Phoenician alphabet seem intended to suggest" (Driver 1976:153). It is also worth noting that all Semitic words, with very few exceptions, begin with consonants (including glottal stop) (Barr 1976:80–81), a fact which surely facilitates using the initial sounds of words in naming the consonant symbols. Although some scholars, including Gelb (1963:140–143), reject the acrophonic origin of the symbols, the data just cited speak in favor of this explanation. As to the symbols themselves, it appears that twenty-two letters of the Phoenician alphabet (shown in figure 25), are either indigenous symbols or borrowed ones adapted to Phoenician usage.

In general the Phoenicians took over from the Egyptians the basic idea of representing only the consonants of their language while jettisoning such other features as the use of determinatives and the representation of two or more consonants by a single symbol. In contrast to the Egyptians, who introduced some vowel signs in the last phase of their writing, "the Phoenicians adhered strictly to the defective spelling" (Naveh 1982:62). The Phoenician script was thus a "pure" consonantal system of writing.

The contrast between the two systems of consonantal writing mani-

Letter name	Phonetic value	Phoenician	Modern Hebrew	Modern Arabic
'Āleph	'A		א	١
Bêth	B		ב	ب
Gimel	G		ג	ج
Dāleth	D		ד	د
Hē	H		ה	ه
Wāw	V		ו	و
Zayin	Z		ז	ز
Ḥēth	CH		ח	ح
Ṭēth	T		ט	ط
Yōdh	Y		י	ي
Kaph	K		כ	ك
Lāmadh	L		ל	ل
Mêm	M		מ	م
Nūn	N		נ	ن
Sāmekh	S		ס	س
'Ayin	A		ע	ع
Pê	P		פ	ف
Ṣādê	TS		צ	ص
Qōph	Q		ק	ق
Rêš	R		ר	ر
Šîn	SH		ש	ش
Tāw	T		ת	ت

Figure 25. Phoenician, Hebrew, and Arabic Scripts

Phoenician writing consisted of symbols some of which have been traced back to pictographic origins. One example is the fourth sign, which is said to have been derived from the picture of a three-cornered tent flap and is related to the Phoenician word of *daleth* 'door.' Some of the signs used in Hebrew and Arabic, two of the main offshoots of the Phoenician system, clearly reveal their Phoenician ancestry. Adapted with permission from A. C. Moorhouse, *The Triumph of the Alphabet* (New York: Henry Schuman, 1953), p. 305.

fested itself both in the forms of the symbols they used and in their functions. The Egyptians used symbols whose form was usually iconic, such as those representing an owl, a hand, and so on. Moreover, they used the symbols sometimes to express the depicted meaning, sometimes merely for the consonant sounds that the symbols evoked. The Phoenicians started out with some iconic symbols but soon stylized these to the point where they were no longer iconic. Moreover, they used the symbols solely for phonetic representation of consonants.

The Phoenicians are generally credited with this major innovation in writing, though there is some question as to whether they or the speakers of Ugaritic were the first to carry it out to the full. Driver (1976:151) gives priority to the Phoenicians, Paper (1982:111) to the citizens of Ugarit.

In the early part of the first millennium B.C., Phoenician was a language of prestige and together with its script enjoyed a certain international status. Its use lasted about a millennium. The latest inscription from Phoenicia proper dates from the first century B.C., when the language was gradually being superseded by other forms of Semitic speech (EBMIC 1988b:392).

One of its chief rivals was the Aramaic language, a Phoenician offshoot which developed a consonantal script that had enormous influence. Aramaic was the ancestral script of the writing systems developed for several Semitic tongues as well as for the languages of India and even more distant languages like Uighur and Mongolian (Paper 1982:111–113).

Hebrew

When the Hebrews first undertook to write, they did so in the Phoenician script. They soon began to modify it and to evolve their own system of writing.

There were two phases in this development. The first was a "Phoenician-Hebrew" phase that began in the ninth century B.C. and was broken off with the dispersion of the Jews in the sixth century B.C., though the early script which resulted from the first modifications continued to be used in some Jewish circles. The second phase that began around the second century B.C. resulted in the development of the familiar "square Hebrew" or "Jewish" script from the Aramaic branch of Phoenician (Naveh 1982:10–11). Both phases adopted the general principles of the ancestral script, but they differed from it chiefly in two ways.

The first is in the shape of the symbols. These, as can be seen from figure 25, have a distinctive angular appearance. Despite the difference in shape, the relationship to Phoenician can be seen from the similarity between a few symbols. The points of similarity would be somewhat greater if the comparison were made with the symbols in Proto-Canaanite.

The second and more important departure from the ancestral model is in the addition of symbols to supply information which it was felt was needed to facilitate reading. One device was to add dots *within* some letters to indicate doubling of consonants (Trager 1974:394). But the most important innovations addressed the major problem inherent in the special nature of the writing system. Ordinarily the script expressed only the consonant roots, and the reader was expected to be able to supply the appropriate vowels by determining what word was appropriate in a given context.

The following are some dictionary examples of contextual variations on the basic root form *ktb/v:*

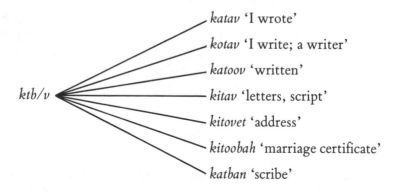

katav 'I wrote'

kotav 'I write; a writer'

katoov 'written'

kitav 'letters, script'

kitovet 'address'

kitoobah 'marriage certificate'

katban 'scribe'

ktb/v

Various expedients were evoked to give more precise information about which vowels to supply in a particular context. One technique involved using the letters *', h, w,* and *y* as symbols for some syllables with vowels, e.g., *'* for *a, ā* (Trager 1974:394–395). A symbol used in this way is referred to as a *mater lectionis* 'reading mother,' and a text so marked is said to have *plene spelling* 'full spelling' (Jensen 1969:309). In the sixth century A.D. a fuller system of vowel indication was developed that made use of dots placed above or below a letter. These are referred to as "vowel points," and a text so marked is said to be "pointed." These diacritical marks are especially used in the teaching of Hebrew and in printed texts of the Hebrew Bible. The complete list of vowel signs (taken from Trager 1974:395) is as follows:

□ *ā, â;* also *o* (short)	ʾ□ *î* or *ī*	□ *u*
□ *a*	□ *i* (short)	□ *ă*
ʾ□ *ê*	ו *ô*	□ *ẽ*
□ *ē*	□ *ō*	□ *ŏ*
□ *e*	ו *û* or *ū*	□ *ə* (shwa), or no vowel

The use of vowel diacritics appears to be much more common than is generally supposed, so much so that it is necessary to draw attention again to the quotation marks in our classification of Hebrew as a "pure" consonantal system. Hebrew and (as we shall see) Arabic are "pure" consonantal scripts only in comparison to Egyptian with its iconic symbols. The actual situation in Semitic writing is nicely summarized in the following quotation:

> It can be *very roughly* said that the scripts of languages like Arabic and Hebrew are 'consonantal' scripts. . . . Actually, however, even the so-called 'consonantal' text of such a Semitic writing commonly includes the marking of *some* vowels. . . . The writing of a text which is absolutely without any kind of vowel indication is actually rather exceptional in the Semitic world [Barr 1976:76–78].

It has obviously often proved necessary to resort to modifications in the script. This suggests that while it may be true that nonindication of vowels is suited to the peculiarities of the Semitic languages, this is true only for skilled native readers who can put up with a graphic system that clumsily conveys a message.

That the users of the script have indeed been more than willing to put up with the system, warts and all, is amply attested by the course of events over the past few millennia. These events have culminated in the last century in the unprecedented creation, unique in the history of human speech, of a colloquial language based on a written language. Hebrew, before 1948 a language limited largely to religious literature, together with its tenaciously surviving script, has been expanded in use to become a national language and a national script.

Arabic

The Arabic script deserves some mention in a general survey because of its widespread adaptation to a host of languages belonging to many different language families. In its basic principles and specific adaptations, however, like Hebrew, it presents no great novelties.

As a Semitic language Arabic displays the same distinctive feature, which we have noted in the case of Phoenician and Hebrew, of consonantal ascendancy over vowels. This common family feature is clearly seen in the following Arabic expansion (taken from Hawkes and Woolley 1963:656; Barr 1976:87) of the basic root form *ktb*[2] that was noted earlier for Hebrew:

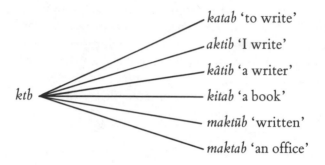

A further indication of the ascendancy of the consonants in Arabic writing is the fact that words are arranged in dictionaries under their roots. Thus *'islam, muslim, salām* are all found under the root *slm* (Yushmanov 1961:5).

Arabic has an even richer inventory of consonants than other Semitic languages. There are 28 of these in the written normative form of the language.

The colloquial dialects of Arabic, spoken in the long stretch of territory from the northwestern corner of Africa to the Persian Gulf, show considerable local variation. Written Arabic, on the other hand, is fairly uniform. Apart from being the language of the Koran, written Arabic serves as the primary form of communication among Arabic speakers of different dialect areas; it is the language of broadcasts over radio and television and of many other public activities.

Arabic is written in a script based on 28 consonant symbols. Of these, 22 are letters that trace their ancestry to the same Aramaic branch of Phoenician from which the Hebrew script is descended. In addition, six letters have been created to represent sounds not found in the other Semitic language (Naveh 1982). Owing to the interpolation of these additional letters, the old Semitic order of signs has not been preserved. Figure 25 shows 22 of the 28 Arabic letters in the same order in which Phoenician and Hebrew are traditionally arranged (Mason 1920:305).

There is considerable uncertainty regarding the transmission of the early Semitic scripts into something that can be called Arabic. The earliest inscriptions claimed to be Arabic date from the sixth century A.D., and there are only a very few of these before the advent of Islam in the seventh century. In the Islamic period Arabic was used in the beginning primarily for recording the Koran in written form. The early form of the script, confined largely to writing on stone, was characterized by straight lines and sharp angles. Later a more cursive style developed which has remained popular ever since (Naveh 1982:161).

Owing, it would seem, to Islam's disapproval of portrayal of the human form, there was a correspondingly greater emphasis on calligraphy, something that is matched only in the case of Chinese. This emphasis on the artistic cultivation of the script has led to the development of numerous styles (Jensen 1969:330–332). The script is also distinguished by the large number of ligatures and by its different shapes for the letters in initial, medial, and final position (Trager 1974:396). Calligraphy has also strongly influenced printed texts. The tendency to imitate manuscript forms has called for precise gearing of the connective elements between symbols and maintaining a large stock of variants and ligatures (Yushmanov 1961:19).

Still another factor that has contributed to the proliferation of forms is the need, as in the case of Hebrew, to add some markers not provided by the consonant-only alphabet. A special symbol is sometimes added to show doubling of a consonant. Other symbols are added to represent vowels, of which (in the standard language) there are three short, *a, i,* and *u,* and the same three long. Long vowels are generally marked, short ones not (Barr 1976:87–89). All this makes for a rather complicated system that works well enough for those who have mastered it, but is not at all easy to learn. It has been estimated that in Turkey, which changed from the Arabic to the Latin script in 1928, children learn to read in half the time with the new script (Gelb 1963:238).[3]

With the expansion of Islam, the Arabic script has spread throughout much of the world. It now stands second only to the Latin alphabet in the extent of its use.

5.

Alphabetic Systems

In the two preceding chapters the material appears in two subsections in which the sequence marks a progression from earlier complex writing systems to later simpler systems of the same basic type. In the present chapter the situation is reversed: The first group consists of alphabetic scripts that are simpler—"purer"—than their descendants. This reversal is of course due to the fact that our basic sequence in each chapter is chronological and, to a certain extent, geneological.

"Pure" Alphabetic Systems

Greek

Greek is presented here first because it is the first fully alphabetic system of writing ever created. It started out as a relatively "pure" system of alphabetic writing. The later scripts based on this principle that directly or indirectly trace their origins to Greek writing include some even simpler than their progenitor, and others so complex that the question has been raised as to whether they really belong to the same category. This mother of alphabets would have difficulty in recognizing her remarkably diverse progeny.

Although the Greeks are well known as the creators of the alphabet to which their name is attached, this was not the first nor the only writing system created by them. Even earlier the Aegean area had produced a number of nonalphabetic scripts whose origin is much disputed. From early in the second millennium B.C. dates a script composed of pictographic symbols. A few hundred years later this gave way to two successive linear scripts which have been labeled Linear A and Linear B and are believed to be related. Both consist of pictographs and other symbols, some of them employed as syllabic signs (Chadwick 1987; Jensen 1969:123–135).

Of these three Cretan Bronze Age scripts, only Linear B has been deciphered. This feat was brilliantly accomplished in 1952 by a young British architect, Michael Ventris, with assistance from John Chadwick, a specialist in Greek. The partially pictographic script includes about eighty-nine symbols that represent vowels or consonant plus vowel. Most syllables were of the CV type. Sequences of two consonants, of which there appear to have been very few, were represented by telescoping two CV syllables, as in the rendering of *tr* in *ti-ri-po-de* for *tripode* 'tripods.' From the decipherment of this meaning-plus-sound script came the discovery of the most ancient form of the Greek language, so far known, written seven hundred years before Homer (Chadwick 1967, 1987; Doblhofer 1961:238–264).

The language was also written by Cypriot Greeks in another syllabic script of a much later date. Generally considered to be related to the earlier linear scripts, and to some undeciphered Bronze Age "Cypro-Minoan" scripts, the Cypriot syllabary was in use from the sixth to the third centuries B.C. (Pope 1975:123). The symbols represented vowels or consonant plus vowel. Consonant-vowel-consonant syllables and clusters of two consonants were represented by telescoping two CV syllables, as in the case of *ka-re* for *gar* and *a-po-ro-ti-ta-i* for *Aphrodite* (Diringer 1968, 1:120–122; Doblhofer 1961:227–237).

Linear B and its predecessors all vanished near 1100 B.C. with the destruction of the civilizations that had produced them. The same fate befell the Cypriot script. It is only in the past century or so that we have known of the existence of such early Greek writing. The Bronze Age syllabic systems were most likely not known even to later Greeks. If they were aware of the scripts, they made no use of their knowledge, for in devising their alphabetic systems they embarked on a quite different approach to writing.

Whereas scholars disagree about the origins of Linear B and other syllabic systems, there seems to be rather general agreement that the Greeks developed their alphabetic system under the influence of the Phoenicians. The Greeks themselves advance this view. Herodotus, the "father of history," recorded in the fifth century B.C. that a Phoenician by the name of Cadmus introduced the "Phoenician letters" when he came to Greece from his homeland (Driver 1976:128). Some modern scholars seem to accept the idea that the Greek acquisition of writing was due to the Phoenicians' having brought their system to Greece (Driver 1976:176–177; Moorhouse 1953:127).

A somewhat different view is presented by L. H. Jeffery, a Greek specialist who appears to have most thoroughly researched the subject. Addressing the highly important matter of precisely how illiterate people might acquire knowledge of writing, she speculates as follows:

> It is, I think, legitimate to postulate that an individual, or a people, learning for the first time a wholly new technical device, is apt to learn it without rejecting or even disputing details, since to try to correct them at this stage implies a previous notion as to what that detail ought to imply; it presupposes a background, a familiarity with the subject, which as yet he is not in a position to have. Thus the illiterate learner may be expected to absorb the letters of the alphabet without deliberate alteration or rejection. He will learn the names and copy the letter-shapes as well as he can. He will accept the sound-value attributed by his teacher to each letter, and will equate it with a familiar sound which occurs in his own language and which seems to him to be more or less the same, though in fact, to a modern philologist's ear, produced by a totally different method of manipulating the breath [Jeffery 1961:3].

Jeffery appears to be dealing with a different kind of borrowing than that engaged in by the Egyptians. As already noted, the Egyptians, who appear to have had only limited knowledge of what was going on in Mesopotamia, borrowed from the Sumerians only the idea of writing. In the application of the idea they made use of indigenous hieroglyphic symbols and introduced the novel acrophonic variation of the rebus principle to represent the consonant sounds of their language. The Phoenicians, on the other hand, while borrowing from the Egyptians chiefly the idea of writing, also appear to have taken over, to a certain extent at least, the Egyptian adaptation of the rebus principle, together with some specific symbols. This suggests a considerably greater contact between Phoenicians and Egyptians than between Egyptians and Sumerians.

Jeffery is envisaging a situation of even closer contact. Applying the approach sketched above to the Greek problem, she presents as the most likely scenario a situation involving close contact between Phoenician merchants and Greek traders living in a Greek settlement which is known to have existed in the Phoenician region on the Mediterranean coast in the eighth century B.C. In contrast to the settled Greeks, traveling Phoenician traders had only tenuous links in the Greek homeland, and they therefore were not part of "the settled intercourse . . . essential to the transplanting of an alphabet." The more firmly rooted Greeks were in a better position to acquire some knowledge, however imperfect, of the local language and the letters in which it was written from their Phoenician trading partners, whose command of their own script was probably also imperfect, since they were not skilled scribes—much less trained linguists. The Greek traders took their knowledge back to their homeland, where it was utilized in the creation of an alphabet to write the Greek language. All this seems to have happened in the eighth century B.C., since there is no surviving example of the Greek alphabet that can be dated earlier than late in that century (Jeffery 1961).

The details of the scenario sketched by Jeffery are important because they bear on the problem of the major modification the Greeks made in the use of the Phoenician letters. For, as is well known, the Greeks took over the 22 consonant letters of the Phoenicians, but in the process used some of them to represent vowels.

Jeffery takes exception to the Greek tradition that this monumental change to vowel representation was "the deliberate, brilliant innovation of a single creator" (1961:2). The idea that the innovation did indeed stem from the brilliant insight of some early Greek inventor is actually held by some modern scholars, including the American linguist George L. Trager (1974:402). But Jeffery's doubts are shared by other scholars. A well-known husband-and-wife team of linguists, in a thoughtful study of types of writing systems, conclude that the Greeks did not precisely understand that the phonetic symbols of the Phoenicians consisted exclusively of signs for independent consonants and so changed the system "without being aware of the fact." They add that the structure of the Greek language, rather than the genius of its speakers, is responsible for the transformation from an "independent consonant" type for Phoenician—a language whose structure permits only consonant-initial words—to the "independent consonant" plus "independent vowel" type for Greek, which includes both consonant-initial and vowel-initial words (Voegelin and Voegelin 1961:63–65). The reasoning of all three scholars in reaching their conclusion is essentially the same. Jeffery's account is much more detailed, however, so I base my nontechnical summary of the matter chiefly on her analysis.

Proceeding from Jeffery's contention that the transmission of the symbols was from Greeks living in Phoenicia rather than from Phoenicians visiting Greece, she speculates on the precise manner in which linguistically unsophisticated Greek traders might hear some alien sounds and see some odd-looking scribblings which equally unsophisticated Phoenicians would demonstrate for them. The Phoenicians write a symbol and say a word that the Greeks hear as starting with a sound similar to what would today be represented by the letter *b*. The Phoenicians tell the Greeks that the letter is called "beth," which the Greeks imitate fairly closely as "beta." The Greeks score well on this because this is a sound familiar to them that is more or less common to most of the languages of the world.

The Phoenicians also write a symbol and utter a word that starts with what we might describe as a kind of "coughed *ah*" sound, made with a sudden closing of the air passage—what linguists call a glottal stop. To the Phoenicians the coughed aspect is important and marks the sound as a consonant. To Greek ears it sounds like a funny way of pronouncing what is to them a sort of *a* sound.

The hypothetical situation sketched here is one that actually happens whenever people are confronted with the sounds of an unknown tongue. An English speaker who knows no French is likely to hear the French pronounce *rue* 'street' as *roo,* whereas the actual equivalent for the latter is the way *roux* 'reddish' sounds. To the French speaker *rue* and *roux* are pronounced in distinctly different ways and are heard as two quite different words. To the untrained English speaker there is no significant difference between them.

The Greek speakers do not need a symbol to represent a coughed consonant, which they probably haven't heard as such in the first place. But they do need one to represent their sound *a,* which occurs initially and in all possible positions, including within clusters of several vowels, so they mechanically use the symbol in question to write their vowel *a.*

The actual order in which the Greeks learn the pair of items is probably the reverse of what I have presented here. They first learn the sound and symbol which the Phoenicians, following the order in which their letters are conventionally listed, refer to as "aleph," and which the Greeks hear as "alpha." The Greeks call the whole series of twenty-two sounds and symbols by the names of the first two, *alpha* and *beta,* from which our word *alphabet* is derived

In much the same way as the vowel *a* came to be represented, so also the symbols for the remaining vowels resulted from the Greeks mishearing Phoenician consonants as Greek vowels. As to the remaining Phoenician consonant symbols, the Greeks simply took all of these over to represent their own approximately equivalent consonant sounds. To take care of some additional sounds not covered by the

Phoenician symbols, the Greeks eventually added a few symbols of their own creation.

The twenty-two Greek letters from alpha to tau, the earliest forms of which are shown in our figure 26, were taken directly from Phoenician. In general the order follows the Phoenician listing of their symbols. The Phoenician names of the letters, which were derived on the basis of the acrophonic principle, were taken over by the Greeks even though the names meant nothing to them. Thus Greek alpha, beta, gamma, and delta correspond to Phoenician aleph, beth, gimel, and daleth, which respectively mean 'ox, house, throw-stick, door' (Driver 1976:181–185).

The Greeks further followed Phoenician practice by first writing from right to left. Later they went in both directions in the manner called *boustrophedon,* literally 'turning like oxen in plowing.' Still later, in the fifth century B.C., writing stabilized at left to right.

Although it is clear that Greek writing derives from Phoenician writing, even in respect to the forms of specific symbols, there are not a few differences between the two. In many cases discrepancies are no doubt because the Greek purveyors of Phoenician writing misunderstood just how the system worked and missed some of the fine points, so that they made unintended changes in copying the symbols. To the changes produced at the first stage of copying the Phoenicians were added others as Greeks from different localities and further removed from the source attempted to apply the symbols to their dialects. The result was a considerable proliferation in forms, a fact which greatly complicates the task of tracing particular symbols to their source.

The local Greek alphabets gradually gave way, first to two main varieties, and later to one. The West Greek alphabet went out of use in Greece but was transplanted westward. The East Greek variety became dominant after it was officially adopted in Athens in 403 B.C. In the middle of the third century B.C. it was improved by the addition of three accent marks. It has come down as the 24-letter alphabet in which Classical Greek is written (Diringer 1968, 1:362–363; Trager 1974:403–404). While there is not exactly a one-to-one correspondence between sound and symbol, the fit is close enough to warrant placing the script far ahead of all previous systems of writing in terms of simplicity.

The Greek idea of writing, though not the precise form that its symbols took, spread in all directions and throughout much of the world. Apart from Latin, the Cyrillic script, used now to write Rus-

North-Semitic	Phoenician	Name	Phonetic Value	Early (Greek)	Classical (Greek)	Name (Greek)	Early (Latin)	Monumental (Classical, Latin)
		'Aleph	'		A	Alpha	A	A
		Beth	B		B	Beta		B
		Gimel	G		Γ	Gamma		C
		Daleth	D	Δ	Δ	Delta		D
		He	H		E	Ĕpsilon		E
		Waw	W			Digamma		F
								G
		Zayin	Z	I	Z			
		Ḥeth	Ḥ		H	Ēta		H
		Teth	Ṭ		θ	Theta		
		Yod	Y		I	Iota	I	I (J)
		Kaph	K		K	Kappa		K
		Lamed	L		Λ	Lambda		L
		Mem	M		M	Mu		M
		Nun	N		N	Nu		N
		Samekh	S					
		'Ayin	'	O	O	Ŏmicron	O	O
		Pe	P		Π	Pi		P
		Sade	S	M				
		Qoph	Q					Q
		Reš	R		P	Rho		R
		Šin	SH—S		Σ	Sigma		S
		Taw	T	X		Tau		T
					Y	Upsilon	V	V
					X	Chi		X
					Ω	Ōmega		Y
								Z

Figure 26. Phoenician, Greek, and Latin Scripts

The genealogical sequence of Phoenician to Greek to Latin is evident in the similarity of some of the symbols, as in the case of the Latin D, derived from Greek delta, which in turn goes back to Phoenician daleth. Adapted with permission from David Diringer, "Alphabet." *Encyclopedia Americana* 1 (1968):622.

sian and many other languages, is the most widely used offspring of Greek; it is based on the capital-letter form of the system. Many other alphabetic systems are more remotely based on Greek symbols. Some owe only the idea of alphabetic writing to intermediaries whose inspiration goes back ultimately to the Greeks.

In a comment that sounds ethnocentric unless one understands it as applying to all existing alphabetic systems, Gelb summarizes as follows:

> The development of a full Greek alphabet, expressing single sounds of language by means of consonant and vowel signs, is the last important step in the history of writing. From the Greek period up to the present, nothing new has happened in the inner structural development of writing. Generally speaking, we write consonants and vowels in the same way as the ancient Greeks did [Gelb 1963:184].

Latin

The ancient region of Latium and its main city, Rome, have both given their name to the alphabet that forms the basis of the greatest number of writing systems now in existence. Differing in form but not in principle from its Greek predecessor, the Latin or Roman alphabet deserves attention here chiefly because of its widespread use—in more than 60 countries and by over 600 million people (Spencer 1969:57).

The Romans acquired their writing through the intermediary of their mysterious neighbors to the north, whom they called "Etrusci" or "Tusci," from which come the names "Etruscans" and "Tuscany." The Etruscans were the leading power in Italy in the first half of the first millennium B.C. At that time they developed a script based on the West Greek alphabet. They have left over 10,000 inscriptions, most of them short but one running to about fifteen hundred words. These inscriptions can be read with ease, since the sound values of the letters are known from Greek, but their decipherment presents a serious problem, as the language of the Etruscans has so far eluded identification. Since almost all of the short inscriptions are funerary or dedicatory, they are so formalistic and repetitive that many if not most are understood. The long inscription remains a puzzle.

The earliest examples of Latin writing are a few inscriptions that have been variously dated at between the seventh and fifth centuries B.C. Following the Etruscan order, these inscriptions ran from right to left or in both directions. Subsequent writing all went from left to right.

The oldest Latin alphabet contained twenty-one letters with forms almost identical to those of the West Greek letters (Jensen 1969:509). Initially the letter *C* was used to represent both *K* and *G,* but later, perhaps in the third century B.C., the two were differentiated by adding a vertical bar to the lower end of *C* to create the new symbol, *G.* This replaced Greek zeta, which was not needed for Latin. However, after the conquest of Greece in the first century B.C., the need to transcribe borrowed Greek words like *zephyros* 'west wind' led to the creation of the new symbol, *Z.* The letter *Y* was created at the same time (Diringer 1968, 1:420–421; Trager 1974:410). Some of the early letters and those in use in Roman times are shown in figure 26.

Much later, in the Middle Ages, the final inventory of twenty-six letters was achieved by adding the letters *J, U,* and *W* as modifications of existing letters: *J* was formed from *I* to differentiate consonant from vowel, *U* was created from *V* to differentiate vowel from consonant, and *W* was formed by joining two *V*'s (Diringer 1968, 1:421). Since *V* originally stood for both the vowel *U* and the consonant *V,* English speakers refer to *W* as "double *U,*" whereas the French call it "double *V.*"

The Latin alphabet was well adapted to the representation of the Latin language. The fit between sound and symbol was in general quite close. For example, spoken Latin had five basic vowel sounds, and the alphabet had five symbols to represent them. The vowels were either short or long, but no graphic distinction was made between them until modern times, when a macron was placed over long vowels (e.g., *ā* versus *a*). There were thirteen consonants, most of them represented on a one-to-one basis by single letters. The few exceptions include the representation of the sound *ks* by the single letter *X* and of *k* by *Q* before a nonsyllabic vowel (i.e., *quo*) and by *C* before a syllabic vowel (e.g., *cum*). Gelb points out that both Greek and Latin were "pretty nearly phonemic" (Gelb 1963:239). As a result of this relatively close fit between sound and symbol, Latin must also be placed in the forefront of simple writing systems.

However, modifications were made when the alphabet was adapted to other languages, as happened especially with the growth of national languages and the spread of Western power to other areas. Italian added a grave accent to show stress on the end of a word, as in *civiltà* 'civilization.' French accents grew up more or less by chance, as in the writing of *tête* for earlier *teste* 'head,' the circumflex being used to point out the loss of an *s*. Some examples of other changes are the use of *ñ* in Spanish, *ü* in German, *č* in Czech, and *ø* and *å* in Scandinavian languages (Trager 1974:407–409).

In contrast to the often unplanned adaptations of the Latin alphabet in the case of the European languages, a more scientific application resulted when trained linguists set about creating new writing systems. Missionary-linguists connected with the Summer Institute of Linguistics are an outstanding example of this development. Their fieldwork conducted among many Indian linguistic groups in Central and South America has resulted in a number of scripts closely fitted to the individual languages.

In the 1920s Soviet linguists applied the Latin alphabet to the creation of many new scripts for previously unwritten languages or as replacements for existing systems, particularly those in Central Asia based on the Arabic script. In the 1930s all these were changed to the Cyrillic alphabet as the primary system of writing throughout the Soviet Union. In many other areas scripts based on the Latin alphabet have been created either as a new official writing system (Turkish), or as an auxiliary system of writing (Chinese and Japanese romanizations).

The adaptation of the Latin alphabet to represent a great variety of spoken languages means of course that the value of specific symbols varies from language to language. This is true both of the European adaptations, which in most cases came about rather haphazardly, and of the more recent creations based on more carefully thought-out linguistic principles. So it is that the French *u* has a different value from that in English. The letter *j* represents one sound in English *jam,* another in German *ja*. The initial sound of English *sure* is written *sz* in Polish and *š* in Czech. The sound represented by English *ts* is written *c* in Polish, Czech, Hungarian, Serbo-Croatian, and Chinese.

In short, contrary to provincial if not chauvinistic objections to any departure from English letter values, the Latin alphabet comprises a flexible inventory of basic symbols whose adaptation should be judged in terms of the fit between sounds and symbols in specific writing systems. In this area, English hardly stands as a model.

"Meaning-plus-Sound" Alphabetic Systems

In the two previous chapters we have seen that meaning is conveyed in "pure" syllabic and consonantal systems (e.g., Japanese and Phoenician, respectively) by symbols used solely for their phonetic value. In "meaning-plus-sound" syllabic and consonantal systems (e.g., Chinese and Egyptian), on the other hand, meaning is conveyed by symbols of two kinds, some used solely for their phonetic value, and others (or the same ones) for their semantic value. A Chinese example is the use of a stylized symbol derived from an early pictograph for a horse to represent both the animal in question and the syllable *ma* applied to several unrelated words. An Egyptian hieroglyphic example is the use of a wavy line to represent both the word for "water" and the consonant sound *n*. These nonphonetic Chinese and Egyptian examples originated from iconic symbols.

In "pure" alphabetic systems such as those which have just been described, meaning is likewise conveyed by symbols used solely for their phonetic value. But in the case of "meaning-plus-sound" alphabetic systems, apart from some symbols used only for their phonetic value, there are other symbols that convey information which is neither phonetic nor iconic, even in origin. Together with iconic symbols they comprise a category of nonphonetic symbols that I have called "mnemonic." The term is admittedly not a very good one, but it is hard to find a good inclusive label to cover the miscellaneous kinds of things that fall under that rubric.

Conveying mnemonic information plays a particularly important role in "meaning-plus-sound" alphabetic systems, but it can be found to varying degrees in all systems of writing. An example that appears to be almost universally applicable is the technique of dividing text into smaller units, most often words, by various devices that include the little vertical wedge used as a word-separating symbol in some cuneiform writing (Gordon 1982:105) and white space in English and most other alphabetic systems. The use of capital letters is another frequently used device. Writing systems differ in the kinds of devices which they employ as well as the extent to which they resort to these techniques.

One device that is common to most alphabetic writing systems is referred to by linguists as *morphophonemic spelling*. The significance of the term *morphophonemic* can perhaps best be brought out by noting that it is one of three levels of sound representation which in strict technical usage are clearly distinguished. These three levels are:

1. phonetic
2. phonemic
3. morphophonemic

In phonetic representation differences in sound are noted regardless of whether or not they affect meaning. Thus a strictly phonetic representation of English would have to distinguish two different *p* sounds, one aspirated (spoken with a puff of air, as in *pot*), and the other unaspirated (spoken without the puff of air, as in *spot*). Aspirated *p* is sometimes written *pʰ;* the unaspirated variety is written simply as *p.*

In phonemic representation differences in sound are written differently only if they make a difference in meaning. The two different *p* sounds noted above are not distinguished in English *pot:spot* because the difference in sound does not involve a difference in meaning. We could pronounce these words with or without aspiration and it would make no difference except perhaps to sound a little odd. But in Chinese the difference *is* significant, and so the two sounds are distinguished in Pinyin spelling by writing the aspirated consonant as *p* and the unaspirated as *b,* as in the pair *pà* 'fear' and *bà* 'dam.' In a purely phonemic system of writing, there is a one-to-one correspondence between phonemes and their written representation.

In morphophonemic spelling, if a basic unit of meaning, called a morpheme, is represented by different sounds, these are written the same way if the different pronunciations are systematic and predictable. Thus in English the plural morpheme is represented by two different sounds in *pats:pads* (the first is like *s,* the second like *z*), but they can be written with the same letter *s* because native speakers will automatically make the distinction in pronouncing the two words.

In the initial stage of investigating an unknown spoken language, linguists first work out a rough phonetic notation, carefully recording whatever sounds their ears can distinguish, since they do not yet know whether or not these differences are significant. From their rough phonetic notation they distill a phonemic representation of the language after they have discovered which sounds are distinctive. Finally they may change the phonemic representation to a morphophonemic spelling in accordance with the structure of the language. Because of this careful, principled approach, new alphabetic writing systems tend to be much more regular, and hence simpler, than old ones.

When linguists speak of a good fit between sound and symbol, they generally have in mind a basically morphophonemic system rather than one that is strictly phonemic. Of the well-established orthographies that are known for their good fit, such as German, Russian, Spanish, and Italian, most fall into this category. Even basically phonemic Finnish, which has the reputation of being a "near perfect" orthography with an almost one-to-one correspondence, has some morphophonemic features (Austerlitz, personal communication, 5/28/87). The same is true of Greek and Latin.

Morphophonemic spelling is the most distinctive feature of "meaning-plus-sound" alphabetic systems. Korean orthography is based on this principle. English spelling makes use of the principle even more extensively and in even more diverse ways.

Korean

In the fifteenth century the Koreans created an alphabetic script based on the innovative adaptation of two borrowed concepts of writing. One of these is the alphabetic principle, borrowed indirectly from India and the Middle East. The other is the syllabic principle, borrowed directly from China. By combining these two principles in a unique way, the Koreans produced a widely praised system which has been described in such terms as "one of the most remarkable scripts in the world" (Ledyard 1975:9) and "perhaps the most scientific system in general use in any country" because it possesses "the advantages of an alphabetic script as well as a syllabary" (Reischauer and Fairbank 1960:435–436).

The creation of this script must be viewed against the backdrop of overwhelming Chinese influence that had probably started two millennia earlier and has continued to the present century. Chinese influence delayed the creation of the script in the first place, helped shape the specific form of the graphic symbols, and loomed over the fate of the system for the next five hundred and more years.

The Chinese system of writing may have been known to the Koreans as early as the fifth century B.C. Chinese power, and with it the Chinese bureaucratic system and its system of writing, became established in northern Korea in the second century A.D. Korean kingdoms throughout the peninsula took over Chinese writing and used it for their own purposes. History books in Chinese were compiled as early as 375 A.D. (Yi 1975:21). Bureaucracies were developed on the Chinese model. This development included the recruitment of officials through a system of competitive examination based on classical Chinese.

When writing in what was called *hanmun,* from Chinese *hanwen* 'Chinese writing,' Korean scribes encountered the problem of how to write the names of Korean persons and places. They solved the problem, as many others have done who borrowed an alien system of writing, by using the borrowed symbols for their phonetic value. Sometimes this resulted in a good rendition of the Korean sounds, as in the case of the Chinese character for 'to add,' whose ancient pronunciation *ka* was the same in Korean. But there were also many Korean sounds which could not be adequately represented by the sounds of the Chinese syllabic characters (Yi 1975:31).

Later the use of Chinese characters was extended in various ways, including rearranging them to suit Korean syntax and having them represent Korean grammatical elements such as case endings. Since Korean, together with Japanese, belongs to a completely different family of languages, this development required changing the sequence of the Chinese characters from the SVO order of Chinese sentences into the SOV order of Korean and adding the grammatical elements just noted.

Out of these developments emerged two systems of writing which represent complex adaptations of Chinese characters to Korean needs. The more important system is known as *idu* 'clerk reading.' In the words of Yi Ki-moon, a leading Korean linguist: "*Idu* can be defined as a mixture of *hanmun* and Korean in which *hanmun* sentences are more or less integrated into Korean syntax, and Korean grammatical markers, sometimes even adverbs, are supplied" (Yi 1975:22). In the idu system the main words were not only expressed in Hanmun 'Chinese writing,' they *were* for the most part borrowed Chinese words, pronounced in the Korean fashion. Such Sino-Korean words have come to comprise more than half of the Korean vocabulary (Yi 1975:25).

The second system is called *hyangchal,* a word of rather uncertain meaning. It is described by Yi Ki-moon as the summation of the efforts of early Korean intellectuals to write their own language with Chinese characters. Extant materials in this script are not only rare but confined to poetry; hyangchal appears never to have been applied to prose (Yi 1975:23). Although the system made extensive use of Chinese characters purely for their phonetic value, it by no means completely ignored their semantic aspect (Ledyard 1975).

In the case of Japanese (see chapter 4), the early use of Chinese characters to represent the sounds of that language led first to the writing of complete texts such as poems in characters used solely for their phonetic value, and later to the simplification of the original characters into the purely syllabic signs called kana. Neither of these developments occurred in Korea.

Why did the Koreans fail to pursue a similar course, using Chinese characters as purely phonetic symbols? Yi Ki-moon explains, "There were many syllables in the Korean language that could not be adequately represented by the sounds of the Chinese characters." He rejects the suggestion advanced by some Japanese scholars that the disparity between Korean and Japanese use of Chinese characters as phonetic symbols is to be explained by the different degree of Sinification of the two countries (Yi 1975:23, 31). I am not, however, convinced that the sole or even the main explanation lies in the purely technical difference between the sound structure of Korean and Japanese, for Korean scholars appear to have been even more enamored of things Chinese than were their Japanese counterparts. This is to be seen even in the new alphabetic system that was created in the fifteenth century.

The date of its creation is itself significant. It took the Koreans more than a millennium after acquiring the art of writing, in the form of classical Chinese, to get around to creating an indigenous phonetic script. The Japanese accomplished that feat after a much shorter interval of exposure to Chinese writing. And the Korean accomplishment, stupendous though it was, appears to have come about not through the efforts of the literati, but through the stubborn insistence of a monarch who, if rulers were ever measured by anything besides military exploits, would surely rank among the foremost of those who have appeared on the stage of history.

Modern scholarship, especially the thoroughgoing study by G. K. Ledyard (1975), on which the present discussion is largely based, suggests that much of the hagiography surrounding King Sejong is in fact justified. The fourth monarch of the Yi dynasty, which began in 1392 and lasted until 1910, Sejong ascended the throne in 1418 and reigned until 1450. Celebrated for his love of learning, he is known to have studied both spoken and written Chinese. Apart from the usual study of the Chinese classics, the area to which most literati confined their attention, he also concerned himself with more practical and utilitarian matters, such as the work of his interpreters' school. His wide-ranging interests centered particularly on phonology and on the promotion of popular education. To this end he encouraged the publication of agricultural and medical books. He also issued an edict in 1434 exhorting his subjects as follows:

> Let everyone, in the capital and out, exert themselves in the arts of teaching and instruction . . . let all of them search everywhere for men of learning and sophistication, without regard to whether they are of noble birth or mean, earnestly encouraging them and urging them to teach people to read, even women and girls [Ledyard 1975:94].

But Sejong was unhappy with the difficulty of promoting such education via the medium of classical Chinese. He was also dissatisfied with the use of the "clerk readings" because of the inability of Chinese characters to represent the exact pronunciation of Korean words, as was especially necessary in referring to indigenous plants that were agriculturally and medicinally valuable. These attitudes, combined with his interest in phonology, led to the creation of a simple Korean alphabet that is generally accepted as being his own brainchild, though he had the help of some middle-level scholars, especially those connected with his interpreters' school.

The system was announced in 1443–1444 in a statement which said, "His Majesty personally created the twenty-eight letters of the Vulgar Script *(onmun)*" (Ledyard 1975:97). It was generally referred to by this name, though various other names were attached to it during the five centuries that have elapsed since its creation. Current usage favors the term *Hangŭl* (or *Hankŭl*), probably an early twentieth-century neologism which some scholars render as as 'great script,' though it is usually thought of simply as 'Korea script' (Martin 1968:85–86).

The alphabet was not officially promulgated until 1446 in a document entitled "The Correct Sounds for the Instruction of the People." King Sejong introduced this document with a short preface which, in its translation from his original version in classical Chinese, schoolchildren now commit to memory:

> The sounds of our country's language are different from those of the Middle Kingdom and are not confluent with the sounds of our charac-

ters. Therefore, among the ignorant people, there have been many who, having something they want to put into words, have in the end been unable to express their feelings. I have been distressed because of this, and have newly designed twenty-eight letters, which I wish to have everyone practice at their ease and make convenient for their daily use [Ledyard 1975:124].

Although details are lacking as to just how Sejong went about creating the alphabet, scholars have been able to suggest the origins of the principles behind it, and even, though with less assurance, of its specific symbols. It appears that the alphabetic principle on which the script is based derives from Korean knowledge of its use in the writing systems of neighboring peoples and even of more distant peoples in India and Iran. All of these writing systems trace back to Aramaic, and ultimately to Phoenician, from which the Hebrew and Arabic scripts are also descended, but they differ from these Semitic scripts in clearly including provision for representation of vowels, though generally in a very clumsy fashion.

The Koreans were in direct contact with the Mongols and were well acquainted with their language in its spoken and written forms, both of which were taught in the interpreters' school. Mongolian was written in two alphabetic scripts. One was the Uighur, borrowed from the Central Asian people of that name, who in turn had based their script on an Iranian model. The other was the Phags-pa, named after a Tibetan lama who developed the script at the request of Kublai Khan on the basis of Tibetan, Tibetan of course being based on an Indian model (Jensen 1969; Ledyard 1975).

The Koreans also became acquainted with the alphabetic principle from Indian Buddhist writings transmitted through the Chinese. The latter transcribed Buddhist terms that were originally expressed in some Indian alphabetic writing by rendering them in very clumsy fashion in the Chinese syllabic script. Sejong's deep interest in Buddhism added a spur to his phonological studies by providing a further incentive to seek a simple solution to the vexing problem of transcribing Buddhist and other foreign terminology.

Although it is fairly obvious that the Koreans derived the idea of alphabetic writing from all these sources, it is less clear that they based their symbols on them. Various attempts have been made to offer a pedigree for individual symbols. One of the latest, that of Ledyard, suggests a relationship with Phags-pa, but only a limited one. The conclusion seems warranted that Sejong took over primarily the idea of an alphabet, and secondarily perhaps a few letter shapes. The other features are due to his own inventiveness (Ledyard 1975).

One of these features was the ingenious adaptation of the syllabic principle used in Chinese writing. Every Chinese character represents a syllable of sound and, regardless of whether it is a simple graph of one or two strokes or a complex one of several dozen, occupies the same amount of square space. Within a compound character it may be difficult to distinguish the component elements, but every syllable-character is clearly distinguished from another by white space on the printed page and even in handwritten manuscripts. What Sejong did was to adapt the Chinese principle of equidimensional syllabic blocks by grouping the letters that comprise a Korean syllable into blocks separated from each other by white space.

The letters are arranged in square spaces in sequences determined by fixed rules. The following examples of modern usage as standardized in the 1930s (adapted from Taylor 1980:70; Gerald Mathias, personal communication, 8/17/87) show the arrangement within the six types of Korean syllables formed by the various combinations of vowels and consonants, namely V, CV, VC, VCC, CVC, and CVCC, which make up the 1,096 different syllables that have been counted as actually occurring in the language (out of a theoretically possible total of 3,520) (Ho-min Sohn, personal communication, 1987). Note that in V, VC, and VCC syllables an unsounded circle must precede a beginning vowel.

Linear Arrangement				Letter	Syllable	Morpheme
C	V	C	C			
	ㅏ			아	V/a/	(suffix);ah
ㄷ	ㅏ			다	CV/ta/	all
	ㅏ	ㄹ		알	VC/al/	egg
	ㅣ	ㄹ	ㄱ	읽	VCC/ilk/	read
ㄷ	ㅏ	ㄹ		달	CVC/tal/	moon;sweet
ㄷ	ㅏ	ㄹ	ㄱ	닭	CVCC/talk/	hen

This technique is comparable to writing the English phrase HANGŬL SYSTEM as follows:

HA GŬ SY TE
N   L   S   M

It is worthwhile to give a bit more precision to the foregoing discussion by noting some generally overlooked details regarding the syllabic aspect of Korean writing. In printed or in carefully handwritten texts, each individual letter is written separately within its own allotted space, as in the case of our printed letters or handwritten block letters. Combinations of Korean letters form syllable blocks that are set off from each other by a minimal amount of white space, little more than what separates our printed letters from each other within a word. The syllable blocks are in turn grouped together to form words, and the resultant syllable groups are separated by a greater amount of white space, the equivalent of our spacing between words. Defining words, that is, determining where to place white space, remains a problem in Korean orthography. It has occupied the attention of no less a person than Premier Kim Ilsong of North Korea, who has insisted that the term for "socialist construction" should be written in a way equivalent to *sahoejuigonsol* and not to *sahoejui gonsol* (Kim 1972: 169). Despite problems, though, Korean orthography offers whatever advantages there are in graphically distinguishing letter, syllable, and word.

Although the writing system is often popularly described as being both alphabetic and syllabic, it is important to note that the designation *syllabic* refers to something quite different from what is intended when that term is applied to Chinese, Japanese, and Yi. In these cases the graphic symbols which form the basis of the writing systems comprise unitary symbols in the sense that they cannot be broken down into phonemic components. In Korean, however, the graphic symbols that represent syllables consist of phonemic letters which are merely grouped into character-like squares instead of being written sequentially. On this basis Korean can be called syllabic only in the same sense that English can be called logographic because it groups its letters into words.

A situation somewhat similar to that of Korean characterizes the writing systems of India, where departures from linear sequencing of phonemic symbols even include instances in which the spoken sequence A-B is actually written B-A.[1] As Smalley and his coauthors point out, such divergence between spoken and written order also characterizes many Southeast Asian scripts developed under Indian influence, as well as the apparently independently created Pahawh Hmong script (which they describe in great detail). In most of these cases of nonlinear sequence of phonemes, the vowels are written around a particular consonant, but Pahawh Hmong is exceptional in that in its CV syllables, the most common, the vowel is the core and the consonant is written as a satellite after it (Smalley, Chia, and Gnia, forthcoming).

The practice of grouping the phonemic symbols into syllables leads some scholars to contend that the Indic scripts should be classified as syllabic (Krishnamurti and Gwynn 1985:32–35). Trager, however, disagrees, insisting that "Indic writing is completely alphabetic, though it is often inconsistent and irregular" (1974:438).

The important thing to remember in all this is that scripts like Japanese are syllabic in the strict sense that they represent syllables by means of unitary syllabic signs, whereas the Korean and Indic scripts are "syllabic" only in the quite different sense that they represent syllables by means of nonunitary signs—graphemes representing phonemes—which are grouped together to form a syllabic bundle. Such scripts must still be classified as basically phonemic systems, though James McCawley prefers to label the Indic scripts as "augmented consonantal" systems: "The term 'augmented consonantal' reflects the fact that in these scripts, while vowels as well as consonants are represented, the consonants are written in fairly strict L–R order, while the vowels are written as graphic adjuncts to the consonants and have a variety of different spatial orientations in relation to the consonant" (personal communication, 11/15/87).

Indian orthographic practices[2] probably exercised at least an indirect influence on Korean writing (Ledyard 1975). In neither case, however, should too much be made of the fact that letters are grouped together to represent syllables. Korean most definitely is a morphemic system of writing. Actually, we need to go further and point out, as Martin stresses (1967:vi–xii), that Korean as written today is more accurately designated as morphophonemic. That is to say, changes in pronunciation are generally not indicated in the spelling if they can be predicted from the environment.

This feature was not incorporated in the initial creation of the script, though there were some examples of morphophonemic spellings that were apparently due to scribal error rather than plan. Thus the word for "to cross" sometimes appeared in a form that can be transcribed as *ket-na,* which is the morphophonemic way, and also as *ken-na,* which is the phonemic way, since syllable-final *t* changes to *n* before *n* (Ledyard 1975:216). What was once sporadic and perhaps accidental has now become standard practice, so that the system must be described as basically morphophonemic.[3]

This practice in writing hangŭl differs from the general practice in transcribing Korean into one of the several romanization systems that have been created for the language (and that have resulted in great inconsistency in the romanization of Korean forms). As Martin has noted, "Most versions of Hankul Korean aim to write morphophone-mically, at least in part, so that a given word or element usually appears in the same shape, provided its alternate shapes can be predicted by a regular set of rules" (Martin 1968:89).

The alphabetic, syllabic, and morphophonemic features that have been described are known to Koreans (not necessarily by their technical designations) and are made use of in ordinary reading and writing. There are other aspects that are not exactly commonplace but have aroused the particular interest of scholars. These have to do with the relationship between graphic shape and graphic function.

In his extensive discussion of these matters, Ledyard notes that in the creation of the symbols (shown in figure 27), an attempt was made to relate letter shapes to the speech organs and to have systematic shapes within each class of consonants. The description of the alphabet that accompanied its promulgation stated that the symbol for *k* "depicts the outline of the root of the tongue blocking the throat," that for *n* "depicts the outline of the tongue touching the upper palate," and that for *m* "depicts the outline of the mouth." The sounds represented by *n,t,tʰ* that are made with the tongue touching the same area of the palate are distinguished by the successive addition of a horizontal line to the basic form in the series, as follows (Ledyard 1975:200):

$$\llcorner \quad \sqsubset \quad \bar{\sqsubset}$$
$$n \quad\quad t \quad\quad t^h$$

The remaining consonants are handled more or less along the same lines, though graphic variations on the basic approach sometimes obscure the intended relationships.

The handling of vowels was also based on a somewhat similar approach but with an added twist. This involved relating the vowel

Consonants

place of articulation manner of articulation			Bilabial	Alveo-dental	Palatal	Velar	Glottal
stop	lenis	voiceless/voiced	p (p, b) ㅂ	t (t,d) ㄷ	c (ch, j) ㅈ	k (k, g) ㄱ	
	aspirated	voiceless	ph (p') ㅍ	th (t') ㅌ	ch (ch') ㅊ	kh (k') ㅋ	
	tensed	voiceless	pp (pp) ㅃ	tt (tt) ㄸ	cc (tch) ㅉ	kk (kk) ㄲ	
fricative	aspirated (h)	voiceless (s)		s (s) ㅅ			h (h) ㅎ
	tensed	voiceless		ss (ss) ㅆ			
nasal		voiced	m (m) ㅁ	n (n) ㄴ		ŋ (-ng) ㅇ	
liquid	lateral flap	voiced		l (l,r) ㄹ			

Vowels

place of articulation lip shape tongue height	front		back	
	unrounded	rounded	unrounded	rounded
high	i (i) 이	ü (wi) 위	ɨ (ŭ) 으	u (u) 우
mid	e (e) 에	oe (oe) 외	ə (ŏ) 어	o (o) 오
low	ɛ (ae) 애		a (a) 아	

Figure 27. The Korean Hangŭl Alphabet
A linguistic chart of the Hangŭl alphabet with accompanying transcriptions—a technical transcription and (in parentheses) the McCune-Reischauer romanization system in general use by non-Koreans. Adapted with permission from Ho-min Sohn, *Korean* (Cambridge: Cambridge University Press, 1988).

signs not only to the place and manner of articulation but to Confucian cosmological concepts. Sejong noted three basic vowels which, from the place in the mouth where they are articulated, are called front, central, and back vowels. The front vowel was related to Man, the central to Earth, and the back to Heaven. The last two were in turn related to Yin and Yang. The front vowel was represented by a vertical line. In Sejong's words, "The uprightness of the outline is a depiction of Man." The central vowel was represented by a horizontal line: "The flatness of the outline is a depiction of Earth." The back vowel was represented by a dot: "The roundness of the outline is a depiction of Heaven." Various combinations of these symbols produced the full repertoire of Korean vowels (Ledyard 1975:203–205).

Ledyard is of the opinion that the Yin-Yang aspect of the vowels was thought up by Sejong as a sop to the Confucian prejudices of the literate class. The purely linguistic aspects, on the other hand, and the treatment of vowels and consonants, were based on careful observation of Korean speech, and the treatment of both of these classes of sounds has elicited admiration from modern scholars. Ledyard's comment on the handling of consonants reflects the general opinion regarding the system as a whole:

> It is really impossible to withhold admiration for this conception of shape–function relationship and for the way it was carried out. There is nothing like it in all the long and varied history of writing. It would be quite enough merely to have the systematic shapes within classes, but for those shapes themselves to be rationalized on the basis of the speech organs associated with their sounds—that is unparalleled grammatological luxury! [Ledyard 1975:203].

Although scholars are in general agreement on the excellence of the Korean alphabetic script, there is not complete agreement about how exactly to describe and classify it. It appears to be the nearly unanimous opinion of linguists that the alphabet is a good morphophonemic system in which, as Ledyard notes, the symbols not only have systematic shape within classes but provide an extra bonus in the fact that their shapes are rationalized on the basis of the speech organs associated with their sounds. But Ledyard's extensive discussion makes clear that only relatively broad categories are distinguished (e.g., consonants versus vowels, stop consonants versus continuant consonants, and so on). Moreover, the relationship between symbols in the same class is by no means regular or obvious. The example given above of n,t,t^h is one of the better examples. In some other cases the relationship among symbol forms is far less clear, and in some cases, as Ledyard notes, there is reason to question whether the letters were actually designed with the relationships in mind, or merely rationalized this way (1975:202).

It is questionable, therefore, whether Sampson is correct in classifying hangŭl as a "featural" system of writing. His approach is based on applying a type of linguistic analysis which purports to break down complex speech units, including phonemes, into their ultimate components, called "distinctive features." These subphonemic features include such phonetic details as nasality, aspiration, tenseness, and so on.

There are at least two objections to classifying hangŭl as featural. The first is that too few of the features, which one scholar (Kim-Renaud 1974) has estimated as numbering nineteen, are actually represented in the system. In contrast, even a bad phonemic system, such as English, and a worse syllabic system, such as Chinese, cover the phonological units in the system to a much more useful degree.

The main objection, however, is one that Sampson himself has pointed out (1985:143), namely that Koreans do not perceive or learn their script in terms of distinctive features but regard the hangŭl symbols as separate individual letters rather than as partially identical components. Korean linguists do not accept the notion that the creation of the script can be said to have been based on a featural approach (Pak 1971:98; Ho-min Sohn, personal communication, 3/6/87). Pak asserts that while perception of distinctive features is implicit in the creation of the earliest alphabets, including that devised by Sejong, "It is remarkable, however, that despite this antiquity and pervasiveness of feature perception . . . no writing system has been subphonemic" (Pak 1971:99). An American specialist in Korean also rejects a classification based on features:

No Korean except the trained language scholar or linguist is even aware that these things exist. Even when they are pointed out to him, the average educated reader has trouble understanding them. The schoolchild learns letters, not graphic relationships. There is no reason to believe that anyone, even in Sejong's day, ever read Hangŭl by referring to the featural relationships between the letters [Ramsey, personal communication, 5/24/88].

As in his overestimate of the communicative potential in the "Yukaghir Love Letter," Sampson has also exaggerated the featural aspect in the Korean system of writing. Sejong's creation is not featural; but it is one of the most ingenious systems of phonemic representation ever created.

This creation was of course vastly superior to the clumsy idu system of using whole Chinese characters to represent Korean sounds. It was to an even greater degree a superior alternative to the alien hanmun system that used Chinese characters to write classical Chinese. One would think, therefore, that Sejong's creation would have been warmly received by his subjects.

This was not the case. As a whole the Korean intelligentsia, especially at the higher levels, were so steeped in the borrowed Chinese culture that they vehemently opposed the new script. A leading intellectual, Ch'oe Malli, memorialized against it. Contemptuously remarking that only "barbarians" like the Tibetans, Mongols, and Japanese had scripts "based on the local speech," he said that "To now separately make the Vulgar Script is to discard China and identify ourselves with the barbarians." Abandoning Chinese was to "give in to the language of the alley rustics." Moreover, he said, "If you put the Vulgar Script into practice, then it will be the Vulgar Script that clerks will exclusively study. They will have no regard for learning." And he feared the results if "clerks can gain positions with the Vulgar Script" (Ledyard 1975:104–108).

The literati were so strongly entrenched that they were able to ward off the threat to their near-monopoly of learning even after the lower classes had access to the simpler script. Because of their opposition, hangŭl had only a limited application in some Buddhist literature, in diaries and biographies by court attendants and women of the royal court, and in poetry and a few prose novels (Blank 1981:82–85). For more than five hundred years they effectively blocked the extension of its use by retaining classical Chinese as the primary means of written communication in virtually all areas—government administration, scholarship, and intellectual life in general.

It was not until late in the nineteenth century that new influences began to to be felt in Korean society. In 1896 Sŏ Chepil (Philip Jason), a member of the Progressive Party who had returned to Korea after a long period of exile in the United States, founded the *Independence Daily* as the first newspaper published exclusively in hangŭl. Christian missionaries who translated the Bible had it printed in hangŭl. Linguists also argued for the adoption of the system, as in the case of Chu Si-gyŏng, who in 1897 wrote four editorials in its favor for the *Independence Daily* (Blank 1981:90–97; Park 1985:4–5).

These promising developments in the waning years of the long-lived Yi dynasty (1392–1910) were frustrated with the imposition of Japanese colonial rule in 1910. Imperial language policy sought to replace the indigenous language with Japanese, a policy which, incidentally, some Japanese later expected would be applied to English after the anticipated victory over the United States (Taylor 1983:217–218). Many members of the Korean Language Society were imprisoned in the 1930s and 1940s. In 1938 it was forbidden to teach the Korean language in any school, public or private; Korean teachers and students were not allowed to speak Korean in the classroom or at public meetings; and Koreans were forced to change their family names into Japanese (Blank 1981:100; Park 1985:2–3).

The defeat of Japan provided the Koreans with new opportunities. In 1949 North Korea officially decreed an end to the use of Chinese characters and their replacement by hangŭl in all areas. The many problems of adapting an old script to new uses were energetically attacked under specific directives issued by Premier Kim Ilsong. He demanded greater reliance on Korean roots in the coining of new terms, the acceptance of Korean alternatives for expressions of Chinese origin, and the compilation of dictionaries and other needed materials. He also requested deferring a decision on whether to abandon, as some proposed, the arrangement of the alphabetic symbols into syllabic groups in favor of a sequential order better adapted to typewriters and other modern means of communication, arguing that such a change now would complicate the unification of North and South (Kim 1972). Free compulsory seven-year education, the first such program adopted in East Asia, was introduced and appears within a few years to have begun to eliminate illiteracy. Hangŭl-only publications soon dominated all fields, including that of the advanced sciences (Blank 1981:101–126).

South Korea presents a different picture. Here policy has fluctuated with each regime, one advocating a hangŭl-only approach, another a policy of mixing Chinese characters for the main words and hangŭl for grammatical items. This mixed system, similar to that of Japanese with hangŭl performing the function of kana, has been standardized by restricting the number of characters, again on the Japanese model, to some thirteen hundred.

Since 1945 South Korean intellectuals have remained divided on this issue. Some modern-day literati, for example, Lee Sung-nyŏng, a well-known scholar at Seoul National University and dean of its graduate school, argues that it is sheer chauvinism to insist on doing away with all Chinese characters. Moreover, he says, a hangŭl-only text would be ambiguous. Such a system simply would not work (Lee 1972). Others argue just as strenuously, and in increasing numbers, against these views. No one appears to have cited what has happened in North Korea as concrete and definitive evidence of what can be expressed in hangŭl-only writing.

Nevertheless, South Korea is inching along in the same direction as North Korea. The effect of a vacillating policy is that successive generations are gradually losing command of Chinese characters and turning more and more to the exclusive use of hangŭl. It appears to be only a matter of time before Sejong's great gift to his people achieves a success that even he may not have dreamed of more than five hundred years ago.

English

The fact that English is the outstanding example of the "meaning-plus-sound" alphabetic category of writing systems is due to the diversity of influences on the spoken language and its written form in the course of their evolution from the fifth century A.D. to the present.

In the fifth century various branches of the Teutonic peoples toppled the Roman empire, seized control of Gaul, and invaded Britain. Jutes, Angles, Saxons, and others from the coastal area extending from northern Denmark to the Low Countries came as invaders and remained as settlers in island areas largely peopled by Celtic tribes. The newcomers, chief of whom were the Anglo-Saxons, largely replaced the indigenous speech with their own diverse dialects. The main one of these was known from the beginning as *Englisc*. Later it was also called Anglo-Saxon, and it is today referred to by scholars as Old English (Baugh and Cable 1978).

This early form of English was a highly inflected language (Baugh and Cable 1978). The definite article "the," for example, appeared in 12 different forms depending on the gender, number, and case of the noun it was used with. The word "stone" was inflected as follows:

Case	Singular	Plural
Nominative	stān	stān-as
Genitive	stān-es	stān-a
Dative	stān-e	stān-um
Accusative	stān	stān-as

A second stage in the evolution of the English language began with the conquest of England by the Norman French in 1066. The new rulers initially spoke mainly French and wrote mostly in Latin. But in time they and their descendants acquired some knowledge of English, especially after ties with the Norman homeland were broken early in the thirteenth century. And large numbers of English in contact with those who ruled them learned French in addition to their native tongue. The result was a massive infiltration of new words into the English language, the beginning of a borrowing spree that has resulted in present-day English's vocabulary having more than half words of French or Latin origin.

In addition to this sort of linguistic change due to foreign influence, there were extensive changes due to internal developments in the language. These consisted chiefly of revolutionary changes in pronunciation and grammar, such as the virtual elimination of declensions, which survive only in the possessive: *people:people's* and the plural: *people:peoples.*

Middle English, whose developments have just been summarized, was followed by Modern English, beginning about 1500. New influences such as the introduction of printing in 1476, the explosion of general knowledge, and the spread of popular education, bore fruit in the areas of vocabulary and orthography.

The writing of English began when the Latin alphabet was applied to Old English thanks to the proselytizing activities of Irish missionaries. Anglo-Saxon converts who acquired literacy along with religion did an excellent job of adapting Latin letters to their native language. Where the sounds of English were more or less the same as those of Latin, there was no problem in the application of an appropriate letter. But where the sounds differed, innovations were introduced. Thus the sound of *a* in *hat* was represented by the digraph æ.

Two distinct sounds, which are still preserved today in the initial consonants of *this* and *thin,* were distinguished by introducing a letter called *eth* (ð) for the first and another called *thorn* (þ) for the second. The use of these symbols declined after the Norman conquest and ended completely with the advent of printing (Jensen 1969:532; Baugh and Cable 1978:54). If we add to *this* and *thin* the proper noun *Thomas,* we now have three different sound values for the digraph *th*—four if we include the zero value in some renderings of the word *clothes.*

The nice fit between sound and symbol that had characterized Old English spelling deteriorated further in the Middle English period because of the great influx of French words that were spelled in the French manner at the time they were borrowed. Thus the pronunciation of the English word *chant* preserves the initial sound of early French *chanter.* Later the pronunciation of French initial *ch* in this and other words changed to *sh.* As a result, when English borrowed words like *chaperon* and *chiffon,* the English lexicon came to possess many words whose initials had the same *ch* spelling but two different pronunciations.

The gap between sound and symbol continued to grow in the Modern English period because of the great changes in pronunciation that the language experienced just at the time when printing was beginning to fix the spelling of words. Chief among these changes is what linguists call the Great Vowel Shift. At the time of Chaucer (1340?–1400) long vowels still had their so-called Continental value—e.g., *a* was pronounced like the *a* in *father* rather than in the *a* in *famous.* The new pronunciation was firmly in place by the time of Shakespeare. Since then more changes have taken place.

One of the most far-reaching changes is the tendency of all sorts of unstressed vowels to change to the relaxed sound at the end of *the* or even to disappear completely. This has happened to the italicized vowels *a e i o u* in the following words: eleg*a*nt, om*e*n, rais*i*n, kingd*o*m, reb*u*s; and break*fa*st has become breakfst.

While some of the shifts are regular enough so that one can predict modern pronunciations from old spellings, there are enough exceptions to cause trouble. In Shakespeare's time *clean* rhymed with our present *lane,* but like most *ea* words it has now acquired the sound of *ee* in *meet.* But there are three exceptions that have retained the pronunciation of Shakespeare's time: *break, great, steak* (Baugh and Cable 1978:238–239).

But historical changes in the pronunciation of both English and French and extensive borrowing are only part of the explanation for the present gulf between sound and symbol in English. Another major factor is the entry of words into our present more or less standardized orthography from a great diversity of individual sources. Specific words were first written down by specific individuals. Given the relatively large number of writers who emerged in England precisely at the time of the greatest shifts in the spoken language, there was tremendous variation in how these individual writers decided to spell a particular word. At that time there were no authority figures such as dictionary makers to promote standardization. Not only that, one and the same writer might well, perhaps absent-mindedly, write a particular word in different ways at different times.

Gelb speaks to these points when he notes that a certain Dr. Crown in a book that he published in the second half of the 17th century spelled his own name indifferently as Cron, Croun, Crone, Croone, Croune. Gelb also notes:

> Modern English spelling is only partially historical, as in the case of 'night' or 'knight,' showing that the older pronunciation was similar to that of the corresponding German words *Nacht* or *Knecht*. . . . Many of our modern spellings are left-overs from a period in which a word could be spelled in several different ways, depending on the whim of the writer [Gelb:1963:224].

The whim of the printer was also a factor. Many early printers received their training on the Continent, especially in Germany and the Netherlands, from which they brought back some peculiar spelling conventions. Two of the most famous printers were not even English. The type brought back to England by Caxton, who introduced printing in 1476, lacked the thorn symbol used earlier to write the initial sound of *the,* so he compromised by adapting the manuscript form of the symbol, which looked something like the letter *y,* to create the contracted form y^e for *the.* Typesetting was erratic, proofreading almost nonexistent, especially on the part of authors, whose manuscripts were left to the tender mercies of printers bound by no manuals of style.

It was not until the middle of the eighteenth century, with the publication of Samuel Johnson's *Dictionary,* that the chaos began to be systematized—not ended, merely codified. For Johnson embraced the principle of "historical spelling" and selected for codification the conventions already adopted by various printers. For example, *debt* was spelled with an unpronounced *b* because the word comes from the Latin *debitus.* There has been little change since this imperious figure presented his arbitrary decisions on how words should be spelled (Vallins 1965).

Among the few changes since his time are those that resulted from a sort of cultural declaration of independence on the part of the nineteenth century lexicographer Noah Webster, who spearheaded an abortive movement to establish a separate "American" language distinct from its ancestral English. This "Schoolmaster to America" pursued an erratic course of spelling reform that finally concluded with the acceptance by the American public of only a few departures from the British originals. Perhaps the most widely accepted of these are the changes of *ou* to *o* as in *labour:labor* and of *re* to *er* as in *centre:center* (Vallins 1965:184–202).

The anarchy in orthographic decision making, coupled with the changes in the language that have taken place in the past few hundred years, created a potential for erratic spelling that was increased almost exponentially by the complex phonetic structure of the English language. Its syllable structure of 1–7 phonemes results in more than 8,000 different syllables, far in excess of any of the other systems we have looked at, and it means that variation in representing individual phonemes multiplies the variations in the syllables and the words made up of these unstable units. The extreme inconsistencies in the representation of individual phonemes can be illustrated in the following list of 11 different spellings for the long *i* sound (from Gelb 1963:224) and 14 for the *sh* sound (from Baugh and Cable 1978:12):

ma*chi*ne	na*ti*on
m*e*	*sh*oe
f*ee*	*s*ugar
s*ea*	is*s*ue
f*ie*ld	man*si*on
conc*ei*ve	mi*ssi*on
k*ey*	suspi*ci*on
qu*ay*	o*ce*an
pe*o*ple	nau*se*ous
subp*oe*na	con*sci*ous
C*ae*sar	*ch*aperon
	*sch*ist
	fu*ch*sia
	*psh*aw

Such extensive vagaries have led some writers to caricature English spelling by making up words with bizarre spellings. Best known perhaps is George Bernard Shaw's rendition of the surname *Fish* as *Ghoti,* with the *gh* of *rough*, the *o* of *women*, and the *ti* of *nation*. Gelb upstages Shaw by citing the perhaps apocryphal story of the foreigner who wrote the same surname as *Ghotiugh*, adding the silent *ugh* of *dough* (Gelb 1963:224–225).

In contrast to the litany of criticism of English spelling, support for the writing system has been expressed by various scholars, such as Venezky in an extensive study of the subject (1970). Shaw's *ghoti*, for example, is rejected as unwarranted because *gh* with the *f* value occurs only at the end of a word, never at the beginning, and *ti* with the *sh* value only occurs in the context *tion*. It is also pointed out that critics, among whom foreigners are perhaps the most vocal, unjustly blame the spelling for problems that actually originate in speech. In many languages the basic pronunciation of words remains unchanged despite the addition of elements such as suffixes or the shift in emphasis from one syllable to another. In English, on the other hand, such additions and shifts are accompanied by widespread changes in pronunciation, as indicated by the *a* in courage:courageous and the *i* in divine:divinity.

The well-known American linguists Noam Chomsky and Morris Halle assert that for such shifts there are rules:

> In the case of *courage*, in isolation, primary stress is placed by the Noun Rule (63); in the case of *courageous*, by the Affix Rule (47), in the familiar way. The second syllable of *courageous* becomes a complex nucleus by rule (70), before the nonlow front vowel followed by another vowel. The consonant *g* then softens to [j] by rule (72), and the final *e* is elided. Vowel Reduction then gives the desired forms. Once again, a quite abstract underlying form, very similar to conventional orthography, accounts for the variant forms by rules of great generality and wide applicability.
>
> There is, incidentally, nothing particularly surprising about the fact that conventional orthography is, as these examples suggest, a near optimal system for lexical representation of English words. . . . It is therefore noteworthy, but not too surprising, that English orthography, despite its often cited inconsistencies, comes remarkably close to being an optimal orthographic system for English [Chomsky and Halle 1968:49].

The defense of English spelling by some linguists seems to rest on their ability to discover explanations, however complicated, for the relationship between conventional spelling and the sound patterns of the language. Some of the hypothetical relationships, which are often not obvious even to trained linguists, much less ordinary mortals, are complex to the point of absurdity. The defense of English orthography is arid and of no value outside the rarefied world of a peculiar school of linguistics. There are many areas of English spelling, such as some of the variants for the *sh* and long *i* sounds noted earlier, that are not covered by any practical set of rules.

A somewhat different slant toward English spelling is presented by the Prague School of linguists with their functional dichotomy between spoken and written language, already touched upon in chapter 2. Since, in their view, writing serves a different function from that of speech, differentiations in writing that are not paralleled in speech (e.g., written *wright:write:right:rite* as compared to the single spoken form) find some justification in the fact that they facilitate the reading process by removing ambiguity that might otherwise result from a common spelling for all such words. These and other graphic conventions not paralleled in speech are therefore defended as having a useful function (Vachek 1945–1949, 1976, 1979).

In their discussion of these matters, scholars in the Prague School tradition emphasize the difference between the needs of readers and the needs of writers. In writing, especially in learning to write a language, as on the part of children and foreigners, it is easiest if there is a close correspondence between sound and symbol. On the other hand, for purposes of reading, greater visual distinctions, such as different spellings for words with the same pronunciation, are considered by some scholars to be desirable, especially for very proficient readers (Bradley 1913).

A good deal of the controversy over English orthography revolves around differences of opinion as to which of the three levels of phonological representation noted earlier should be selected as the basis for the writing system. The decision is likely to be heavily influenced by the kind of users for whom a script is intended.

For some limited purposes, such as noting for foreign learners precisely how an English expression is pronounced, it is sometimes considered helpful to have a purely phonetic notation, at least as an adjunct to the regular orthography. There has been a more widespread demand that use should be made of purely phonemic spelling, as in spelling *is* as *iz* and even extending this approach to writing the plural of *pad* as *padz*. This was the position taken by George Bernard Shaw in calling for a new alphabet that would involve a complete restructuring of English orthography. Another well known figure who embraced this approach was Sir Isaac Pitman, creator of the Pitman shorthand system, which was itself a scientifically constructed system of considerable merit. English and American Simplified Spelling Societies, which were organized in 1876, sought reform along the lines of strictly phonemic spelling (Wijk 1959:20–26).

Perhaps the high point of these efforts was the promotion of a simplified orthography known as the Initial Teaching Alphabet (ITA). It was at one time fairly widely used, as the name suggests, as the initial alphabet to teach children to read. The assumption was that achieving quick literacy in a simple script would facilitate acquisition of standard English orthography. It appears, however, that support for this and other proposals for phonemic or near-phonemic writing reform is virtually moribund. The same is true of proposals for much more modest changes like those proposed in *Regularized English* (Wijk 1959).

Most linguists argue for a morphophonemic approach to writing on the grounds that the primary purpose of a writing system is to serve the needs of native speakers. These, unlike foreigners, do not need to be reminded of distinctions in pronunciation if they would automatically make them anyway. As already noted, native speakers of English do not need to be told that the finals in *pats* and *pads* are pronounced differently—they will automatically pronounce the first with an *s* and the second with a *z*. Hence the two pronunciations of the plural morpheme can both be written "morphophonemically" as *s* for native speakers.

Some linguists include under the rubric of morphophonemic spelling something much broader than the principle of using the same spelling for different sounds if these are predictable, as in the case of the *s* in *pats:pads*. A. A. Hill, who was for many years the Secretary of the Linguistic Society of America, extends the term to cover cases where the same sound occurs with different spellings: "Whenever there are varying spellings for individual morphemes, and these spellings are fixed in accord with the morpheme that is being spelled, the writing is morphophonemic." Illustrating the point with some regular and systematic examples from German, he continues: "A more pervasive type of morphophonemic spelling is that which occurs when a series of different phonetic spellings are merely used to identify differing morphemes. This is the general practice in English, where a given sequence such as /sayt/ is spelled *sight, site,* or *cite*" (Hill 1967:98).

Among existing writing systems, English is probably the outstanding example of a morphophonemic system which functions by the extensive use of devices that strictly speaking do not directly represent either meaning or sound. That is to say, the distinction between *site* and *cite* is not conveyed by the disparate meanings of different iconic symbols, as would be the case with Egyptian hieroglyphic symbols. Nor is it conveyed by any difference in sound, since the pronunciation of the two words is exactly the same. For want of a better term, I have called this technique *mnemonic,* since it has the function of jogging the reader into remembering that there is some sort of difference between the two, though without clearly picturing or sounding out what that difference is.

English is not the only writing system that is characterized by the extensive use of the mnemonic technique. Danish has the reputation of being almost as complex in its spelling. In French, too, there is a poor fit between sound and symbol. However, in French, speakers of the language have a good chance of being able to pronounce correctly any sequence of letters they may meet, though they cannot automatically spell out correctly whatever they might say. English has the unenviable distinction of being bad in both directions.

There are a number of scholars who have interpreted the technique which I have labeled mnemonic, or the total English orthography of which it is part, as actually being akin to the Chinese system of writing. It has already been mentioned in chapter 2 that one writer classifies English as "ideographic" (Zachrisson 1931:5), another as "logographic" (Kōno 1969:85). Hill presents a similar view:

> Morphophonemic spelling, when it goes as far as it does in English, brings the linguistic systems full circle back to morphemic writing, so that it is just about as true of English that we spell our morphemes by selecting strokes and placing them in the right order according to partially logical rules, as it is of Chinese [Hill 1967:98–99].

There is an element of truth in such views insofar as they emphasize that Chinese and English orthographies have in common a greater divergence from strict phonological representation than do most other systems, and that both compensate for this by relying on the extensive use of other techniques to convey meaning. But scholars who promulgate these views are seriously at fault in failing to stress that both systems are still, in the final analysis, phonologically based, one as a syllabic script, the other as an alphabetic system. Both share the essential feature common to all full systems of writing.

III
WRITING IN
COMPARATIVE
PERSPECTIVE

6.

A Critique of Writing about Writing

When the Greek historian Diodorus Siculus propounded the thesis in the first century B.C. that the Egyptian hieroglyphs functioned as symbols of meaning rather than of sound, he became the first whose name we know of countless purveyors of misconceptions about the nature of writing. The material presented in the preceding chapters provides, I hope, a basis for readers to make their own assessments about writing. As a further aid toward this end I should like now to take up some of the more pervasive errors and their perpetrators.

In assessing what writers say about writing in general and about individual systems, it helps to approach the task in terms of a three-tiered analysis based on three overarching aspects of writing which are often confused but should be clearly distinguished. These aspects are:

1. graphic principle
2. representational level
3. graphic symbols

The first aspect involves a choice between two principles of graphic representation, one depicting or otherwise symbolizing physical objects and thoughts, the other representing the sounds of spoken utterances. The second aspect involves a choice among several putative representational levels that are universally acknowledged as including alphabets and syllabaries. The third aspect involves the choice of a set of graphic symbols from among the virtually unlimited number of such symbols that can be created for whatever representational level is selected.

The three aspects are ranked in order of importance. The first is crucial: Only by choosing to represent sounds, and not merely relying on pictures themselves, do we get full writing, real writing. The second is less crucial but still important: We usually get a simpler and more flexible system with phonemic representation, though syllabic systems can also serve quite well. The third aspect is least important, one is tempted to say completely insignificant, except insofar as it has to do with matters of aesthetics and efficiency.

We need to add a fourth aspect which, strictly speaking, lies outside the writing systems themselves but is intimately connected with the first three aspects. This is how we view the mental processes involved in deriving meaning from visual symbols. Now let us see in fairly specific detail how all these aspects of writing have been mishandled in the literature devoted to writing.

Graphic Principle

The primary and most pervasive error having to do with the graphic principle is the failure to distinguish between partial and full systems of writing. This failure is particularly apparent in discussions dealing with the origins of writing and with the expressive potential of various systems of representation, most especially pictographic symbols.

Most treatments of pictograhic symbols do not discriminate between significant symbols and symbols that have little if any bearing on the evolution of writing. Thousands of attempts at pictographic representation have been made, but in a discussion of full writing systems only three are of any interest or importance: Sumerian, Chinese, and Mayan. Discussions of other pictographic "systems" should be limited to works dealing with partial communication. They do not belong in a study of full writing. In a general history of communication, yes; in a history of writing, no. Their inclusion in a study of writing can only lead to misunderstanding.

Students of writing, in their fascination with dead-end pictographic symbols, often neglect to explore the details of how Sumerian, Chinese, and Mayan made the transition to full writing. The relevant details may not be fully available or readily understandable except perhaps to specialists in various early writing systems. But anyone who has the temerity to discuss the origins of writing must have the perseverance to dig out what is known.

In discussions of writing there is often an indiscriminate lumping together of all pictographs on the presumption that they could have developed into a full system of writing. Also, belief in the potential of pictographic symbols frequently leads to uncritical handling of them. Diringer let his daughter's inaccurate drawing of the "Yukaghir Love Letter" stand, and Sampson relied on it. His thesis of full semasiographic writing has no sound basis upon which to rest.

These are not minor academic lapses; they are serious and quite revealing failures which take on particular significance precisely because of the stature of the scholars committing them. Diringer has to his credit an indispensable reference work on writing. Sampson has produced several important works, especially *Making Sense,* which combine proficient scholarship with a humanistic approach unusual in linguistic literature. Even his *Writing Systems,* my criticisms aside, has much of value for discriminating readers.

But these otherwise first-rate scholars, like many others, are betrayed by their naiveté about and desire to believe in the power of pictographs. This has led to much slovenly scholarship. Even scholars whose intent is to be honest have gotten away with an academic equivalent to malpractice in the area of writing, and they must be called to account.

Roy Harris' *Origins of Writing* (1986) (see negative review by Alexander George [1987]) attacks anonymous scholars for allegedly thinking that creators of the alphabet were committed to setting up a science of phonetics. He asserts that "writing 'as writing' had been for many centuries previously independent of the spoken word" (p. 110). He also considers possible "the development of graphic systems which are independent of oral communication altogether" (p. 150), and he objects to approaches in which "the capacity of the system for indicating pronunciation is elevated into the criterion for recognizing writing as such" (p. 122), a point of view diametrically opposing the one presented above. Harris does not recognize that this is precisely the criterion which distinguishes full writing from partial writing, real writing from pseudowriting, from nonwriting. And it is precisely the use of the rebus, despite his devaluation of it, that marks the transition to real writing. It is also factually untrue that writing was ever independent of the spoken word, unless one counts as writing productions such as those of the Yukaghir and North American Indians.

Railing against Plato, Aristotle, Bloomfield, and others because they "treated writing simply as a representation of speech" (pp. 25–27), Harris echoes the criticism advanced by Prague School writers like Vachek and others against the idea that writing "merely" records language. In their justified questioning of the word "merely," Harris and his predecessors throw out the baby with the bath water by appearing to suggest that writing systems are possible which do not record language.

Harris actually devotes remarkably little space to a direct discussion of the origin of writing, his ostensible subject. He does assert that the invention of writing "almost certainly" was related to the move from a "token-iterative" to an "emblem-slotting" system for recording numerical information. What he is referring to is the change from token counting (e.g., one sheep, one pebble; one sheep, one pebble; one sheep, one pebble; . . .) to a technique which involves a number and an enumerated item (e.g., 3 sheep). This is an interesting idea, but Harris does not provide much factual support for it. Of the extensive literature about the numerical systems of the Sumerians and the Maya, Harris cites little besides the work of Schmandt-Besserat (whose limited value was noted above, in chapter 3).

This is a pity, for in raising a new factor that might be related to the origin of writing, Harris skirts but does not pursue one of the major unsolved mysteries in this area. That mystery is, to what factor or factors must we ascribe the emergence of writing from primitive pictographs in the cases where this did happen, as against the countless other cases where it did not? Leaving aside the Mayan script because it is still perhaps inadequately deciphered, and the Chinese case because its earliest extant form is already too advanced for our purposes, leaves Sumerian as the best candidate for solving the mystery.

Was there something special about Sumerian society, such as its complex bureaucracy, which required the use of writing and therefore led to its invention? The implication in this question that necessity is the mother of invention is rejected by the author of *Ancient Mesopotamia.* "It should be kept in mind," he asserts, "that the use of writing is not absolutely necessary for recording and controlling complex bureaucratic transactions" (Oppenheim 1977:230). This view is supported by the highly complex bureaucratic structure developed by the Incas without benefit of writing.

Was there then something special about Sumerian prewriting that led to the emergence of full writing? Schmandt-Besserat thinks she has found a positive answer to this question in the early use of clay tokens for recording purposes. It appears, however, that the early symbols at best simply explain the origin of a few later pictographic symbols still used merely as pictographic symbols. They do not explain the use of pictographic symbols used as phonetic symbols, as in the case of *gi* 'reed' used for *gi* 'reimburse.' Hence they do not throw any significant light on the origin of writing.

Sumerian pictographs seem to me to differ only in insignificant detail from their Amerindian counterparts. Yet in one case the pictographs led to full writing through their use as rebus symbols, while in the other case, like the symbols developed by countless creators of pictographs, they never got beyond being employed as mute signs.

I also fail to see a significant difference between Amerindian totems and the Shang and pre-Shang clan symbols which Boltz (1986:432–434) provocatively suggests may have led to "a moment when someone recognized a relation between the drawing of a clan emblem and the *name* of the clan. This would have been the point at which the pictograph changed from being 'nonphonetic' to 'phonetic,' and could then be considered a form of writing." If this suggestion turns out to have merit, we have another example of where similar symbols in one case led to full writing but in other cases never got beyond the prewriting stage.

Perhaps further excavations and further research by Sumerologists will eventually solve one of the key puzzles in the origin of writing. Pending a better solution, I incline to the belief that the emergence of writing was accidental.

It is perhaps misleading to speak, as is frequently done, of the "invention" of writing. Invention presupposes a conscious search for the solution to a clearly perceived problem. A classic example is Edison's search for the filament that enabled him to invent the electric light bulb. My impression of the earliest stage of writing, not only among the Sumerians but also among the Chinese and Maya, is that it looks more like an accidental discovery than a conscious invention.

Hence to my mind the term *invention* is misused when a Chinese author relates neolithic pottery marks to Shang writing and claims that "the invention and development of writing in China was a continuous process covering a period of no less than 6000 years" (Chang 1982:22, quoted in Boltz 1986:432). This view of "invention" as a long-drawn-out process is simply wrongheaded, whether it is applied to Sumerian or to Chinese. As Boltz aptly remarks,

> Writing systems do not evolve in that way. If a potential for writing arises in the form of graphs or marks standing for names or words, no matter of what kind or how limited, that potential must either fulfill

itself apace, culminating in a viable full-fledged system, or wither and die. A 'half-way' writing system is no system at all, and there is no way it could remain in a kind of 'limbo' or 'suspended animation' for such a long time. If it did not develop into a real writing system reasonably expeditiously, there would be no reason for people to preserve its embryonic bits and pieces. As a practical matter a writing system is something that is achieved either relatively quickly, or not at all. . . . Writing is an invention, not the end product of evolutionary development. . . . The invention itself was a kind of realization, and must have been a punctual event [Boltz 1986:432].

But discovery can also be a punctual event, that is, one happening at a moment in time. I believe that this term accounts better for what appears to be the slow pace at which writing evolved. If the process of conceiving the idea of writing were part of the mental process of invention, one would expect a quicker and more thorough elaboration of the idea. Instead, the development of the rebus principle from its inception to its refinement into a full system of writing seems to have required several hundred years in the case of Sumerian.

To be sure, the Mayanists Prem and Riese (1983) speak of the "incredibly short time-span of 400 years" that it took the Maya to develop their writing system into a full-fledged script. From this perspective, Sumerian writing appears to have developed at an even more rapid pace. Yet it seems that the early creators of writing, as discoverers rather than as inventors, did not immediately realize the full potential inherent in using pictographs as phonetic symbols.

This is, of course, hardly to be wondered at. If modern inheritors of writing have such difficulty in sorting out the relationship between spoken words and written symbols, it is hardly surprising that early scribes groped their way to full writing.

The failure of scholars today to emphasize the central role of sound in the emergence of writing is well illustrated by the case of G. R. Driver. Here is an unquestionably erudite scholar who is the author of highly regarded scholarship on the writing systems of Near Eastern origin. However, his attention is so narrowly focused on details that he fails to give due credit to the Sumerians for the revolutionary idea that the principle of using signs to depict concrete objects, already extended to express similar concepts and analogous activities (e.g., expressing 'to go' by the sign for 'leg'), might be further extended to represent sound. "This principle," he says, "was seriously strained when the use of a sign was stretched to make it serve for something with which it had no semantic or logical connection but of which the name had a similar sound. . . . The defects of such a system are obvious: ambiguity is unavoidable and the range of expression gravely restricted" (Driver 1976:57). Instead of hailing the use of the rebus principle as an epoch-making breakthrough leading to the first true system of writing in human history, Driver belittles it as "this abusive employment of a sign" and sees only defects in a system which uses pictographs in both phonetic and semantic functions.

More serious than Driver's ambivalence toward the use of the rebus principle is the lack of understanding of the relationship between speech and writing on the part of those who think writing can be divorced from speech. Particularly astonishing is the failure of linguists to insist that writing—real writing, full writing—first and foremost represents speech, however well or badly it may do its job, even if its role is acknowledged as not being limited to representing speech.

The basis for my insistence is no mere assumption of the primacy of speech. The historical reality is that all full systems of writing have been based on speech, and that no set of nonphonetic symbols has ever shown itself capable of conveying anything more than an extremely limited range of thought. It will not do merely to assume, or to argue from evidence of the "Yukaghir Love Letter" type, that such symbolization can be expanded to express any and all thought. The burden of proof rests with those who propound a thesis that goes so against the historical record. Before their claims can be taken seriously, they must be able to find or create a nonphonetic system of writing capable of unambiguously representing any and all thought.

The failure of linguists in this area comprises a major dereliction of duty that reflects very badly on their discipline. This is evidenced both in the careless handling of the relationship between speech and writing by Sampson and Harris and in the misguided efforts to score a point by juggling with words in a misleading way. An example of the latter is Householder's eye-catching chapter title "On the Primacy of Writing" (1971:244–246). The primacy turns out to be little more than the superior ability in English to predict pronunciation from spelling as compared to predicting spelling from pronunciation. The effect, however, is to suggest a secondary role for speech.

The claim of linguists to any authority for their discipline is seriously compromised by such irresponsible scholarship. The primacy of speech and the primacy of the graphic principle based on speech need to receive the categorical support of scholars concerned with the nature of writing and the progress of linguistic science.

Representational Level

Claims have been made for a variety of levels of representation that can be summarized as follows:

1. pictographic
2. ideographic
3. logographic/morphemic
4. syllabic
5. phonemic
6. featural

Terminological differences aside, this list does not differ much from the evolutionary stages of writing that we have already noted were propounded in the last century by Isaac Taylor and have essentially been followed by most writers since then. It is my contention that these writers are in error in considering that it is possible for a writing system to be based on a representational level other than the phonemic or syllabic.

A common error is the failure to make a clear distinction among the various levels by specifying the distinguishing features of each, a problem that is at its most acute for the first four levels. The last two, namely the phonemic and the featural, present few if any problems, because these are the areas of linguistic analysis that have received the most attention and the most agreement as to their linguistic status. Their symbolic representation is also fairly clear, as witness both the featural charts that have been developed by linguists and the various scientific notations that have been applied to individual languages, which can easily be related to their conventional orthographies. Such notations as [+vocalic] and *lock*/lak/ are distinctive enough so that there is little confusion with other levels of representation. The existence of alphabetic systems representing speech at the phonemic level is well attested. I have argued earlier for the nonexistence of systems representing speech at the featural level.

The other four levels present special problems and are fruitful sources of confusion and error. At the pictographic level, inadequate attention is paid to sorting out the two possible aspects of pictographic symbols, namely that they represent either concepts divorced from sound, or sounds at one of the various levels of speech. Of course, a specific symbol may be used in both ways, but a set of symbols must be classified in one or the other category.

If a set of pictographic symbols does not represent sound, then it should be dismissed as at best a limited system of writing. If it represents some level of spoken utterances, then it should be classified as belonging to that level, regardless of the incidental pictographic shape of the symbols or the added use, however extensive, of nonphonetic supplements such as semantic determinatives.

Hill's classification of Amerindian pictographs as iconic symbols representing speech is a variation on the notion held by many scholars, as well as by the public at large, that the discourse level of speech, that is, stretches of speech beyond words and sentences, can be represented by pictographic symbols. The limitations of such symbols have been amply demonstrated and should be clearly acknowledged in discussions of writing systems by dismissing them as not really relevant to the subject at hand. Yet even Gelb, despite his rejection of pictographs as true writing, misleadingly presents them as "forerunners of writing." In his words: "Under 'Forerunners of Writing' are included all the various devices by which man first attempted to convey his thoughts and feelings" (1963:190).

This is like including as "Forerunners of the Automobile" all the various devices by which humans have attempted to transport themselves. But English dog-carts, Russian droshkies, and Indian bullock carts preceded the automobile only chronologically and were definitely not its forerunners or precursors in the sense of being conceptually related in some fundamental way. Such a direct relationship is implicit in these terms. But in fact horseless carriages were only superficially related to horse-drawn carriages, since the basic driving force was completely different in the two cases. Granted that all those other conveyances share with motor vehicles the ability to transport people, nevertheless it would be ludicrous to include them in a history of the conveyance that has set a land speed record of 740 miles per hour. In a general history of transportation, yes; in a history of the automobile, no. Only Sumerian, Chinese, and Mayan pictographs can be considered as forerunners of writing, since only they incorporated the conceptually new technique of sound representation that made it possible to go beyond expressing a few limited ideas to conveying any and all thought. Amerindian, Yukaghir, and other pictographic systems were forerunners of nothing. Such real writing systems as were created by American Indians like Sequoya had as their forerunners the writing systems of white men with whom the Indians came in contact.

On a par with inflating the expressive potential of pictographic symbols such as those of the Yukaghir is the error in viewing some actual full systems of writing as based on the pictographic principle. Egyptian hieroglyphs have long been misrepresented in this fashion. The same is true of Chinese.

The first Westerner to comment on Chinese writing, the Dominican friar Gaspar da Cruz, wrote in 1569 that each thing was represented by its own character. He gave three examples, namely those referring to "man," "Heaven," and "earth" (Boxer 1953:161–162). In the traditional system of classifying Chinese characters the three graphs in question are indeed placed in the category of pictographic symbols, and rightly so, since the earliest forms in the Shang inscriptions can be interpreted as more or less iconic symbols.

But remember that the category to which the three symbols referred to by da Cruz belong comprises only about one percent of the characters in the total Chinese lexicon. From this one percent the friar extrapolated to the totality of Chinese characters. This is comparable to the blind man who felt the tip of an elephant's tail and identified the creature as a snake.

In the more than four hundred years that have elapsed since this initial error was made, the blindness toward the reality of Chinese writing displayed by da Cruz has been manifested with disheartening repetition by subsequent writers. A recent example is one that brings to mind an incisive comment made by A. E. Housman, who besides being poet-laureate was also an outstanding classical scholar. His scholarly writing was edged with sarcasm and cold contempt for inferior work, as in his remark that "When X has acquired a scrap of misinformation he cannot rest until he has imparted it" (Untermeyer 1942:103).

In a widely reviewed work R. K. Logan (1986) imparts the misinformation that "the Chinese writing system, basically unchanged from its original form, is still purely pictographic." It "is non-phonetic." The category to which it belongs "is logographic or (pictographic) writing in which each spoken word is represented by its own unique visual sign, which denotes or depicts the word symbolically or pictorially" (1986:20, 25, 30–31). Logan's misinformation was given wide publicity in a *New York Times* review by Christopher Lehmann-Haupt, who sees the book "as an often absorbing review of the evolution of written language" marred by the fact that "for all the plausibility of its detail, Mr. Logan does not really prove anything." The reviewer summarizes Logan's work by stating, "He dramatizes how progress to a phonetic alphabet in the West (as opposed to China's pictographic system of writing) yielded such breakthroughs as the Copernican revolution, a triumph of abstract thinking over common sense, and eventually led to the wonders of the modern age, when Occidental logic had presumably 'triumphed' over Oriental intuition."

If it is an error to call Chinese writing "pictographic" because it neither currently consists of recognizable pictures nor differs from other full systems in ultimately tracing its ancestry back to pictographic symbols, what then of the frequent use of the term *ideographic?* This term refers to the representation of ideas by symbols that are not necessarily pictographic but may be symbolic in some other way, as in the case of placing a dot above a horizontal line to convey the idea "above." Quite ironically, the term was coined in 1822 by Jean François Champollion when he announced his decipherment of the Egyptian script. The irony lies in the fact that while many of the hieroglyphic symbols are recognizable pictures whose original meaning might be guessed at, Champollion achieved success precisely because he discovered that the pictures also functioned as phonetic symbols, and that this was their primary function. Yet the term has stuck as an overall designation for the kinds of writing represented by Egyptian, Sumerian, and Chinese.

Writers who refer to Chinese characters as "ideographs" can be divided into several groups. One consists of those who are essentially innocent of any knowledge of Chinese and really believe that the characters represent ideas and not sounds. Another group consists chiefly of specialists in Chinese who recognize in varying degrees that Chinese characters represent sounds but consider this to be immaterial on the grounds that they can directly convey meaning to the eye. One well known representative of this group is Herrlee Creel, who several decades ago engaged in a sharp polemical exchange with Peter Boodberg; Boodberg clearly emerged victorious, though knowledge of the matter has been largely limited to specialists in the field (DeFrancis 1984a). Another representative is the French scholar Georges Margouliès, author of *La Langue et l'écriture chinoises* (1957), a work that was written for a popular audience and has gone through two editions.

Still another group includes many people who use the term *ideographic* because it is the most popular designation for the characters, just as *sweetbread* is used as the common designation for an item of food that is neither sweet nor bread. To my intense chagrin, I used to belong to the third group, on the rather unthinking grounds that I should go along with whatever was common usage. It was only on reading Margouliès that I was awakened to the error of my ways.

Margouliès presents an extended essay extolling the superiority of Chinese "ideographs" as symbols which convey thought directly to the mind without having to rely on the phonetic information they contain, and do so so well that they could function as a universal system of writing. I was much annoyed by the book. In the first place, as one writer has pointed out in dealing with the criteria for calling a script "logographic" or "ideographic," the status of a writing system "does not depend on what its users do when they read" (Coulmas 1984:63). That remark applies not only to Chinese but also to English, which it is widely believed is also read as whole words without any use of the alphabetic information contained in the writing.

But the chief reason for my annoyance at the book is that it is an almost exaggerated example of a work that pontificates about Chinese, or about writing in general, with high-sounding verbiage that takes the place of fact-based analysis. For 274 pages Margouliès rings the changes on his theme that the characters are like our Arabic numerals. Not once does he cite a single character or even a single transcription. Nor does he illustrate with a single example how Chinese can serve as a model for a system capable of solving "le problème d'une langue internationale."

To counter the nonsense purveyed by writers like Margouliès, and to expiate my own sin in this area, I have dealt at length with the issues involved in various works. One chapter in *The Chinese Language: Fact and Fantasy* deals specifically with the ideographic myth. The present work extends to writing in general the refutation of the widely held notion of ideographic writing. The concept of logographic writing is also rejected both here and there.

Chinese writing was designated *logographic* in 1838 by the Franco-American scholar Peter S. DuPonceau to counter its characterization as an ideographic script. The term was revived in the 1930s by Boodberg and has since been taken up by many scholars. It is often replaced by the term *morphemic* on the grounds that Chinese writing represents spoken language at the level of morphemes rather than of words.

The use of either term is actually quite misleading. The major error is the failure, already discussed in the section "Full/Unlimited/Real Writing" in chapter 2, to distinguish adequately between grapheme and frame (or lexeme). Focusing their attention on the characters that comprise either the modern lexicon of 4,000–7,000 characters or the more comprehensive historical lexicon of 25,000–50,000 characters, most writers make the error of equating these lexemes with the writing system itself.

This is true even of specialists in Chinese, who are generally quite aware that phonetic elements exist in the system but tend to focus their attention on the characters as wholes. The main reason for this myopia is that the characters are the units that generally receive the most attention, as in dictionaries, where they are traditionally listed without regard to their sound but by order of the "keys" to which they are traditionally assigned. The phonetic element gets very short shrift in general sinological work. Moreover, the designations generally given to Chinese characters—*ideographic, logographic,* and *morphemic*—seem better suited as general labels than more accurate jawbreakers like *morphosyllabic* or *syllabomorphemic,* which, if used at all, tend to get buried in specialized publications. Hence specialists in Chinese, including myself, share a good part of the responsibility for the failure of the general public to understand the real nature of Chinese writing.

It is not surprising, therefore, that many people seem unaware of the fact that the overwhelming majority of graphs are of the SP type made up by combining a semantic element with a phonetic element. Hence they often look upon Chinese characters as unitary symbols. That seems to be the case in Logan's previously mentioned references to Chinese characters as nonphonetic symbols that depict an entire word with one sign. Other writers appear to be aware that Chinese characters contain phonetic as well as semantic components, but they tend to minimize the former and overemphasize the latter. Such confusion and misjudgment is to be found both in general statements about writing systems and in the specific examples cited to illustrate particular systems.

General statements often fail to sort out the differences in meaning among the terms *pictographic, ideographic, logographic,* and *morphemic.*

The terms are often used more or less interchangeably, and so loosely that it is difficult to ascertain exactly what a writer has in mind in using one or another of them. Here are some quotations that reveal the confusion in the thinking of the authors. All ignore or minimize the phonetic aspect in Chinese writing:

1. Ferdinand de Saussure, one of the founders of modern linguistics:

> There are only two ways of writing:
> 1) In an ideographic system each word is represented by a single sign that is unrelated to the sounds of the word itself. Each written sign stands for a whole word and, consequently, for the idea expressed by the word. The classic example of an ideographic system of writing is Chinese.
> 2) The system commonly known as "phonetic" tries to reproduce the succession of sounds that make up a word. Phonetic systems are sometimes syllabic, sometimes alphabetic, i.e., based on the irreducible elements used in speaking.
> Moreover, ideographic systems freely become mixtures when certain ideograms lose their original value and become symbols of isolated sounds [1959:25–26].

2. I. J. Gelb, author of perhaps the most important book on writing:

> The great majority of signs in the Sumerian, Egyptian, Hittite, and Chinese systems of writing are simple pictures of objects found in the surrounding world [1963:97].

> In Chinese . . . a phonetic complement or indicator, once added to a word-sign, remains with it always to form one word sign composed of two elements. The great majority of Chinese word signs belong to this class [1963:104].

3. Paul A. Kolers, a prominent psycholinguist:

> Although derived from pictures, contemporary Chinese logograms have little of their pictorial origins still visible; and as they are not phonetic either, learning them requires a protracted process of memorizing [1969:353].

4. A popular elementary textbook of linguistics:

In *logographic writing systems* each character that is used represents either a concrete or abstract concept or idea. (For this reason, they are also called ideographic.) [Geoghegan et al. 1979:131–1].

5. A work dealing with symbolic expression generally:

In Chinese writing, which goes back some four thousand years, primitive customs live on to this day, for Chinese writing never pro gressed to the syllabic stage. It depicts the complex word in the form of a complex image [Giedion 1966:90].

Perhaps even more revealing than these general statements are the specific examples cited by various authors to illustrate one or another system of writing. Gelb (1963:17) illustrates what he calls "word-signs," his less technical equivalent for "logographs," with the fol lowing five symbols and their explanations:

> † = 'dead, died'
> 2 = 'two, second'
> ° = 'degree'
> & (originally Latin) *et* = 'and'
> &c = '*et cetera,* and so forth, and so on,' and the like

Note that the first four examples are unitary symbols explained as having word meanings. The last is a sequence of two symbols each of which is likewise explained as standing for a word. The implication that these are typical of so-called word-syllabic or logographic writing is false. As we have seen, the word *mā* 'mother' in Chinese is written with a phonetic element to represent the sound *ma* and a semantic determinative to hint at the meaning as related to females.

That logographic writing is widely believed to involve no sound representation at all is indicated by an article devoted to teaching "logographic reading" to trainable mentally retarded adults who were taught "a set of 16 logographic signs" consisting solely of picturable objects or figures (House, Hanly, and Magid 1980).

A similar approach is taken by Sampson (1985:33) in an attempt at inventing "a logographic system for English" which he illustrates by presenting seven signs (one repeated) to represent "The cat walked over the mat." Each of the morphemes *(the, cat, walk, ed, over, the, mat)* is represented by its own symbol, e.g., a pointing index finger for

'the,' a bewhiskered feline for 'cat.' No element of sound is represented in the symbols. Thus the kind of phonetic similarity that exists
between *cat:mat* in English and *mǎ:mā* in Chinese is completely sup-
pressed in the illustration. Again the impression is conveyed that logographic or morphemic writing is characterized by a complete absence
of any phonetic component.

Later in the same book (1985:145–146) Sampson starts his discussion of Chinese by citing two completely unrelated graphs which can
both be transcribed as *cuān* and have the respective meanings 'parboil'
and 'leap.' Of these he says:

> The two graphs do not look similar to the untutored eye, and this
> impression is correct—there is no relationship between them. The
> European expectation that homophones, such as English *can* 'be able
> to' and *can* 'metal box,' will normally be written alike, and that a spe-
> cial explanation is needed when homophones such as *meet* and *meat,* or
> *doe* and *dough,* are written differently, is alien to the Chinese method of
> writing. This is not to say that similarities between the shapes of Chi-
> nese graphs never correspond to similarities between the pronuncia-
> tions of the morphemes they represent; we shall see that correspon-
> dences of this kind do play a part in the organization of Chinese
> writing. But although it not infrequently happens that morphemes
> which sound the same or similar are written with partly similar graphs,
> there is nothing regular in this; very often, as in the case just illus-
> trated, there is no relationship between the graphs for words which are
> perfect homophones. The European idea that from a knowledge of the
> pronunciation of a word one should be able to make at least a good
> guess at how to write it would seem bizarre to a Chinese.

Sampson makes the poor phonetic aspect of Chinese writing seem
even poorer than it actually is by selecting his examples from among
the one-third of the characters which provide no phonetic clue, instead
of from the two-thirds which have clues of the varying degrees of utility indicated above in figure 18 and the related discussion. And while
willing to put up with the fact that "a special explanation is needed"
for differences of spelling in English, he is unwilling to do so in the
case of Chinese because "there is nothing regular about this." Sampson stresses how bizarre it is to think of guessing writing from pronunciation. He glosses over the idea that from a knowledge of the
writing of a character one might be able to make a good guess at its

pronunciation. This idea also might seem bizarre to him and the Chinese because both he and the Chinese have been brainwashed into believing that the phonetic aspect is unimportant. The reality is that this aspect, poor as it is, is by no means as useless as Sampson's discussion implies.

Fuller expositions of the theoretical basis of Sampson's views appear in several works by William Haas and have been taken up by a number of scholars (Haas 1970, 1976, 1983). Haas goes to great lengths to refute the notion that what have generally been called logographic or morphemic scripts might conceivably be syllabic. At one point he downgrades the phonetic aspect completely by stating that Chinese, like other scripts of the same sort, "can serve a wide variety of phonologically distinct dialects and languages, precisely because it does not provide phonological information, leaving it up to the reader to supply this information from his knowledge of any one of the languages or dialects" (1983:21).

At another point Haas does note that phonological information is indeed provided by phonetic elements such as *mǎ* 'horse' in *mā* 'mother' (1983:18). And he also notes the phonetic use of characters to represent foreign names, as in the case of three characters that lose their meaning of 'horse,' 'overcome,' and 'think,' respectively, and are used merely for their pronunciation *Mǎkèsī* to render the name *Marx*. But he refuses to interpret such occurrences as instances of syllabic writing: "Instead of speaking of syllables with reference to Chinese or Sumerian writings, it would be less misleading to speak of defective morphs or words—defective, that is, in their being deprived of morphemic or lexical values" (1976:199). This is reminiscent of Driver's reference, cited in the preceding section, to the "abusive" use of Sumerian pictographs. Moreover, Haas says,

> *Ad hoc* cancellation of morphemic or lexical values affords no reason for crediting writers or readers with a syllabic analysis of their language; on the contrary, we have every reason to suppose they did not conceive of the idea of an inventory of syllables to represent all their utterances [1976:200].

Another scholar of the same school of thought emphatically rejects the idea that Modern Standard Chinese (MSC) might be syllabic for somewhat similar reasons: "That the Chinese writing system is nevertheless *not* a syllabary is suggested by the fact that almost 80 percent of the syllables of MSC are written in more ways than one" (French 1976:105). This is a curious argument coming from a writer of English, in which *100 percent* of the phonemes are spelled in more ways than one. Does that make English a nonphonemic system of writing?

The lack of a systematic inventory of syllabic signs is no proof that the Chinese were unable to make at least a rough syllabic analysis of their language and to create a written system based on the syllabic principle. Their use of phonetic elements like those shown in figure 18, their creation of the "reverse-cutting" syllable-telescoping technique, their compilation of rhyme-books, and their extensive writings on phonology amply demonstrate their capacity for linguistic analysis. As early as 420–581 Chinese scholars had analyzed their language as consisting of syllables composed of three elements, namely an initial consonant, a final (vowel or vowel plus consonant) and one of four possible tones (Lin 1988:187; McIntosh and Halliday 1966:1). Traditional Chinese scholars, an elitist group seeming actually to revel in the complexities of their esoteric script, cannot be expected to have sought anything so banal as simplifying their writing system by creating a nice regular syllabary. It is a serious error to equate *unsystematic* syllabic representation with *absence* of syllabic writing.

Hill's treatment of Chinese is a somewhat more subtle example of the downgrading of the phonetic aspect. He notes, correctly, that in some of what he calls morphemic scripts, which he lists as those of Egypt, Mesopotamia, China, and Central America, "the basic device in the system" consists of "giving two components for each sign, one semantic, the other phonetic, thus identifying the morphemes precisely by the intersection of the two." Then he goes on to state:

> The system could be illustrated in English by a hypothetical word-character made by drawing two strokes for the semantic indicator, and a fruit for the phonetic indicator. The composite symbol would be a sort of puzzle, like saying 'think of something which has to do with the number two, and sounds like a fruit' [1967:95].

Note that he is very specific about the semantic indicator: 'think of something which has to do with the number two'—that is, not one or three or just any old number, but quite specifically the number two. But he is quite vague about the phonetic indicator: 'think of something which . . . sounds like a fruit.' So we guess: apple? plum? orange? persimmon? pear?—That's it, pear = pair.

Hill's example stacks the cards against the phonetic element and in favor of the semantic element. "Two" is actually a key (no. 7) in Chinese, but few of the three dozen or so characters listed under this key turn out to have anything to do with the number. Among Chinese semantic indicators—whose utility in general is far inferior to that of phonetic indicators—this key ranks particularly low. As for the phonetic indicator, a fairer set of instructions would be "Think of something which has to do with the number two, and sounds like *parc* or *pier* or *pore* or something of that sort."

As a final illustration of the pervasive misrepresentation of Chinese, I cite an example taken from a popular work on writing by Robert Claiborne. The author states that in Chinese the symbol for "mouth" combined with the symbol for "door" means "to inquire." He adds that this illustrates the extension, first by the Sumerians and today by the Chinese, of picturing concrete objects and actions by combining two signs to form a third with a different meaning (Claiborne 1974:16).

The character Claiborne is discussing is the eighth derivative under phonetic no. 635 *mén* in figure 18. The character is indeed made up of the two components for "mouth" and "door," but as should be apparent, the "door" character is used not for its semantic value but as a fairly close phonetic element: *mén:wèn*. The two were near-homophones in Old Chinese: *mwən:mิwən* (Karlgren 1940:441), and both are now still pronounced with an *m* initial in Cantonese.

Such examples could be added to almost endlessly. They are enough, however, to alert readers to the kind of misunderstandings and obfuscations about the representational level of writing that they are likely to encounter in much of the literature on the subject. Together with the discussion in earlier chapters they are also enough, I hope, to drive home the point that there never has been a system of writing that represents language on the pictographic, ideographic, logographic, morphemic, or featural levels. The only writing systems that have ever been created, and the only ones that I believe ever can be created, are those that represent language on the syllabic or phonemic levels.

This does not mean that a writing system is necessarily either purely syllabic or purely phonemic. For purposes of classification these broad categories will do. But because there are no pure systems of writing, there is sure to be some mixing of levels. Numerals and a few other symbols such as those commonly found on typewriter and word-processor keyboards are obvious examples that do not belong to the major set of symbols defining a representational level. The major set itself may include some admixture. A case in point is the Chinese Phonetic Alphabet created in 1913 under the influence of the syllabic "reverse-cutting" technique. It consists of some three dozen simple character-like symbols, of which two-thirds represent single initial consonant phonemes, and one-third final phoneme clusters—diphthongs or combinations of vowels plus *n* or *ng*. This is still primarily a phonemic script, though it is worth noting that Smalley, Chia, and Gnia (forthcoming) have set up a separate category of "demisyllabic" scripts which represent "each of the halves of the syllable, initial and final."

Graphic Symbols

One of the main sources of error about graphic symbols is the failure to distinguish between form and function. The outward appearance of symbols is, of course, the first thing that strikes the eye when we look at a sample of writing. Egyptian hieroglyphs consist of pictures and are therefore (naturally, at first) thought to comprise a symbolic system of writing; Chinese characters are complex symbols that can be traced back to pictorial origins and are therefore thought to comprise a pictographic system of writing.

We forget that the English letter *A* originated from the picture of an ox head, *D* from that of a triangular tent-flap, and *F,* according to Bloomfield (1933:284), from the depiction of some sort of horned creature (the horns are more apparent if the letter is rotated thus: ᴚ). In fact, proportionately speaking, English is perhaps more "pictographic" than Chinese. We recognize that *A, D,* and *F* now represent sounds and that the origin of our letters, if known at all, is irrelevant. But we fail to acknowledge that in Chinese and other "pictographic" systems we also have to distinguish between form and function and place our main emphasis squarely on function.

Since the primary goal of writing (reservations from Prague School critics and others notwithstanding), is to represent speech, those who discuss the subject should concentrate their attention on just how, and how well, the symbols do their job. It is not difficult to state what we must know to make the assessment, though actually getting the information may be another matter.

In an alphabetic system of writing, since what is represented is phonemes, we should start by asking how many phonemes there are, and what symbols are used to represent them. In the case of English, we know that there are about 40 phonemes of various kinds (consonants, vowels, stress, pitch, and others). We also know that there are 26 letters and a few other symbols available to represent those 40 phonemes —or at least those we choose to represent, as against those we ignore —in our writing system. There is a huge literature dealing with the relationship between sound and symbol in English now and in the past.

In a syllabic system of writing, since what is represented is syllables, we should start by asking how many syllables there are, and what symbols are used to represent them. In the case of Japanese, the answer is fairly clear, despite some differences of opinion among specialists. There are 105 or 113 syllables and 46 syllabic symbols to represent them. The 46 symbols are juggled around in various well known ways so as to handle all of the syllables, in somewhat the same way that we combine *t* and *h* to represent the sounds in *this* and *thin*.

Some of the problems involved in creating a set of graphic symbols and adapting them to a particular language can be illustrated by trying to do this for a specific language. Let us attempt the task by taking as an example a phonologically simple language—Hawaiian.

Hawaiian can be analyzed as having 8 consonants and 5 vowels, which may be either long or short. The syllable structure is very simple, V or CV syllables only. There are 45 possible basic syllables, or 90 if we account for those with long vowels. Words consist either of single vowels (e.g., *a* 'and'), single syllables (e.g., *ma* 'at'), or combinations of syllables (e.g., *mahimahi* 'dolphin'). I have no idea how many morphemes there are in the language, nor how many words, but since even a small dictionary of Hawaiian contains thousands of entries, I assume that it is impractical to think of providing Hawaiian with a morphemic or logographic script. That leaves only syllabic or phonemic codes as reasonable alternatives.

If we were to write Hawaiian syllabically, we could do so with only 45 symbols to handle the basic syllables. Syllables with long vowels could be represented by incorporating length within the symbol, as in the Yi approach to tones, and would add another 45 symbols. Long syllables could be handled more economically by using the Vai approach to tones and giving a single separate length sign to each basic syllable sign.

The precise form of the symbols we select would be of quite secondary importance. We could use Cherokee, Yi, Chinese, kana, or completely arbitrary miscellaneous symbols, as in the following examples of the rendition of the syllable *ma:*

	Chinese	Kana	Miscellaneous
ma	馬	ㄞ	& ! 16

Since American missionaries arrived in Hawaii some years before the Chinese and Japanese did, Hawaiian was provided with a simple alphabetic script based on the Latin alphabet rather than one based on the syllabic principle. As a result, the sounds of Hawaiian are rendered as follows:

Consonants	Vowels
1 p	9 a
2 k	10 e
3 h	11 i
4 l	12 o
5 m	13 u
6 n	
7 w	
8 ' (glottal stop)	

Again it would be possible to create other symbols to represent the 13 phonemes (14 if we count length for vowels). The Russian alphabet would be just about as efficient as our Latin alphabet. Less efficient, but still effective, would be to adapt Chinese characters by using only the initial sound of the syllables they represent, as in the case of *m* from the pronunciation of the character for *mǎ* 'horse.'

The point of all this is to stress that the precise shape of the symbols is less important than the fact that all sorts of symbols can accurately represent the sounds of a language. But while it would be possible to represent Hawaiian syllables or phonemes on a one-to-one basis with any of the previously mentioned symbolic codes, practical considerations of course also need to be taken into account. This suggests that, given the realities of the present-day world, a simple phonemic system based on the Latin alphabet is the best solution for Hawaiian. In fact, the American missionaries who created the Hawaiian orthography in the early nineteenth century did a very commendable job from both the technical and more general points of view.

In this century missionaries associated with the Summer Institute of Linguistics have been in the forefront of creating writing systems for previously unwritten languages. Their approach is largely based on the following principles, laid down by a leading member of the group:

> A practical orthography should be phonemic. There should be a one-to-one correspondence between each phoneme and the symbolization of that phoneme.
> Some orthographies are based on the syllable and have a one-to-one correspondence between each syllable and the symbol representing it. Syllabaries have proved to be effective, and in areas where syllabaries are traditionally acceptable a syllabary may still prove to be the most adequate solution [Pike 1947:208].

But most writing systems, especially the early ones discussed in this book, were created in premodern times, long before the advent of the science of linguistics. They were created by scribes who obviously, from the results of their work, had some glimmerings of the phonemic and syllabic structure of their language, though they were hardly equipped to approach the matter in a fully systematic and scientific manner. We therefore need to look especially carefully, not at the sometimes crude outer form of the symbols they created, but at the function that they intended those symbols to have.

Here, however, many students of writing fail us. Elaborate and ill-founded theories about the origins of writing and the evolution and classification of writing systems abound. A case in point is the rejection by many scholars of the notion that the function of the symbols used in the Sumerian, Chinese, and typologically similar systems of writing might warrant their being called syllabic rather than morphemic, logographic, ideographic, or pictographic. Haas, for example, dismisses the matter by arguing against a line of thought that suggests "implausibly, that the Chinese system of writing is predominantly syllabic" (1976:183).

Many scholars evade the most cogent factors in comparing the symbols used within particular systems of writing and in different systems. One writer states that the Japanese kana syllabaries "involve deliberate phonological derivation, while kanji does not follow the phonemic principle" (Scinto 1986:48). But the opposite of "deliberate phonological derivation" is not Scinto's "phonemic principle"; it is undeliberate—unsystematic, haphazard—phonological derivation, in this case at the syllabic level. The opposite of phonemic is not nonphonetic, but syllabic. The opposite of nonphonetic is phonetic—either at the phonemic or at the syllabic level.

The greater complexity of the kanji symbols, compared to the simpler form and more obviously syllabic function of the kana, lead many observers to disregard the shared element of syllabic representation. A more thoughtful approach might suggest that the kanji symbols represent a very bad morphosyllabic system and the kana symbols a very good "pure" syllabic system.

The literature on writing not only often leaves the reader in the dark about the relationship of sounds and symbols; it also fails to place the creation of a system in a perspective which would help to evaluate the accomplishment. A good example is Sequoya's Cherokee syllabary. His principal biographer (Foreman 1938) and other writers constantly refer to his "invention." He is described as "the only man in history to conceive and perfect in its entirety an alphabet or syllabary" (Foreman 1938:3).

But Sequoya's syllabary should be sharply distinguished from the three true inventions or discoveries of writing by the Sumerians, the Chinese, and the Maya. Much has been made of the fact that he did not know English, but it is clear that he had a good deal of contact with the English-speaking and English-writing world about him, either directly or indirectly. His achievement consisted not of independently conceiving the idea of writing but of adapting the idea to Cherokee by creating a new symbolic system specifically for his own language.

This was no small achievement, and my comments are intended solely to place Sequoya's work in the proper perspective, not to deny him credit. It is a pity that his adaptation is not treated with more understanding by those who have written about him and his syllabary, for the vignettes that we have give fascinating glimpses into the creation of one specific set of graphic symbols.

On learning that whites were able to convey messages by symbols written on paper, Sequoya conceived the idea of using the technique for his own language. First he tried to make a character for each word. He pursued this approach for about a year but, not surprisingly, abandoned it when he had put down several thousand characters. He then hit upon the idea of dividing the words into parts or syllables. Not being confident of his own ability to discriminate sounds, he called on the help of the more acute ears of his wife and children and finally arrived at what he thought were all the sounds of his language.

After making an inventory of the sounds, Sequoya set about the task of devising symbols for them. From an English spelling book in his possession he took over a number of letters, which he adapted to represent syllabic sounds, as in the case of the letter *H* for the sound *mi.* At one point he had about 200 symbols in his syllabary, but later, as noted in the earlier discussion of Sequoya's work in chapter 3, he reduced the number of symbols to 85.

There is much lacking in the information provided by the various writers who have dealt with Sequoya and his work. For one thing, they do not tell us whether Sequoya ever considered a phonemic rather than a syllabic approach. Nor do they inform us why he abandoned something approaching a one-to-one correspondence between sound and symbol and opted instead for a smaller number of symbols with multiple phonetic values. While we do have some useful glimpses into the creation of a simple syllabic code that provided a highly effective means of writing the Cherokee language, the sketchiness of the available data points up the failure of observers to appreciate what is really involved in creating a set of graphic symbols.

Another case in which we need to look more closely at the form and function of graphic symbols involves the Naxi or Moso, one of the minority peoples in southwestern China. The Naxi are said to have two separate traditions of "writing," one primarily pictographic, the other syllabic (Ramsey 1987:264–270; Li 1957; Li, Zhang, and He 1953; Fu 1986a, 1986b). Thousands of manuscripts of the first have been found, but under a dozen of the second. Many of the symbols in the syllabic script were borrowed from Chinese and Yi writing. The pictographic symbols have served chiefly as mnemonic devices to remind shamans of the details of stories they already know by heart. In this respect the symbols are reminiscent of the pictographs used as memory aids by American Indians in chanting their songs. They are, however, much more aesthetically appealing, as they comprise daintily drawn pictographs that, like Egyptian hieroglyphic symbols, depict clearly recognizable objects.

An intriguing aspect of the Naxi pictographs that has been widely noted is the fact that they sometimes represent sounds. For example, a drawing of a pair of eyes is sometimes used for the idea *fate,* because the Naxi words for "eye" and "fate" are pronounced alike. Yet the

Naxi have made little use of such rebus symbols. Does this mean we are confronted here with another invention of writing, one which, uniquely among writing systems, started on the road to full writing but never got there?

In answering this question one should keep in mind that the Naxi have long been surrounded by Chinese and can therefore be supposed to have gotten the idea of writing from their literate neighbors. It is also useful to pay particular attention to the chronology that can be pieced together for the two systems.

There is general agreement that the pictographic symbols go back many hundreds of years. The earliest extant document using the symbols dates from 1668, but their prior existence is attested by a stone monument of the twelfth or thirteenth century, and some Chinese scholars believe that the symbols were already in use in the eleventh century (Fu 1986a:95). There is less agreement on the syllabic script. A recent source states, without elaboration, that it was created in the thirteenth century (Wang 1986:347). A longer and seemingly more authoritative study, noting that most if not all manuscripts of this type are attributed to a single shaman of the late nineteenth and early twentieth centuries, says the syllabic script most likely does not predate the Qing dynasty (1644–1911) (Li, Zhang, and He 1953, 2:xi).

The main question, however, is when the Naxi began to use their pictographs as phonetic symbols. In this connection it is useful to note the sequence of events as summarized by a leading Chinese specialist on the Naxi language and writing:

> 1. First a stage of pictographic symbols called Tomba. [This is the same designation as that for the shamans.]
> 2. Next a stage of syllabic writing called Geba, a term meaning 'disciple, follower' that is explained as referring to the fact that the system was created later than the pictographic symbols. Some of the Geba symbols were created by simplifying Tomba symbols, others were derived from Chinese characters.
> 3. Finally a stage, very late in developing, in which pictographic symbols are used for their phonetic value. This was done under the influence of the syllabic writing [Fu 1986b:133].

The key thing to consider in the foregoing observations is the context and timing involved in the adoption of the pictographs as phonetic symbols. These suggest that the very late and sporadic application of the rebus principle by the Naxi is not particularly striking or innovative. Their use of pictographs as phonetic symbols came *after* their creation of a purely syllabic script, and therefore differs fundamentally from the Sumerian, Chinese, Mayan, and Egyptian use of the rebus principle to create phonetic systems.

The limited use of the rebus principle by the Naxi seems to have led nowhere. As for their syllabic script, although it provided the Naxi with the means to write all of their own language, they did not make much use of it. Nor have they shown much interest in a script based on the Latin alphabet that was created for them in the 1950s. Because of their close contact with the Chinese, many Naxi use Chinese writing.[1]

The dearth of truly illuminating discussion of the relationship between writing systems and the languages they represent, a lack illustrated by the examples of Cherokee and Naxi, is only occasionally relieved. One satisfying bit of scholarship is the incisive account of the syllabic script that was developed early in this century to represent the Njuka language spoken in Surinam. The problems involved in representing 336 (counting tones) or 168 syllables (not counting tones) by using a syllabary of only 56 signs are succinctly dealt with in a publication which, perhaps significantly, is somewhat outside the mainstream of linguistic literature (Huttar 1985).

Even more exceptional than the article just cited is a fascinating study which presents the first fully documented case in the history of writing of an illiterate's creating an alphabetic script of amazing sophistication. It tells the story of the enigmatic Shong Lue Yong, a messianic Hmong figure described by his biographers as "apparently a genius, with extraordinary insight and ability to analyze, a man with a sharp linguistic sense" and revered by his followers as "Savior of the People, Mother of Writing" (Smalley, Chia, and Gnia, forthcoming). This account of the remarkable achievements of an illiterate mountaineer stands in welcome contrast to the lack of understanding shown by many scholars.

In all of the extensive literature devoted to writing, one of the most astonishing examples of the failure to understand the workings of a particular set of symbols is the statement by the well-known linguist Morris Halle to the effect that learning Chinese characters is like remembering so many arbitrary telephone numbers (Halle 1969:18). This idea can be tested by examining a situation in which the characters are indeed more or less equated with phone numbers, because it happens that the sending of Chinese telegrams is done by converting almost 10,000 characters into a four-digit code. Thus the five characters used to write *míngtian zhōngwǔ dào* 'arriving tomorrow noon' would be sent as 2494 1131 0022 0582 0451. The dispatching and receiving clerks have available a code book listing the characters and their numerical codes.

However, the clerks have also memorized quite a few of the numbers. I have no idea how many. In any case, the method whereby ordinary Chinese memorize characters certainly cannot be equated with the feats displayed by the very special category of telegraphic code clerks. A Chinese critic has gently chided Halle with the comment that to suggest that learning Chinese characters is like remembering so many phone numbers "is to compliment the Chinese for memory feats of which few mortals are capable!" (Wang 1980:200).

But something far more serious than an exaggeration of Chinese capacity to memorize is involved in Halle's equating of Chinese characters with telephone numbers. His analogy reveals a belief that Chinese characters are like a table of random numbers, that they bear no relationship to the sound structure of the language they represent. And it is this belief in the possibility of writing systems divorced from the sounds of spoken language (as I have said before) that makes so unsatisfactory much of the literature on all aspects of writing—from graphic principle to representational level to graphic symbols.

Writing, Reading, and Thinking

A common error in dealing with the problem of how we derive meaning from various kinds of writing is to confuse the nature of the script with the process of reading. The error is compounded when the nature of the script is itself misunderstood.

Many writers assume that a symbol which is not overtly phonetic is read nonphonetically. This particularly applies to the reading of numbers. But numbers do not normally occur in isolation. In an English phrase like "2nd floor" the symbol *2* is as much an English phonetic symbol as its more overtly phonetic representation, "second floor." The phrase "2ᵉ étage" can only occur as an alternate way of writing the French expression "deuxième étage." Similarly the symbol for a horned creature was just as much a phonetic symbol for *f* in Egyptian as is that letter in present-day English.

Symbols in a writing system have whatever phonetic value the users of that system agree to assign to them. The symbol *2* has the value *two* or *second* in English and *deux* or *deuxième* in French. The symbol *c* has certain assigned values in English *cant* and *cent,* but a different value in Chinese *can,* where it is to be pronounced as *ts.*

How we actually read all these symbols is quite another matter. Conceivably speakers of English might pronounce Chinese *can* as if it were the name of a metal container in English. Or they might read the number *2* as "two" on the spine of a French book. Or, according to some reading specialists, they might read without regard to sound at all. This is the thesis of American reading specialists who espouse the "whole word" method of teaching children to read, an approach which objects to the stress on "phonics."

The question of how we actually read, specifically whether we engage in any phonetic encoding or bypass that stage completely, deriving meaning from written symbols directly without regard to their sound, is the subject of extensive research and sharp differences of opinion. Not being a reading specialist, I specifically distance myself from this debate except for one major aspect, which I have discussed elsewhere (DeFrancis 1984a). This is my strong disagreement with those specialists who seek to support their approach to reading by citing Chinese as an example of a nonphonetic system of writing which is, necessarily, read without phonetic encoding. It is additionally disquieting that their mistaken assumptions about the nature of Chinese writing further leads them to overlook or minimize research findings which not only clearly document the existence of phonetic clues in Chinese characters, but also suggest that Chinese readers make use of these clues (Tzeng, Hung, and Wang 1977; Tzeng, Hung, and Garro 1978; Tsao and Wang 1983).[2]

Another group of specialists who have seized hold of Chinese characters to sharpen their own axes are certain psycholinguists concerned with reading disabilities. Here too there is an extensive literature dealing with such subjects as specialization in left and right brain hemispheres and the results of injuries to one or another area of the brain. In this literature some psycholinguists, especially some Chinese and Japanese scholars, have claimed that Chinese characters are processed differently from alphabetic systems. Suzuki Takao, a leading exponent of this point of view, supports this position by asserting: "It is well-known that Chinese characters, as a writing system, signify meaning independently of sounds." He further points to the semantic elements in Chinese characters as providing etymological clues that help to derive meaning directly (Suzuki 1975).

That the etymology of Chinese characters is immediately apparent to the eye is true only of some characters and only, obviously, for those readers who have accomplished the not inconsiderable task of mastering these complex symbols. It is doubtful if even in those cases etymology is any more useful in Chinese than it is in English. As Bolinger points out, knowing that *insult* comes from Latin "jump on" and *hyperbole* from Greek "throwing beyond" does not automatically lead to understanding the meaning of the terms (1968:111). Also suspect are the claims for superiority of Chinese characters on the grounds that they are allegedly processed by the brain in a significantly different way than are alphabetic scripts, and that their use is not accompanied by the reading disabilities prevalent among Western children. An extensive study conducted among children in the United States, Japan, and Taiwan concludes that "differences in orthography do not provide a sufficient basis for explaining the occurrence of severe reading problems. Such problems occur regardless of whether children are reading a language represented by an alphabet, logographs, or a combination of logographs and a syllabary" (Stevenson et al. 1982). A careful and comprehensive review of the literature on reading disabilities concludes that the claims that have been advanced by various psycholinguists cannot be sustained (Paradis, Haguwara, and Hildebrandt 1985).

Similarly spurious are the widespread claims that Chinese characters rescue speakers from difficulties in expressing their thoughts in speech. In a passage chock-full of misinformation, Logan says, "Virtually every Chinese word is a homonym with an average of ten words for each sound. There are 2,365 different Mandarin words, each with its own pictogram or character, that are all pronounced *shih*" (1986:44). Compounding the pervasive Western ignorance of the role of tones in Chinese, which are as important as vowels in English, Logan is engaging in something about as stupid as suppressing the vowels in *pap, pep, pip, pop, pup* and then complaining about the horrendous ambiguity of the five "words" *pp*.[3] What Logan calls a word is actually the pronunciation of a character which perhaps represents only a bound morpheme, like the *er* in *teacher*, a dead morpheme last used two thousand years ago, or a syllable that conveys meaning only if combined with some other syllable, parallel to the case of *cor* and *al* in English *coral*.

Another example of misplaced concern regarding the ability of Chinese to express themselves appears in an article by Edward S. Klima, a very competent student of sign language who is fascinated by a perceived problem of homonyms in the Li Jiang dialect of Mandarin. This dialect spoken in southwest China has 550 distinct syllables—"only" 550 (though it should be noted that this is still about ten times more than in Hawaiian). Trapped by his assumption that as a dialect of Chinese the Li Jiang syllables must always represent morphemes, and that speakers must be conscious of the syllables as such, Klima concludes, "The amount of homophony is enormous." He echoes the usual rationale of how speakers of the Li Jiang and other Chinese dialects can make up for the phonetic poverty of their speech: "It appears that in these Chinese dialects, the greater the homophony, the more abundant the compounding" (Klima 1975:262–267).

The compounding, or in any case the concatenation of syllables, is even greater in phonetically simple languages like Japanese and Hawaiian. Indeed, perhaps it is a universal rule that the simpler the phonology, the more extensive the compounding. In any event no one is concerned about the need to combine syllables in order to avoid ambiguity in these languages, but because Chinese is not approached as rationally, there is endless discussion.

The reason for such discussion is the pernicious influence of the idea that the traditional Chinese system of writing directly reflected speech rather than being only loosely based on it. From that notion came the view that the Chinese speak and write entirely in morphemes which, if not clearly differentiated, lead to "this hazardous—and, in the case of the Li Jiang dialect—intolerable potential for ambiguity" (Klima 1975:265). In fact, however, the average Li Jiang speaker speaks in syllables, not in morphemes, just as the average speaker of English utters the syllables *in-sult* without any awareness of their individual meanings.

It seems to be the inveterate habit of many who write about Chinese to consider syllables, morphemes, words, and characters in isolation rather than in context and to worry about the homophony which allegedly results from having only a small inventory of syllables. This approach is largely due to the fact that the greater distinctiveness of individual Chinese characters has conditioned people to demand— unreasonably—that isolated spoken or written items should be clearly distinguishable despite their isolation. In every language and in every writing system words and other units acquire definite meaning only from their context. And ordinary people ordinarily handle such items contextually, as against scholars, who artificially atomize them and then worry about the problems conjured up by the process.

A Li Jiang inventory of 550 syllables can be expanded to over 300,000 items by the simple device of combining two syllables in the way we do with English *breakout:outbreak, income:come in, warlike:like war,* and so on and so on. Even the minimal context of two juxtaposed syllables is enough to avoid most ambiguity. Broader context will take care of the rest.

Concern about the hazardous potential for ambiguity in the Li Jiang dialect is part of a wider syndrome that sees the Chinese language in both its spoken and written forms as presenting special problems for the expression of thought. The idea that "language shapes thought" has fascinated people ever since the linguists Edward Sapir and Benjamin Lee Whorf advanced the view that the structure and categories of a language might impose certain forms on how its speakers think. The Chinese system of writing is a particularly fertile field for those who see thought as conditioned by its means of expression.

In view of the fact that the notion of linguistic determinism has increasingly fallen into disfavor among scholars, some writers are at pains to disassociate themselves from the idea, but their basic acceptance of the concept comes through clearly nevertheless. One such case is a sinological study by Alfred E. Bloom entitled *The Linguistic Shaping of Thought: A Study of the Impact of Language on Thinking in China and the West* (1981). In the same vein is a study by the sinologist Chad Hansen, *Language and Thought in Ancient China* (1983). Both works argue that Chinese think less abstractly than do Westerners because of differences in the languages involved.

These views have been rejected by several linguistically oriented students of Chinese, including William G. Boltz (1985) and Mary S. Erbaugh (1988), as based on factual errors and incautious scholarship. Hansen, for example, confuses spoken and written language, accepts the idea of a "model of language . . . that is 'pictographic' or ideographic," and contends, "The Chinese can rely on picturing or representing as the method of tying language to things without having to invent a detour through the mind and mental images." Despite the academic tone employed by Bloom and Hansen, they present little more than variations on the popular misconceptions regarding Chinese.

This is not to say that all languages and all writing systems are always equally effective means of communication, or that they have no influence on thinking. Although all spoken languages have the potential of being used to express any and all thought, they do indeed vary in how well or how simply they can express it, and some may need to be doctored (e.g., by addition of new vocabulary) to adapt to new needs.

A case in point is the transition from French to Vietnamese as the medium of intellectual communication in Vietnam after World War II. Prior to that time all instruction beyond the primary grades had been in French. After the Vietnamese declared their independence in 1945, the attempt of political leaders to replace French with Vietnamese encountered strong objection from academics, especially in the sciences, who said they simply could not deal with these subjects in their own language. The demand of the government to effect the transition within a year was accompanied by a crash program to prepare materials in a number of areas. The poor professors, who needed only a few hours to prepare a French lecture on an advanced scientific subject, had to labor for days to put it into Vietnamese. At the end of one year all university examinations were conducted in Vietnamese, and subsequently the native language became the primary means of intellectual communication at all levels. The Vietnamese success stands as a model that deserves study by many Third World countries with a similar need to adapt their languages to modern needs following colonial attempts at what Haugen has called "linguistic genocide" (Haugen 1973).

All written languages also have the potential of being used to express any and all thought, but here too there may be differences in efficiency. Chinese characters, for example, are extremely clumsy and time-consuming when it comes to indexing written materials, and there can be little doubt that in many other ways they retard Chinese progress. This complex character script falls far short of the efficiency of alphabetic systems, which is one reason why Pinyin is being used more and more for alphabetic classification even of materials written in characters.

As for the influence of language and writing on thought, there is doubtless some relationship between the complex Chinese system of kinship terms and the Chinese view of family relationships. Sexist language also surely affects thought. This is documented in my mind by an episode reported by the mother of a four-year-old girl, who excitedly told of her trip to the park and her encounter with "the policeman riding a horsie." To her mother's offhand remark that when she grew up she too might be able to join the mounted police and help patrol the park, the child angrily replied that she would not be able to because "You have to be a boy to be a police*man*" (Rao 1977:21). Yet this child, and others similarly conditioned, need not be permanently fettered by the sexist language bequeathed to them. There are many speakers of English who are quite capable of thinking in terms of sexual equality, as witness their efforts to degender the language (e.g., by replacing *policeman* with *police officer*) and to obtain equal treatment in other areas (Miller and Swift 1980).

The key question here is how far one wants to push the idea of the interrelationship of thinking and the means of expressing thought. In a pointed discussion of the Whorfian hypothesis through a comparison of Chinese and English, Charles Hockett refuses to go very far. He reaches the following conclusions which he feels "probably hold for languages in general":

1. "The most precisely definable differences between languages are also the most trivial from the Whorfian point of view. The more important an ostensible difference is from this point of view, the harder it is to pin down."
2. "Languages differ not so much as to what *can* be said in them, but rather as to what is *relatively easy* to say."
3. "Scientific discourse can be carried on in any language the speakers of which have become participants in the world of science . . ." [Hockett 1954:122–123].

In particular I strongly reject the attempts to find in language and writing facile answers to enormously complicated problems regarding differences among various societies. A case in point is an influential article by Goody and Watts (1972) that attributes the emergence of "logico-empirical modes of thought" to the "widespread diffusion of writing throughout the Greek world" thanks to the invention of a simple consonant-plus-vowel script. While all literate societies are said to think differently from strictly oral societies,

since the first methods of writing employed were difficult to master, their effects were extremely limited, and it was only when the simplicity and flexibility of later alphabetic writing made widespread literacy possible that for the first time there began to take concrete shape in the Greek world of the seventh century B.C. a society that was essentially literate and that soon established many of the institutions that became characteristic of all later literate societies [1972:352].

Sumerian, Egyptian, and Chinese writing, in this view, inhibited the emergence of "the logical methods" developed by the Greeks. Even the consonant-only scripts of the Near East were unsuited to this end.

There is in this approach no concrete analysis of why a consonantal script of 22 letters is so much more difficult than a 24-letter script which represents vowels as well as consonants that the consonant-plus-vowel system should be singled out as the primary factor in the intellectual ascendancy of Greece over its Near Eastern neighbors, who had achieved their inferior literacy half a millennium earlier. As to the ascendancy of "alphabetic literacy," those who employ this term fail to make the legitimate contrast with "syllabic literacy" and instead improperly oppose it both to nonliteracy and to the restricted literacy of China, which they misrepresent by accusing the Chinese script of being "a virtually nonphonetic system of writing" and saying that "full literate proficiency" requires mastery of "a total repertoire of some 50,000 characters" (Goody and Watt 1972:330, 336, 349, 352).[4]

But the difficulty of a script cannot inhibit innovative thought, since such thought is initiated not by society as a whole—however much it might provide conditioning factors of one sort or another—but by individual thinkers like Aristotle, Confucius, and Einstein, who surely were smart enough to have been able to cope with any kind of script. And granted that full phonemic alphabets are somewhat easier than consonantal scripts like Phoenician and Hebrew, and far easier than clumsy morphosyllabic systems like Sumerian and Chinese, only a superficial analysis of writing systems and an unprovable belief in their restrictive influence on thought can justify an analysis that fails to pay adequate attention to the many other factors which, either singly or in concert, might better account for differences among various literate societies.

Joseph Needham, the foremost Western student of Chinese science, in commenting on the commonly held notion that the Chinese system of writing "was a powerful inhibiting factor in the development of modern science in China," expresses the belief that "this influence is generally grossly overrated" (1964:106). Another prominent historian of science, Nathan Sivin, warns that invidious comparisons regarding uneven development among different societies are "so burdened by suspect assumptions that they do not encourage clear explanation" and should therefore be suspended in favor of much further study and reflection (Sivin 1982).

Sivin's remarks apply with greatest force to the previously mentioned work by R. K. Logan. To begin with, Logan misrepresents Chinese as "pictographic." Moreover, while "not suggesting a direct causal connection between the alphabet and the other innovations" which he mentions as emerging exclusively in the West, such as "codified law, monotheism, abstract theoretical science, formal logic, and individualism," his whole book does make such a connection in his only superficially altered claim that "the phonetic alphabet played a particularly dynamic role within this constellation of events and provided the ground or framework for the mutual development of these innovations." All this came about because "Eastern and Western thought patterns are as polarized as their respective writing systems."

The nonsense about Chinese purveyed by Logan has already been dealt with in this book and elsewhere (DeFrancis 1984a). As to his work in general, the highly involved problem of causality in human affairs cannot be reduced to explanations that are simplistic to begin with and are further vitiated by being shot through with error.

Logan bases his thesis primarily on such allegedly different "Eastern and Western Cultural Patterns" as ideographic versus alphabetic, analogical versus logical, inductive versus deductive, concrete versus abstract, right-brain oriented versus left-brain oriented, and so on. Compare with these differences between East and West one that was pointed out years ago by Berthold Laufer, an eminent student of Chinese culture:

> We observe that the Chinese, like all the peoples of eastern Asia, have never produced any epic poetry. Epic poems are met with among all Indo-European nations, among the Finno-Ugrians, the Turkish, Tibetan, Mongol, and Tungusian tribes; and it is a peculiar coincidence that all these peoples of epic songs are also milk-consumers, while those abstaining from milk are deficient in epic poems. I do not mean to say that there is an interrelation between milk and epics, but merely wish to point out the fact of this curious coincidence [Laufer 1914:170].

The "curious coincidence" noted by Laufer was particularly apparent in the formative era of Chinese civilization but has persisted into present times. In ancient China "milk and milk products were apparently not used," and "to this date have not taken a prominent place in the Chinese cuisine" (Chang 1977:7, 29). The curious correlation between Westerners' drinking milk and thinking scientifically—the Milk Diet Effect rather than Logan's Alphabet Effect—should be noted. Correlations are not causes, and can be meaningless. We must resist the temptation, to which many observers of the Chinese system of writing succumb, to see in mere correlations simple solutions to the complex issues of language, writing, and thought.

7.

The Essential Oneness of Full Writing

Linguists have devoted a great deal of attention to what they call "universals of language"—features or properties shared by all languages (Hockett 1963:1). They also have reached a considerable area of agreement regarding what these features or properties are. In contrast, there is little discussion, and even less consensus, regarding universals of writing. The lack of agreement is manifested even in such a basic matter as whether phonological representation of utterances in spoken language comprises one of the defining features or properties of writing.

In this concluding chapter I should like to suggest a few universals of writing which seem to me to be particularly helpful in illuminating the nature of writing and the classification of writing systems. Three such universals are discussed below.

Writing as Visible Speech

The concept of writing as visible speech summarizes the insistence throughout this book that the primary defining feature of writing is the representation of speech. The dichotomy between full and partial writing is intended to sort out graphic symbols which are capable of conveying any and all thought from those which can convey only limited areas of thought, chiefly ones that are picturable. No end is served by lumping the two kinds of symbols together. The pervasive confusion which has resulted from doing so needs to be cleared up by stressing the empirical fact that all full systems of writing are based on representation of sounds, and that no sets of symbols not based on representation of sounds have been shown capable of conveying anything more than a limited range of thought.

Just how a particular writing system goes about making sound visible is a secondary matter. That all sorts of symbols can serve to represent sounds is shown by the variety of writing systems depicted in the frontispiece. These are all representations of the opening words of the Gettysburg Address and can be summarized as follows:

1. Acoustic wave graph of voice of Professor William S.-Y. Wang.
2. Linguistic transcription of Wang acoustic wave graph.
3. Conventional English spelling.
4. Russian alphabetic transcription.
5. Hindi alphabetic version, followed by the linguistic transcription of the Devanagari symbols.
6. Korean alphabetic version, followed by the conventional transcription of the hangŭl symbols.
7. Egyptian consonantal version, based on a late phase of the writing with some representation of vowels, followed by the English equivalent for the hieroglyphs.
8. Arabic consonantal version, followed by the linguistic transcription of the symbols.
9. Japanese syllabic version, followed by the conventional transcription of the kana symbols.
10. Yi syllabic version, followed by the standard transcription of the Yi symbols.
11. Cuneiform syllabic version, (mixed Sumerian and Akkadian sign values), followed by the conventional transcription of the cuneiform symbols.
12. Chinese syllabic version, followed by the Pinyin equivalent for the characters.

These twelve representations of the same utterance can be classified as follows:

1	acoustic
2–6	phonemic
7–8	consonantal
9–12	syllabic

The acoustic wave graph of Wang's speech is the most direct example of visible speech. Accurate though it is as the representation of an actual utterance, this sort of symbolization will hardly do as a practical system of writing, as it is limited to the close phonetic representation of a particular individual's way of speaking, cannot be generalized to phonemic representation of a language, and requires great skill to decipher, even approximately, the sounds that are represented. On the other hand, the linguistic transcription of the sounds given immediately below the wave graph simply and accurately represents the sounds of the utterance on a one-to-one basis. It is a much more systematic orthography than the conventional spelling presented in the third item.

The Russian alphabet used to transliterate the utterance in the fourth item has an advantage over the Latin alphabet in that it possesses half a dozen additional symbols. It works well for the Russian language and serves, with some modifications, to write the scores of languages spoken in the Soviet Union.

The Korean alphabet effectively represents the Korean language and our sample utterance as it might be approximated by a native speaker of that language. It could readily be supplied with a few additional symbols to represent English sounds not present in Korean. It is doubtful that there would be any advantage over our present system if English adopted the practice of writing syllables in the Korean style, as in the previously cited example of

HA GŬ SY TE
N   L   S   M

English could be written quite well with Egyptian hieroglyphics, especially if, as in the frontispiece, we adopted those of the late stage of the system, when the use of vowel signs had become more common. Teachers of reading who have made use of pictographs as rebus symbols might even argue that such symbols have an advantage in the initial learning stage in that a limited number of pictured figures is easier to memorize than abstract symbols. This would of course be more true if the original symbols, which acrophonically represented Egyptian words, were replaced with symbols related to the sounds of English. Thus the Egyptian symbol for a horned creature (the English name of which would not be informative) might be replaced with a picture of a fish to represent the letter *f*. Some American reading specialists have experimented with this in using pictorial symbols in the initial stage of teaching children how to read (Woodcock 1968; Woodcock, Clark, and Davies 1967–1969).

The relatively simple syllabic scripts presented as items 9–11 serve quite well for the languages they represent, but they would be ill-adapted to English, with its huge number of different syllables. This is, of course, even more true of the last example, Chinese characters used for their syllabic value, since they are so much more complex. Nevertheless, if we leave considerations of difficulty and practicality aside, it would be quite possible to write English using Chinese characters. If the characters were used the way they have been used to write Japanese, the result would be no more absurd for English than it is for Japanese itself (DeFrancis 1984a). If the characters were adapted more nearly along Chinese lines, with a single character representing a syllable of English, by resorting, as is the case in Chinese itself, to a certain amount of under-differentiation (e.g., by not making such distinctions as *cat:cats* and *sit:sits*) it would be possible to write English with only 3,000–4,000 characters. It would be a difficult system, but then so is Chinese.

Despite the great diversity of form of the symbols presented in the frontispiece, they all share the common feature of representing sound on either the phonemic (including consonantal) or syllabic level. If we concentrate attention on function rather than on form, it will become readily apparent that within the two categories of phonemic and syllabic writing there is no basic difference between the two. Both are utilized for the purpose of making speech visible.

The essential oneness of full writing is also demonstrated by the way only minor variations in principle underlie the use of quite disparate symbols used in several syllabic systems of writing. In previous chapters we have seen how the Sumerian, Chinese, Mayan, Japanese, and Cretan and Cypriot Greek syllabic scripts all made use of what I have called the syllable-telescoping technique. All these systems were essentially variations on a single theme. Leaving aside the Chinese application, which is somewhat similar to the Sumerian approach, because it has had only limited lexicographical use and does not form part of the writing system itself, the other four cases can be summarized as follows:

	Formula	Example
Sumerian	$C_1(V_1 + V_1)C_2 = C_1V_1C_2$	da + am = dam
Mayan	$C_1V_1 + C_2(V_1) = C_1V_1C_2$	ma + ca = mac
Greek	$C_1(V_1) + C_2V_1 = C_1C_2V_1$	ti + ri = tri
Japanese	$C(i) + yV = CyV$	ki + yo = kyo
	$C(u) + wa = Cwa$	ku + wa = kwa

Note that all four cases follow the general rule: reduce by one the number of vowels in parentheses. Only specific details distinguish the four.

If we equate *i* with *y* and *u* with *w*, the Japanese version of the technique can be said to be closest to the Sumerian. It is, however, more restrictive, since apart from *kwa* only the signs for eleven CV syllables ending in *i* are combined with signs for syllables consisting of *y* followed by a vowel, always *a*, *o*, or *u*.

In the case of Greek, one of the problems that had to be solved was how to represent consonant clusters like *tri* without proliferating syllable signs. The solution that was arrived at in the Linear B system called for telescoping the two syllables *ti* and *ri* as indicated. The problem was not very serious in Greek, for it had only a few consonant clusters.

The Sumerians and the Maya were confronted with a much more serious problem because their languages had many CVC syllables. Sumerian's 4 vowels and 16 consonants made for 1,024 theoretically possible CVC syllables. In comparison, there were only 64 each of the CV and VC type (plus 4 consisting of single vowels). By combining the CV and VC syllables in the way indicated, the Sumerians could reduce their theoretically needed CVC symbols from 1,156 to 128. In actual fact the number of syllable signs used in any one period was much closer to the minimum of 128 than to the maximum of 1,156.

Thus we have four ingenious solutions to a basically similar problem of how to represent syllables containing more than just a single consonant and a vowel. It was lucky that the languages involved did not have syllables of still greater complexity—compare English with its more than 8,000 different monosyllables. Using half a dozen syllabic signs representing *si-pi-ri-ni-ti-si* for *sprints* would scarcely be economical!

On the surface the symbols used in the Sumerian, Mayan, Japanese, and Cretan Greek systems of writing are so disparate that it is not readily apparent that they have anything in common. Yet they clearly do, for their variations of the syllable-telescoping technique are aimed toward the common goal of representing the syllables of the languages with which they are identified. More generally, they share with the other symbols depicted in the frontispiece, and with those in all other full systems of writing, the primary function of making visible the sounds of the languages they represent.

The Duality Principle

The second universal of writing is the application of a duality principle (mentioned in the section "Full/Unlimited/Real Writing" in chapter 2), whereby a writing system uses nonphonetic, generally noniconic, devices of a largely mnemonic nature. The importance of the nonphonetic aspect of writing differs from one system to another. The better a system represents speech phonetically, the less it uses nonphonetic devices.

This duality concept is limited to its application within specific writing systems. Gelb applies the concept, though not the name, to individual systems. But he goes further and distinguishes among systems on the basis of this concept. The following passage summarizes his thoughts on these matters:

> Full systems of writing express language on two levels, morphological (logography) or phonetic (syllabary, alphabet). This gives rise to three basic types of full writing systems: logo-syllabic, syllabic, and alphabetic. The latter two types are phonetic while the first combines morphological elements (logograms) and phonetic elements (syllabograms). Even so, the syllabic and alphabetic systems usually contain morphemic elements to a greater or lesser degree [1974:303–304].

The central thesis of this book runs counter to Gelb's establishment of a separate category of logographic writing on a level with syllabic and alphabetic. As he himself points out, what he identifies as three separate systems all contain both morphemic and phonetic elements. What then is the basis for setting up "logo-syllabic" as a separate type from "syllabic"? I contend that Chinese and other so-called logo-syllabic scripts are not a separate type but a subcategory of syllabic, which I have labeled *morphosyllabic* to distinguish them from the "pure" syllabic subcategory to which Japanese and Yi belong.

I similarly disagree with Sampson's making a major division between "*logographic* and *phonographic* writing." He does this on the basis of what the French linguist André Martinet has called the "double articulation" of language (Sampson 1985:32–33, 38–39).

Martinet states that all languages are characterized by a "first articulation" consisting of "a succession of units each of which is endowed with a vocal form and a meaning." For these units he coins the term *moneme* in preference to the usual designation *morpheme*—"Monemes are the smallest segments of speech that have some meaning attached to them." All languages are also characterized by a "second articulation" derived from the analysis of "every moneme into a succession of distinctive units, the phonemes." In any given language the phonemes are a small closed list, the monemes a large open list; and the "second articulation" is absolutely essential since "the progress of mankind would have been unthinkable without the tremendous economy" obtained by breaking up monemes (morphemes) into phonemes (Martinet 1962:22–30; 1964:22–28).

Martinet limits his application of the concept of "double articulation" to spoken languages. Other scholars have applied his concept to writing (Holenstein 1983; Coulmas 1984), chiefly to explain the inner workings of individual systems. Sampson uses the concept as a basis for classifying writing systems in general into logographic or morphemic on the one hand and syllabic, phonemic, or featural on the other.

In their similar approaches to the classification of writing systems, both Gelb and Sampson, along with most other students of the subject, fail to come to grips with the problem that Martinet dealt with when he noted the absolute necessity of breaking up spoken morphemic units into smaller phonemic units. To paraphrase Martinet, a logographic or morphemic system of writing is unthinkable without somehow breaking up the large number of logographic or morphemic units into a smaller number of phonetic units. Chinese and other morphosyllabic systems do precisely this and thus achieve the requisite "economy" by making use of a smaller number of syllabic units. The number of syllabic units is small (in the hundreds) relative to the morphemic units (in the thousands) but large relative to the number of symbols (in the dozens) of simple syllabic systems such as Japanese. Simple syllabic systems have rigidly closed syllabaries whereas Chinese and other morphosyllabic systems have only semi-closed systems—limited by accidental practice rather than by deliberate standardization.

One could also speak of "double articulation" within a specific writing system. In that case the "first articulation" would comprise the written units that represent morphemes—in Chinese, chiefly single characters with some of two characters (e.g., *shānhú* 'coral'); in English, strings of letters, such as the *teach, er,* and *s* of *teachers.* The "second articulation" would of course then be the phonetic elements in Chinese characters and the letters or groups of letters in English.

Although Martinet does not explicitly mention the fact, it is worth noting that all native speakers of a language know all of the closed set of items in the second articulation (phonemes and syllables) and how they are used in speech. No native speakers of English, for example, would accept *tli* or *tsan* as indigenous spoken forms. But few if any speakers of a language are likely to know all of the open set of items in the first articulation. The number of morphemes is well over 8,000 in Chinese. A limited analysis of English turns up almost 6,000 in a pocket dictionary (Trnka 1968). In failing to take note of such facts, those who misapply Martinet's idea to writing fail to tell us how it is possible for people to cope with a huge open-ended set of graphic symbols not based primarily on the limited set of sounds known to them as native speakers of a language.

All systems of writing, like all systems of speech, necessarily have both a "first articulation" and "second articulation." But the duality principle requires only that a writing system convey meaning by representing speech at the phonemic or syllabic level. It does not require it to convey meaning by nonphonetic means. In practice it seems to be a universal phenomenon of writing systems that they do make use of nonphonetic devices, but in contrast to phonetic symbolization these are not essential.

Just as there are many ways of conveying phonetic information, the precise manner in which nonphonetic information is conveyed also takes many different forms. A few of these are worth noting.

The earliest stages of writing appear always to comprise a mixture of pictographs used for their semantic value and pictographs used for their phonetic value. In subsequent stages the symbols may become stylized to the point where all connection with the earlier pictographic forms is lost, but the use of symbols in the two indicated values continues. In current systems the use of nonphonetic symbols is illustrated by the examples of numerals and a few other symbols such as the ampersand and asterisk.

At some point or other in the use of all writing systems for recording spoken utterances, it is apparently considered desirable to break up the continuum of speech into smaller visible segments. Apart from having to pause for breath, most speakers can go on at some length with a concatenated sequence of sounds that run the gamut from phonemes to syllables to words to phrases to sentences, and so on and on. In speech the stream of sounds is somewhat segmented, apart from obvious pauses, by such features as intonation and tempo, but the written version of spoken utterances rarely represents such features.

Whatever segmentation of written text that does take place is usually more or less ad hoc and unsystematic. This has led one student of writing to the following not completely accurate conclusion:

> The division of words and sentences, which we take so much for granted, developed only gradually. The majority of ancient scripts—the Egyptian, the cuneiform script of Mesopotamia, the syllabic script of the Aegean, at times also some Indian scripts (especially the two classical languages of the sub-continent, Sanskrit and Tamil)—did not divide words and sentences. In those societies writing was done by specialists who were completely immersed in writing conventions and who could therefore dispense with such aids to legibility. This lack of word division is also a feature of early European manuscripts, no doubt for similar reasons; the monastic scribes knew not only the intricacies of their script, but, since most manuscripts dealt with religious matters, they also knew the text [Gaur 1984:55–56].

In actual fact, some segmentation of text is apparent even in the earliest Sumerian writing. According to one authority, two techniques are in evidence: "One involved clustering small groups of signs; the other involved structuring the tablet surface into a regular series of compartments—'columns' and 'cases'—separated by straight dividing lines" (Green 1981:349).

Another writer notes that in Egyptian the convention of ending words with determinatives or terminal symbols "provides a good criterion for dividing the continuous stream of the script into individual words. The resulting 'word signs' contribute much to the legibility of hieroglyphic texts" (Schenkel 1976, quoted in Meltzer 1980:55). Apart from such aids, word separation appears not to have been a common practice in Egyptian (Cohen 1958:245). Though not universal, the practice of word division using blank space or dots or wedges or other devices was common in West Semitic writing systems from very early times and is normal in major living languages like Hebrew and Arabic (Barr 1976:89; Gordon 1982:105; Naveh 1982:62).

In contrast, word division developed only very late in Greek (Jensen 1969:470), and it did not become general in Europe until about the year 1000. Punctuation also increased in use but was not regularized until book publication surged forward in the sixteenth century (Cohen 1958:423).

A scholar who helped in the decipherment of Linear B makes an interesting analogy between capital letters, which are common in scripts based on the Greek and Latin alphabets, and earlier sense-determining techniques, commenting that they comprise "a very simple form of determinatives" (Chadwick 1967:33). In German, except for sentence-initial words, capital letters determine the category of nouns. This is a bit of information that is very useful for nonnative readers of German, but native readers have no need for this crutch, and as writers they often complain about capitalization because it makes their writing more difficult; hence there have been demands to end the practice (LPLP 1985:284–285). In English, capital letters are used only for proper nouns; this helps to distinguish visually such isolated phrases as

> the White House
> the White house
> the white house

The many ways in which English orthography segments text and provides supplementary visual information is well summarized by one writer (Waller 1980:248) in the following list of functions of what he calls micro- and macro-punctuation:

	Micro-level	*Macro-level*
Delineation	initial capital full point comma semicolon colon	headings title pages space rules
Interpolation	parentheses dashes commas	footnotes boxed inserts marginalia indentation
Serialization	commas semicolons oblique strokes bullets numerals	headings, numerals tabular format regular spacing/styling
Stylization	quotation marks exclamation marks question marks	size variation style variation layout variation

Many of the practices in the preceding list are of relatively recent development. Some of them have spread to other writing systems. Both historically and at present still other techniques are to be found in various scripts. Syriac consonant texts had the rudimentary practice of indicating certain grammatical categories (Barr 1976:90–91). Japanese mixed texts roughly distinguish content words (e.g., nouns) from function words (e.g., case markers and verb suffixes) by generally writing the former in kanji and the latter in kana (see Unger 1987). Nonnative readers find this a great help in coping with written Japanese.

The current writing system with the reputation of providing the most nonphonetic information is of course Chinese. Although the system lacks aids comparable to the capital letters in English and the kanji-kana division in Japanese, it is frequently cited for the semantic information provided at the level of individual characters. The keys or so-called radicals are commonly believed to play a particularly important role in determining the meaning of the characters of which they form part.

The Chinese keys are a more elaborate application of a visual disambiguating technique that has some parallels in other writing systems. As has already been noted, Sumerian and Egyptian both employed semantic determinatives. Even English makes some use of a technique which is roughly parallel to that of the earlier scripts.

In English dictionaries what might be called "numerical determinatives" distinguish two or more entries that have the same spelling but different meanings, as in the following example:

[1]can *vb* to be able to
[2]can *n* a metal container for holding liquids
[3]can *vt* to put in a can

These several *can*'s, if used in the Chinese way, would appear in sentences such as the following:

We [1]can do it.
Please open the [2]can.
We'll [3]can the peaches.

In our dictionaries each of the entries for *can* is glossed as having several different meanings. Apparently the differences in meaning within each entry are not deemed to be sufficiently great to warrant setting up separate entries, such as [4]*can,* [5]*can,* and so on. Yet one wonders whether it is justified to include under [3]*can* the subdefinition "to discharge from employment," or whether it might not be better to include it as the definition for a new entry [4]*can.* Similarly it might seem more reasonable to list

[1]fire *n* the phenomenon of combustion
[2]fire *vt* to kindle
[3]fire *vt* to shoot

rather than follow the usual dictionary practice of including the third item as a subdefinition of [2]*fire* 'to kindle.'

While these questions may appear academic if not nonsensical in English, they are anything but that in Chinese, where there has been a tendency historically to proliferate the use of determinatives and separate out homophonous syllables which enter into the formation of words of various meanings, as in the case of the syllable *hú* in

珊 瑚 *shānhú* 'coral' (In the second character, *hú,* the element on the left is the 'jade' determinative, and that on the right is the phonetic *hú.*)

鵜 鶘 *tíhú* 'pelican' (In the second character, *hú,* the element on the left is the phonetic *hú,* and that on the right is the "bird" determinative.)

Neither of the characters pronounced *hú* is used independently or in combination with other characters than those indicated in the preceding examples. Yet the Chinese insist on adding a separate determinative to each *hú* phonetic and providing a separate dictionary listing for the resultant combinations of phonetic and determinative. That is as if our dictionaries had an entry

[4]can *n* pelican.

Not only are determinatives in Chinese often unnecessary, they are also often useless and even misleading. This can be seen by glancing across the row of characters with the 'person' key in the semantic-plus-phonetic matrix in chapter 3.

But one thing that determinatives in Chinese do help to do is to enable the Chinese to indulge in their favorite pastime of playing games with their characters. They can, for example, write a string of similar-sounding characters which, when pronounced, mean nothing to the ear, but when taken in by the eye, convey a meaning of sorts. Thus a bogus sentence which can be made maximally ambiguous, as is often done, by writing it without tones, for example, *ma ma ma,* can be triumphantly presented as meaning "Mother is scolding the horse" by writing it in characters:

媽 罵 馬

An example that is cited by some Chinese to prove the superiority of their system of writing is one in which 24 different characters all pronounced with tonal variations of *xi* are strung together to produce a bit of doggerel that is unintelligible to the ear but is more or less meaningful to the eye (DeFrancis 1984a:196). This sort of game is similar to our playfully writing

FIRST SOLDIER: Did he say: "³Fire!"?
SECOND SOLDIER: No, he said "¹Fire!"

In point of fact, the numerals in the English examples are not too different from the traditional 214 Chinese determinatives or keys, which no longer have any real iconic value and can be considered as little more than vaguely mnemonic symbols comprising thesaurus headings that could be replaced by their equivalent numbers. (Many non-Chinese students memorize the numbers of the most common keys, which enable them to look up words faster than native Chinese.) If we were to replace the Chinese keys by their equivalent numbers, ambiguous *ma ma ma* could be unambiguously written in the English fashion as ³⁸*ma* ³⁰*ma ma* by attaching the numbers for the keys meaning 'female' (no. 38) and 'mouth' (no. 30) to the transcription of the phonetic element *ma* 'horse' (no. 255). Or the sentence could be written with characters as

38   30
馬   馬   馬

The function of disambiguating homonyms that is served by semantic determinatives in Chinese and by numerical determinatives in English is also served by morphophonemic spellings like *hair:hare.* The existence of spelling differences and other disambiguating techniques is widely viewed as an indispensable aid to reading (Bradley 1913).

All of these techniques, together with the various nonphonetic devices noted earlier, comprise an aspect of the writing universal, which I have labeled the duality principle, whereby writing systems convey meaning by nonphonetic as well as phonetic means. Apart from the techniques just mentioned, the duality principle is also manifested in many symbols' having both a phonetic and a semantic function. This can be illustrated in English by the following multiple uses of the simple symbol x. The examples also incidentally illustrate the point that written symbols, whether letters, syllabograms, or combinations of these such as words, only "mean" something in specific contexts.

X as a phonetic symbol:

    1. *z* in *xenophobia.*
    2. *ks* in *excel.*
    3. *gz* in *exist.*
    4. *kris* in *Xmas.*
    5. *cross* in *Xing.*
    6. *ten* in X^{th}. (Compare *dix* [diz] in French X^e = *dixième.*)

X as a semantic symbol:

    1. The concept '10,' *ten* in English, *dix* in French, *shí* in Chinese, etc.

    2. The twenty-fourth item in a serial arrangement based on the twenty-six letters of the Latin alphabet.

    3. An unknown quantity, as in $x = (A + B)^2$ and 'Mr. X.'

    4. Signature of an illiterate.

    5. Command not to do something, as in a symbol of a cigarette overlaid with an x.

    6. Wrong, as in marking answers to examination questions.

    7. Pornographic, as in X-rated movies.

    8. Location of an object, such as a dead body in a detective story.

    9. Times, multiplied by, as in $2 \times 3 = 6$.

The duality principle is implicit in Gelb's dictum that there are no pure systems of writing. Gelb's point should be carried further to include the idea that writing systems can be incredibly "impure" and still work, especially for native speakers and readers, who have a full command of their language. We could make a bad system even worse and it still would work, *so long as it at least minimally represents speech:*[1]

> Th nglsh lngg cld b wrttn lmst wtht vwls.
> wecouldrunthewordsinasentencetogetherandnotbotherwithpunctuation
> It ——— even be -ssible ——— guess ——— -unciation ———
> mean- ——— meny words that ——— either miss- ——— Miss
> Peld.

The omission of vowels in the first sentence has its parallels in Hebrew and Arabic. Running words together reflects an earlier stage of writing in the West and is paralleled by Chinese, with its equal spacing between syllables and no further segmentation of text except by punctuation marks. The indication of only part of spoken utterances is endemic to all systems of writing.

To the extent that writing systems depart from a simple one-to-one correspondence between sound and symbol, they bear less resemblance to carefully constructed schemes for representing spoken languages than they do to a hodgepodge of mnemonic clues that adept readers can use to arrive at coherent messages. Many of the writing systems that have been developed are indeed wonders of improvisation that are characterized by complex mnemonicity rather than simple phoneticity.

But whether these jerry-built structures work well or badly is generally a secondary matter. Efficiency is the concern only of the few who can conceive of tinkering with a script with this consideration in mind. Simplicity is the concern primarily of those who consider it essential to extending literacy and raising the cultural level of the masses. Most people do not think to question systems that have been handed down to them.

The Dead Hand of the Past

In suggesting the "dead hand of the past" as a third universal that is particularly helpful in illuminating the subject of writing, I have in mind two main aspects. The first is the conservative nature of writing. The second is the persistence of ossified attitudes about the subject.

The conservative nature of writing stands in sharp contrast to the constant changes in speech over time. All spoken languages are in a constant state of flux. They change in pronunciation, in vocabulary, in grammar. Shakespeare rhymed *clean* with *lane* and said *more better.* Our modern *blockhead* has replaced his *clotpoll.* Americans no longer end letters with *Your obedient servant.* The word *scientist* was condemned as an "ignoble" new coinage in 1890. Yesterday's slang is today's anachronism.

But English spelling has changed only a little since its standardization in the earliest dictionaries compiled centuries ago. Danish spelling was fixed even earlier than English, about 1200 A.D. (Haugen 1984). Chinese inscriptions on stone monuments dating back two millennia are composed of characters identical in form to those in current use. In all three writing systems the fixed orthographies have lagged behind the changes in speech, more so in Chinese than in English and Danish. These cases illustrate the universal tendency of speech and writing to become separated by gaps that widen continuously with the passage of time.

The most extreme example of rigor mortis in the area of writing is the continued use of entire writing systems (e.g., Latin and classical Chinese) for centuries and even millennia after the demise of the spoken languages on which they were originally based. Less striking but more widespread are the gaps, mentioned above, in which outdated written forms are still used to represent elements of living languages.

Such gaps are inevitable unless steps are taken periodically to bring writing up to date with the changes in speech. But it is a rarity among writing systems to experience such updating. It would be hard to find other examples to match the Swedish practice, as reported by Gleason (1961:434), of undertaking a revision of the orthography "about once each generation," though his characterization of the revisions as "reasonably thorough" is disputed by a leading Swedish student of language policy (Björn Jernudd, personal communication, 10/28/87).

The persistence of outmoded practices is apparent even in the earliest stages of writing. When the Sumerians adopted the practice of using pictographic symbols for their phonetic value, the use of such symbols for their semantic value was no longer necessary, since a simple set of phonetic symbols sufficed to write the whole language. Yet the use of earlier symbols continued in Sumerian, as in Egyptian, long after they had become obsolete. Some of the shorthand practices of earlier temple accountancy also persisted in the style of Sumerian writing that occasionally omitted such spoken items as verbs and case relations and continued. a fortuitous word order probably unrelated to that of speech.

Because of their long history, Chinese characters present a particularly striking example of the huge gap that can develop between the spoken and written forms of a language. The divorce between the two most likely goes back to the earliest known stages of Chinese writing. Shang oracle bone inscriptions exhibit a terseness of style that is probably less a direct reflection of speech than of the need to save space on the precious bones and shells and the familiarity with the subject matter that obviated the need for the verbosity of speech.

The Confucian and other texts that have come down from the Zhou Dynasty also exhibit a striking terseness. When such texts are read aloud in the current pronunciation of the characters, they are unintelligible to modern ears. There is a difference of opinion among scholars as to whether they were even intelligible to Zhou ears. The sinologist Bernhard Karlgren is a leading exponent of the view that the Zhou texts reflected the speech of the time and were intelligible when read aloud because of the greater complexity of the sound system of that era. The texts are said to have later become unintelligible when spoken because of the increase in the number of homonyms that resulted from simplification of the sound system (Karlgren 1929). Karlgren's views have been sharply attacked by another well known sinologist, George A. Kennedy (1964).

On the other hand, the thesis has been advanced that early Chinese literary texts were of a "basically nonverbal nature" and "were dominated linguistically by semantic rather than phonetic or syntactic considerations" (Rosemont 1974). This thesis is largely a restatement of earlier views advanced by Creel and other sinologists, who claimed a semantic interpretation for elements that scholars like Boodberg and Kennedy insist had a phonetic value.

My own view, which has been heavily influenced by those of Boodberg and Kennedy, is that early Chinese writing basically reflected contemporary speech but departed from it considerably in somewhat the same fashion as has been documented in greater detail for Sumerian. In all likelihood scribes purposely left out many words and morphemes to conform to a style which has always placed great store on terseness. In both cases what made such a style feasible was, first of all, the availability of disambiguating determinatives to supplement the unsystematic phonological clues contained in the characters, and second, the specialized training of scribes who devoted a lifetime to mastering such systems of writing.

Regardless of the precise relationship between speech and writing in early Chinese, it is incontestable that for more than a millennium there has been a huge gap between the two. In that long period of time spoken Chinese was represented, more or less, only in what the literati who dominated China's intellectual life considered to be vulgar productions, such as some novels of the sixteenth century.

Around the turn of this century a movement grew up, partly under Western influence, to reform the Chinese system of writing. One group of reformers sought to replace the characters with an alphabetic system that would be based directly on the spoken language. Another group sought only to change the literary style from one based on a dead earlier stage of the language to one that would reflect some form of spoken Chinese. Exactly what form should be taken as a model was disputed. The most influential reformers urged the inclusion of the early novels as a model, advice that is equivalent to urging a modern writer in English to emulate the language of Shakespeare rather than that of King Arthur. This is the position that won out, with the result that a hybrid style has emerged in which there are varying degrees of admixture of elements from the dead stage of classical Chinese (DeFrancis 1950, 1985).

The full flavor of the currently dominant hybrid Chinese style can be better savored in the following example of a parallel hybrid English style derived by mixing obsolete Old English elements with those found in contemporary speech:

> Four score and seven years ær ūre fæderas brought forth in thissum lande a new nation, conceived in liberty and dedicated to the proposition that all men sind created equal. Nu we sind engaged in a michum civil wige, testing hwæder sēo nation, or any nation, swā conceived and swā dedicated, mage long endure.

One of the features of the Chinese hybrid style not reflected in this English analogy is the fact that it often involves abbreviations of spoken items. In an analogy presented by Kennedy in his attack on the idea that such abbreviations represented earlier spoken forms, it is as if we wrote *gar* with a smoke ring for 'cigar' and *gar* with a trellis for 'garden' (Kennedy 1964:114–116). We could then list the two "words" in dictionaries as ^1gar 'cigar' and ^2gar 'garden.' And that would enable us to write a Hybrid English sentence such as "Who is that man smoking a ^{1}gar in the ^{2}gar?"

The pervasiveness of the hybrid style in Chinese is such that it affects all areas of writing, even the preparation of radio scripts, which have been criticized as sometimes leading to incomprehension on the part of listeners because of the extensive infiltration of elements from the dead literary style (Lin 1983). But the baneful influence of this style goes even further than that. It seriously undermines efforts of Chinese language reformers to promote a system of writing in a necessarily more colloquial style as a consequence of the use of the Pinyin alphabetic system. A mental outlook which sees nothing amiss in a hybrid style based on characters is hardly likely to look with favor on proposals to do some writing in a more colloquial style based on Pinyin. It is only the Soviet Dungan writers, third- and fourth-generation descendents of mostly illiterate refugees from China, who in writing Chinese in their Cyrillic orthography have been able to escape the crippling influence of the characters, and this only because of their complete ignorance of this script.

The inheritance from the past, both the characters themselves and the mental outlook based on them, is also having a negative influence on the increasingly important area of information processing. Among Chinese and Japanese as well as Westerners there is a good deal of grandiose talk regarding artificial intelligence (A.I.) as a panacea. The Japanese in particular have been making great promises of a new generation of computers which will solve currently intractable problems, including the efficient handling of Chinese characters. This view has been roundly criticized in J. Marshall Unger's recent *The Fifth Generation Fallacy* (1987), in which the author demonstrates the ultimate incompatibility of the script with existing computer technology and the futility of the hope that A.I. will come to the rescue.

The imminent death of writing itself is proclaimed in a book which sees writing as spanning 20,000 years and concludes, without examining current practice, that "it has become increasingly obvious that information can once again be stored, quite effectively, without writing" (Gaur 1984:7, 210). But Gaur ignores the fact that most information storage is based on writing, and that it is precisely this fact that causes special difficulties for information processing in China and Japan with their inability to shake off the incubus of their character scripts.

In word processing, to take perhaps the most familiar form of information storage, we normally input alphanumeric symbols and print out text expressed in the same symbolic code. This is very simple and highly efficient, especially when the operator is a skilled touch typist.

There is not, and I believe never can be, as efficient a system for inputting and outputting Chinese characters. In actual practice today, most Japanese type kana syllabic symbols into a word processor programmed to convert the input into the traditional kanji-cum-kana orthography. Whenever the kana input evokes more than one kanji symbol on the screen (e.g., the dozen or so evoked by typing the isolated syllable *ko*), the operator has to select the desired kanji. A similar approach is used by those Japanese (the minority) who prefer to work with rōmaji rather than kana. Few Japanese would go so far as to consider bypassing kanji completely by shifting over to outputting as well as inputting kana or rōmaji without any regard whatsoever for the kanji symbols.

Perhaps even fewer Chinese would consider a similar break with the past, despite the greater need to do so. Most Chinese do not command an equivalent of the Japanese kana and rōmaji. To them, Pinyin is an alien script. Although some Chinese favor inputting Pinyin to specify characters, most prefer to work exclusively with characters. This involves exceedingly clumsy techniques of inputting characters by such devices as typing in the Chinese telegraphic code equivalents, punching successive keys to compose characters by graphic components, and using drawing and pattern recognition. While any system of computer-assisted word processing is superior to traditional methods of handwriting and ordinary character composition, character-only Chinese word processing is, and must always be, vastly inferior to the use of Pinyin. Pinyin is superior both in its limited application for inputting text and in its more efficient use for outputting as well an inputting, completely without regard to characters.

The unsuitability of some scripts for word processing suggests the need to reevaluate writing systems on the basis of their ability to serve the needs of the people who use them. This was not much of an issue in the past, when writing was largely limited to specialized groups of scribes and scholars. It is a much more serious problem in an age when mass literacy and general efficiency are viewed as at least socially desirable, if not actually vital for survival.

If we ranked past and present writing systems from the vantage point of these new concerns, we might construct a scale like the following:

1. Finnish, Pinyin, rōmaji, kana
2. Greek, Latin, Russian, German, Spanish
3. Hangŭl
4. French, English
5. Cherokee, Vai, Yi
6. Phoenician, Hebrew, Arabic
7. Egyptian hieroglyphics
8. Japanese kanji-cum-kana, Akkadian
9. Chinese characters
10. Sumerian, Mayan

There is obviously room for disagreement in this rough ranking of scripts. Thus although I place the traditional Japanese orthography slightly ahead of Chinese, in part because the use of kana helps to segment text, I would hesitate to dispute Sir George Sansom's previously quoted contention that the Japanese system surely has no inferiors. Finer distinctions in rank would necessitate placing French slightly ahead of English and Finnish at the head of the lot.

Of course, simplicity and efficiency, though to my mind the most important aspects, are not all that is involved in comparative rating of writing systems, and even they comprise many factors that should receive individual consideration. Moreover, systems need to be evaluated primarily in terms of their ability to serve specific languages. Kana is an excellent system for Japanese, but a script based on the same graphic principle would be a very poor one for English. Some writing systems serve readers better than they do writers; French is a case in point. Adaptability to computer technology gives alphabetic scripts an edge over even the simplest of syllabic scripts; complex syllabic scripts like Chinese are completely out of the running. But even among alphabetic scripts some are more easily adapted to computers than are others (e.g., those with diacritics). This is due in part to the fact that the technology has been largely geared to English, which exercises a sort of linguistic and economic imperialism.

Giving priority to one factor over another results in quite different rankings. Aesthetically Chinese characters should undoubtedly be given first place. Global functional considerations suggest putting the Latin alphabet at the top of the list. If familiarity with a script and emotional attachment are taken into consideration, it is likely that all conventional orthographies would be ranked first by the people who use them.

Leaving aside simplicity and efficiency, all writing systems are on an equal footing as far as their ability to convey any and all thought is concerned. From this point of view, there are no primitive or inferior systems of writing. Alphabetic systems are not necessarily superior to syllabic systems. Chinese is not inferior to English in expressive potential. I do not believe that there is any significant correlation between ways of writing and ways of thinking.

One could go on at great length with the multiple aspects of writing that should receive detailed consideration in any serious treatment of the subject. However, recent works on writing have generally failed to throw any real light on these aspects. Instead, by packaging old ideas in new verbiage, they continue to inhibit the clear understanding that is essential for any rational approach to problems of writing. Much recent writing about writing has tended to reinforce traditional views of writing as something esoteric, sacrosant, not to be tampered with.

The Apache Indian Silas John heard about writing from God in 1904 and created his own system, knowledge of which he restricted to a few "elite ritual specialists" (Basso and Anderson 1975). In traditional China, Heaven was said to have rejoiced when writing was invented. Pagodas for Cherishing the Written Word were to be found in almost every village. In them carefully collected waste paper with writing was burned with the solemnity of a sacrifice (Smith 1983:82). Korean literati would have nothing to do with the Vulgar Script that their king created for the use of "even women and girls." Some American linguists believe that English orthography comes remarkably close to being an optimal system for the language.

With attitudes like these, it is small wonder that many people, including many otherwise able scholars, are unable to look at writing with the detachment to make a sober assessment of what it involves and to consider attacking hitherto intractable problems with new approaches, such as the demand by some Chinese for the previously mentioned policy of digraphia and digraphic literacy. The dead hand of the past has our minds in its rigid grip.

Enough is enough. After two thousand years, it is time to correct the misconception that Egyptian—or any other writing system—can consist of symbols divorced from sound. After four and a half centuries, it is time to end the nonsense that the Chinese express their thoughts with pictures of things. It is high time to acknowledge that all writing is a graphic extension of the uniquely human attribute of speech.

NOTES

Chapter 1. *Kinds of Communication*

1. I owe the ideas, and much of the phrasing, in this paragraph to S. Robert Ramsey (personal communication, 5/24/1988).

Chapter 2. *What Is Writing?*

1. *Horse* and *hoarse* are homophonous in my dialect. But Ramsey (personal communication, 5/24/1988) says they are not homophonous in his speech, and he also notes that the two words are given separate pronunciations in Webster. He further notes that the differences in spelling reflect earlier differences in pronunciation. Hence the disambiguating techniques involved in the spellings for *horse-hoarse* and in the characters for *mă-mā* may not be completly analagous.

2. The relationship between graphemes and frames or lexemes, and the way they are handled in dictionaries, are complicated matters that merit special attention. Detailed study of these matters would throw much light on the workings of individual systems of writing. It is important to note, for example, that the lexemes in English dictionaries, as in those of most other languages, are arranged by their graphemes (that is, by the letters that comprise their graphemes), whereas the lexemes in Chinese dictionaries are arranged not by their graphemes but by their secondary semantic keys or radicals. The dictionary handling of lexemes in Chinese is a major factor leading to the common error of minimizing the phonetic aspect and exaggerating the semantic aspect in the Chinese system of writing (DeFrancis 1984a: 93–97).

Chapter 3. *Syllabic Systems*

1. Edzard (personal communication, 5/20/1988, here and in the following notes) comments on Driver's statement as follows: "*ME* is no pluralizer. It is the copula 'to be,' and affixed *-me* stands for the syllable *me(š)*, including the plural element *-(e)š*. When someone wrote *ME* for the plural, it was meant for *ME.EŠ*."

2. Driver's *TAM.KAR* should be rendered as *dam-gàr* (Edzard).

271

3. Edzard prefers replacing Kramer's "roots" with "bases." He states: "Sumerian bases (rather than 'roots'—a term conjuring up Semitic or Indo-European 'roots') are by no means invariable. They are frequently reduced in reduplication, and there seem to be Ablaut-like variants, too."

4. Edzard notes that although *plow* has the wood determinative, GIŠ, *plowman* usually is just spelled *engar*, without any determinative.

5. Ramsey (5/24/1988) suggests that this was not really a guessing game, except perhaps at the time the graphic combination was first coined, as long as the combination was accepted as a convention. This method, he notes further, is just like the kanji-kana mixed script of the Japanese (as will be seen in the discussion of that system).

6. Edzard suggests the following corrections for this paragraph: " 'God' in general is the sign *AN* read *dingir*. "Sky" is *an*, identical with the name of the sky god. There is no 'to be high.' Akk. read *šamû*. *AN* as a Sumerogram for *šamû* is next to exclusively spelled with an an additional sound-indicating vowel, i.e., *AN-ú* = *šamû*, *AN-e* = *šamê*."

7. It may be of interest to note briefly how phoneticity in Japanese and Korean compares with that in Chinese. There will naturally be differences, because, when the Japanese and Koreans borrowed Chinese characters, their pronunciations of the characters resulted in the so-called Sino-Japanese and Sino-Korean variations from the original. For example, two characters pronounced *shāo* and *shēng* in Chinese both became *shō* in Sino-Japanese.

Horodeck (1987:23) summarizes the results of studies of the utility of the phonetics in 1,240 different Sino-Japanese readings or pronunciations of characters as follows: "Almost 58% of these readings can be predicted with 100% accuracy from the pronunciation of the phonetic contained in the kanji. Another 27.7% can be predicted with 50% or more accuracy."

In the case of Korean, a study developed for pedagogical purposes by Alloco (1972) found that about 400 phonetics predict with 100 percent accuracy the pronunciation of half of a small dictionary's 2,200 characters. (This is almost twice the number in general use today.)

The foregoing figures are, of course, not directly comparable with mine, since the characters studied and the methodologies employed are not identical. Nevertheless, they show incontestibly that the phonetics in the characters borrowed by the Japanese and Koreans also have predictive value in their writing systems.

8. The reader may wonder why I do not base my analysis on the more scholarly work of Karlgren, such as his *Grammata Serica* (1940), a standard tool for the study of Chinese characters. The Soothill material, less scholarly though it is, is nevertheless arranged in a way that makes it relatively easy to handle with the aim of arriving at statistical results such as those which I have presented. To do the same with the Karlgren material would require far more effort, perhaps by a crew of researchers operating with a good-sized budget. I would heartily endorse an attempt to improve on my analysis along these lines, especially since I am convinced that such an attempt would reveal an even greater phonetic aspect in Chinese writing than I have been able to document.

9. Textbooks of standard Chinese published in China, on which figure 19 is based, usually present 398 nontonal syllables. It may be of interest to note how they are con-

structed. If we let capital V stand for a vowel nucleus and small v for an on-glide or off-glide, the vowel content of the syllables can be summarized as follows:

V   vV   Vv   vVv

The following table, in which bold-face **V** stands for any of these vowel types, illustrates the kinds of Chinese syllables and notes the number in each category and the percentage of syllables ending in vowels or in consonants:

V	(e.g., *u, yu=ia, ao, yao=iao*)	17	} 56 percent
CV	(e.g., *la, lia, lao, liao*)	207	}
VC	(e.g., *an, yan=ian*)	15	} 44 percent
CVC	(e.g., *lan, lian*)	159	}

The proportion of syllables ending in consonants was probably considerably greater in earlier stages of Chinese, when there was a richer inventory of final consonants. The same is true today of Cantonese and other varieties of speech subsumed under the umbrella term "Chinese." The number and complexity of syllables in Chinese is now and has been in the past less than in English, but greater than in Sumerian.

10. Ramsey (personal communication, 5/24/1988) adds the following useful information regarding the term *hiragana:*

> The term was not coined until the Edo period [1600–1867]. For the greater part of its history hiragana was called just *kana* (or, sometimes, "women's hand" in contrast with Kanji, which were "men's letters"). (Hira)gana was always the basic system of writing Japanese, while katakana was a special system for annotating pronunciations, e.g., in dictionaries, Buddhist texts, or the libretti of Nō plays. The recognition of a parallel status between hiragana and katakana was a Meiji period [1868–1912] decision.

11. Ramsey (personal communication, 5/24/1988) notes that this convention was introduced by the Portuguese.

12. In explanation of this series, Ramsey (personal communication, 5/24/1988) notes that [h] developed from an original [p].

Chapter 4. *Consonantal Systems*

1. Gardiner (1927:27) has "eagle owl" in place of Budge's "horned owl" for *m,* and "stool" instead of "door" for *p.*

2. Although I have repeatedly hedged on my use of the word "pure" in labeling some of the writing systems discussed in this book, it is useful to reinforce my caution with the following warning by one of the readers of the manuscript: "Careful about Arabic as 'pure consonantal.' There is more to Semitic scripts (when vowelless): *ktb* can mean 'wrote' or a noun, depending on where in sentence it is found: guess by position. Position in sentence gives phonetic information, as Author may put it. (In *ritual* texts, vowels ARE indicated in Arabic, Hebrew, etc.)"

3. The disparity in time needed to attain literacy on the basis of a simple reformed script as compared to a difficult traditional system is even greater in the case of Chinese. Chinese children can become fully literate in Pinyin, that is, they can learn to read and write anything within their range of knowledge in two-and-a-half months to a year of schooling. This is considerably less than one-tenth the time it would take to achieve a comparable level in the traditional characters (DeFrancis 1984a: 212, 268–269, 282–283).

Chapter 5. *Alphabetic Systems*

1. The example in the frontispiece of the Devanagri script as used in Hindi illustrates this reversal in the word transcribed as *saivina*. The spoken sequence transcribed as *vi* appears in the Devanagri written version in the sequence *iv*, the curved loop above and below the horizontal line being the equivalent of the letter *i* before that for *v*, so that a letter-by-letter transcription (which is never done) would produce *saiivna*.

2. As these practices included indication of vowels, and as the Indic scripts are generally traced back to consonantal Aramaic (Gelb 1963:x–xi), the question arises as to where the idea of full phonemic writing came from. The answer is unclear. Perhaps the idea came from the use in Aramaic and other Semitic scripts of the *mater lectionis*, "reading mother" symbols noted earlier in the discussion of "pure" consonantal systems. Perhaps there was some influence from the Greek creation of separate vowel signs. Or perhaps we have here an indigenous development that might be considered a second invention of phonemic writing. These various possibilities suggest that the previously cited statement by Gelb (1963:184) to the effect that after the Greeks "nothing new has happened in the inner structural development of writing," while strictly accurate as far as the principal of full phonemic representation is concerned, should not be interpreted as meaning that all phonemic systems of writing unquestionably trace their ancestry to Greek.

3. I am indebted to Ramsey (5/24/1988 and 5/26/1988) for leading me to this formulation of the evolution of hangŭl from a morphemic to a morphophonemic stage. It corrects my original understanding (or misunderstanding) of Ledyard's discussion of the matter.

Chapter 6. *A Critique of Writing about Writing*

1. Ramsey (personal communication, 5/26/1988) adds an interesting note to the discussion of Naxi in remarking, "The reason I would like to believe that the Naxi independently discovered the rebus principle is . . . because I think the discovery of the rebus represents a kind of natural human progression. People who use visual symbols associated with words can't help but stumble onto such connections, not once or twice but many times. They may not get past the stage of punning and word games, and thus not develop a full writing system, but the potential is always there. We human beings are tied so inextricably to speech, word associations are as close to us as the air we breathe."

The suggestion that many people may have discovered the rebus principle deserves to be explored. To that end it would be helpful if scholars interested in pictographs would stop concentrating on them as symbols with inherent meaning and instead would search for instances of their abortive use as phonetic symbols in punning, word games, and other areas short of full writing.

2. My disquiet extends also to the mistaken assumptions regarding the Chinese characters used in the Japanese and Korean writing systems. It is likely that the way characters are processed in all three systems is similar; thus there is general significance in a recent extensive and seemingly definitive study of the Japanese situation that concludes "kanji typically function as symbols for sounds when Japanese read and write" (Horodeck 1987:188).

3. In point of fact, there is not a single word pronounced *shih* in Chinese, since that transcription properly represents only a nontonal syllable, and toneless syllables do not function as independent words. Moreover, one-fifth of the 1,277 different syllables of Mandarin have no homophones at all and hence are uniquely represented by a single character usually conveying a single meaning (Chao 1968:185).

4. These views by Goody and Watt were originally published in 1963 in a journal article that was reprinted in 1972. Some of the views expressed by the two authors have been modified by Goody in a recently published book the readership of which is, however, unlikely to match that achieved by the two other works. The following quotes indicate the major qualifications in his views: "Chinese characters *(hanzi)* make more use of phonetic elements than is commonly supposed." ". . . the earlier types of writing may have had some of the liberating effects that certain authors (including Watt and myself) attributed to alphabetic literacy. . . . [W]e may need to modify our ideas not only about the uniqueness of the techniques available to the Greeks (i.e., the alphabet) but also about the uniqueness of their achievements in other respects." "[What we] suggested with regard to 'logical reasoning' was highly specific. . . . Logical reasoning as such was never at stake." "It is a gross ethnocentric error to attribute too much to the alphabet and too much to the West" (Goody 1987: 37, 56, 64, 219).

Chapter 7. *The Essential Oneness of Full Writing*

1. This point is supported by the results of unpublished research by Raymond C. Gordon involving readers of English and the American Indian language Crow. His conclusions are summarized by Horodeck (1988:13) as follows:

> He concludes that even a radical reduction of the linguistic features encoded by an orthography will not automatically render that orthography "inadequate": with practice, readers in his experiments were able to achieve a high degree of recovery even at levels of encoding reduction that initially crippled their reading fluency to less than 50% of normal (Gordon 1981:76–77).

GLOSSARY

The following are nontechnical explanations for some of the technical terms used in this book.

Acrophonic. Refers to the principle in which a certain sound is represented by a symbol the pronunciation of which begins with that sound. Example: representing *h* with the picture of a house.

Alphabet, alphabetic. Terms referring to symbols, like our English letters, which represent phonemes. Examples: the letters *p, a, t, b,* and *d* in *pat, bat, pad, bad.*

Aspirated. Marked by release of a puff of air. Example: English *p* is aspirated in *pie,* unaspirated in *spy.*

Bilingual text. A text written in two languages with identical or very similar content.

Bound form. Two kinds of nonfree syllables, semibound and completely bound. A semibound syllable has meaning but must be joined to another syllable. Example: *er* in English *teacher* and *yuán* in Chinese *jiàoyuán* 'teacher.' A completely bound syllable has no meaning and must be combined with another syllable, as in the case of *cor* and *al* in English *coral* and *shān* and *hú* in Chinese *shānhú* 'coral.'

Boustrophedon. (lit. "turning like oxen in plow.") Refers to writing alternate lines in opposite directions.

Cartouche. An oval or oblong frame used in Egyptian hieroglyphics to enclose personal names.

Cuneiform. Wedge-shaped symbols used in Sumerian and other writing systems. (Derived from Latin *cuneus* 'wedge.')

Cyrillic alphabet. An alphabet widely applied to the Slavic languages, as in the case of the thirty-three-letter Russian alphabet. Since the 1930s it has also been used for most of the languages of the Soviet Union. (Named after St. Cyril, a ninth-century apostle of the Slavs.)

277

Demotic script. (lit. "people's script.") Egyptian writing that evolved from the hieroglyphic and hieratic scripts into a linear script tending strongly toward alphabetic representation.

Determinative. An element added to an ambiguous written symbol in order to remove the ambiguity. If the ambiguity comes from the multiple meanings of words with the same sound, a semantic determinative is added. For example, the English word *plant* is ambiguous. To remove the ambiguity, we could add the picture of a tree to represent something growing, or a smokestack to represent a factory. If the ambiguity comes from multiple pronunciations for different words with the same written form, a phonetic determinative is added. We could write *bow(oh)* for the thing used to shoot arrows and *bow(au)* for lowering the head or inclining the body.

Diacritic. A distinguishing mark added to a letter or syllabic sign modifying it in some way. Examples: Chinese tone marks and French cedilla and circumflex.

Dialects. Mutually intelligible varieties of a single language.

Digraph. Two letters used to represent one sound. Example: *ph* in *phase.*

Digraphia. Use of two different scripts for the same language, such as Latin and Cyrillic for Serbo-Croatian, Devanagari and Arabic for Hindi-Urdu, and (the proposed) Pinyin and characters for Chinese.

Digraphic literacy. Literacy in two scripts used for the same language.

Double articulation. Thesis propounded by the French linguist André Martinet, stating that all spoken languages have a "first articulation" which represents morphemes and a "second articulation" which represents phonemes.

Duality principle. A statement of the two aspects of all writing systems: (1) the phonetic representation of speech at either the phonemic or syllabic level; (2) the provision of additional nonphonetic information, such as the use of capital letters to represent proper nouns in English.

Feature, featural. Terms referring to the various phonetic qualities which characterize a phoneme, such as voiced, aspirated, vocalic.

Frame. A basic written unit (corresponding to a free morpheme in speech) singled out for special treatment, such as being surrounded by white space on the printed page and being listed in dictionaries. Also called 'lexeme.'

Glottal stop. A sudden release of air through the glottis, as in a cough.

Glyph. Name given to the symbols used in the Mayan system of writing.

Grammatology. The "scientific" study of writing systems.

Grapheme, graphemic. Terms referring to a basic unit of writing analogous to the phoneme or syllable in speech. The graphemic representation of a phoneme in English is a letter or group of letters. Example: $\int$ and *ph* in *faze* and *phase*. The graphemic representation of a syllable in Chinese is a character. Example: the symbol for *mǎ* 'horse' used either as an independent character or as a phonetic element in compound characters such as that for *mā* 'mother.'

Hangŭl. Korean alphabetic system of writing created in the fifteenth century (see fig. 27).

Hiragana. Cursive form of kana (see fig. 21).

Hieratic script. (lit. "priestly script.") A cursive form of Egyptian writing intermediate between the hieroglyphic and demotic scripts.

Hieroglyph, hieroglyphic. Terms applied to the picture symbols used in (e.g.) Egyptian writing.

Homonyms. Words which have the same pronunciation and written form but different meanings. Examples: *can* 'be able to,' *can* 'metal container.'

Homophones. Words having the same sound. Examples: *right, wright, write, rite; to, too, two.*

Iconic. Pictorially representing some object.

Iconicity. Degree of correspondence between symbol and thing it depicts.

Ideogram. Same as *ideograph*.

Ideograph, ideographic. Terms referring to symbols that represent meaning without indicating pronunciation. Often opposed to *phonetic*, q.v. (It is a central thesis of this book that while it is possible to have some *individual* symbols that might be called ideographic—e.g., "No Smoking" and "No Parking" signs—it is not possible to have a *system* of writing based only or even primarily on ideographs.)

Input. The process of entering data into a computer, usually via a typewriter-like keyboard.

Kana. Japanese syllabic signs derived from Chinese characters. There are two varieties, hiragana and katakana (see fig. 21).

Kanbun. Japanese term for texts in classical Chinese, or an approximation of that style, read according to fixed rules for permuting the word order and glossing the characters.

Kanji. Japanese term for Chinese characters.

Katakana. Angular form of kana, roughly parallel to our block letters (see fig. 21). It is used much like English italics.

Key. One of the (traditionally) 214 semantic elements in Chinese characters. Examples: 'water' (no. 85) and 'vegetation' (no. 140). Also called 'radical,' 'signific,' and 'determinative.'

Latinxua ("Latinization"). Alphabetic scheme for Chinese based on Latin letters. Created in the early 1930s and widely used for about a decade.

Lexeme. The written unit singled out for listing in dictionaries.

Linguist. One devoted to scientific study of language. (To be distinguished from *polyglot,* a person who speaks several languages but, as in the case of most native speakers, is largely ignorant of such technical details as the phonemic and morphemic structure of a language.)

Logograph, logographic. Terms referring to graphic symbols that represent words. Thus *&* is a logograph representing the word *and.* The terms are often equated, incorrectly, with *ideograph* and *ideographic.*

Matrix. An array of information set up in rows and columns.

Mnemonic. Graphically providing nonphonetic information, either iconically or noniconically.

Mnemonicity. Provision of mnemonic information.

Moneme. Alternative term for *morpheme.* (Coined by the French linguist André Martinet.)

Morpheme, morphemic. Terms referring to the smallest meaningful units of speech. English *teachers* consists of three morphemes, *teach, er,* and *s.* Chinese *jiàoyuán* consists of two morphemes, *jiao* 'teach' and *yuán* 'one who does something.'

Morphoconsonantal. Term referring to a writing system (example: Egyptian) that basically represents consonants but also makes extensive use of nonphonetic techniques, such as semantic determinatives, to suggest the meaning category to which a given symbol belongs.

Morphophonemic. Term referring to a writing system that is basically phonemic (represents sounds below syllable level by letters) but also takes meaning into account. Example: English plural indicator written *s* even though sometimes pronounced as *s (pots)* and other times as *z (pods).*

Morphophonic, Morphonic. Inclusive term referring to morphosyllabic, morphoconsonantal, and morphophonemic systems of writing.

Morphosyllabic. Term referring to a writing system (example: Chinese) that basically represents syllables but also makes extensive use of nonphonetic techniques, such as determinatives, to suggest the meaning category to which a given written item belongs.

Orthography. A conventional writing system used for a specific language.

Output. The process of producing information, usually in printed form, from a computer.

Phoneme, phonemic. Terms used in reference to the smallest units of speech that distinguish one word from another. Examples: the *b* and *p* of *bat* and *pat;* the *t* and *d* of *bat* and *bad.* Can be thought of, very roughly, as the sound represented by a letter, as long as one remembers that the existence of the sound historically and psychologically precedes its representation by a letter.

Phonetic. Term referring to sounds. Here I list three different usages. (1) To distinguish phonetic symbols (symbols representing sound) from non-phonetic symbols (symbols that do not represent sound). (2) To make a distinction from phonemic writing. Phonetic writing represents the two *p*'s in *pot* and *spot* differently, since the first is aspirated and the latter is not. Phonemic representation is based on the premise that since the *p* in *pot* is always aspirated and the *p* in *spot* is always unaspirated, there is no need to differentiate them, because native speakers will always pronounce them correctly. (3) As a short form of 'phonetic element,' the basic symbol that represents sound in Chinese.

Phoneticity. The fit between symbols and sounds.

Phonology, phonological. Having to do with (1) the study of speech sounds, and (2) the sounds used in a particular form of speech.

Pictograph, pictographic. Terms applied to symbols which depict things or actions.

Pinyin. (lit. "spell sounds.") Name given to the alphabet based on Latin letters that was adopted in the People's Republic of China in 1958.

Primitive. The part of a Chinese character that remains after the key (or determinative or radical) is detached. Also called a phonetic or a phonetic element. Some primitives also function as keys.

Quipu. Knotted cords used by the ancient Peruvians for recordkeeping.

Radical. Popular (but misleading) term for the key or determinative in Chinese characters.

Rebus. Representation of a word or syllable by pictures of objects whose names resemble the sounds of the words or syllables. Example: a picture of a bee representing the syllable *be.*

Schwa. (1) A sound, very common in English, that appears at the end of *the* when the next word begins with a consonant, in the second syllable of *raisin,* and in many other occurrences. (2) The symbol ə (an upside-down *e*) that is used to represent this sound, which in ordinary English orthography is spelled in many different ways.

Segments, segmental phonemes. Vowels and consonants. (That is, phonemes other than such "suprasegmental" phonemes as tones and intonation.)

Semasiographic. Ideographic.

Signific. See 'key.'

Syllabary, syllabic. Terms referring to symbols used to represent whole syllables.

Syllabogram. A graphic symbol representing a syllable. A set of syllabograms comprises a syllabary in the same way that a set of letters comprises an alphabet.

Tone. The pitch of an utterance. A "tone language" is one in which words are distinguished by tonal differences. Example: Chinese *ma* spoken with the pitch of English *Yes?* means 'hemp'; spoken with the pitch of *Yes!* it means 'revile.'

Vocalic. Of or having to do with vowels.

Voiced. Characterized by vibration of the vocal cords. In English, all vowels and some consonants are voiced. Example: voiced *b* in *ban* contrasts with voiceless *p* in *pan.*

REFERENCES

Alisjahbana, S. Takdir. 1965. "New National Languages: A Problem Modern Linguistics Has Failed to Solve." *Lingua* 15:515–530.

Alloco, Vincent Anello. 1972. "Phonetic Method of Organizing Chinese Characters Used in the Republic of Korea: New Alternative to Rote Memorization." Ph.D. diss., United States International University.

Amiot, J. J. M. 1776. [Comments on Chinese writing]. In *Mémoires concernant l'histoire, les sciences, les arts, les moeurs, les usages &c des Chinois, par les missionaires de Pékin.* 1:282–285. Paris: Nyon.

Barber, F. J. W. 1974. *Archaeological Decipherment. A Handbook.* Princeton: Princeton University Press.

Barnard, Noel. 1978. "The Nature of the Ch'in 'Reform of the Script' as Reflected in Archaeological Documents Excavated under Conditions of Control." In David T. Roy and Tsuen-hsuin Tsien, eds., *Ancient China: Studies in Early Civilization.* Pp. 181–213. Hong Kong: Chinese University Press.

Baron, Naomi S. 1981. *Speech, Writing, and Sign.* Bloomington: Indiana University Press.

Barr, James. 1976. "Reading a Script without Vowels." In William Haas, ed., *Writing without Letters.* Pp. 71–100. Manchester: Manchester University Press.

Basso, Keith H., and Ned Anderson. 1975. "A Western Apache Writing System: The Symbols of Silas John." In M. D. Kinkaide et al., eds., *Linguistics and Anthropology, in Honor of C. F. Voegelin.* Pp. 27–52. Lisse: Peter de Ridder.

Battison, R. 1978. *Lexical Borrowing in American Sign Language.* Silver Spring, Md.: Linstock Press.

Baugh, Albert C., and Thomas Cable. 1978. *A History of the English Language.* 3d ed. Englewood Cliffs, N.J.: Prentice-Hall.

Bazin, Louis. 1983. "La Réforme linguistique en Turquie." In István Fodor and Claude Hagège, eds., *Language Reform. History and Future.* Vol. 1, pp. 155–177. Hamburg: Buske Verlag.

Bellugi, Ursula, and Edward S. Klima. 1975. "Aspects of Sign Language and Its Structure." In J. F. Kavanagh and J. E. Cutting, eds., *The Role of Speech in Language.* Pp. 171–205. Cambridge: MIT Press.

Blank, Lenore Kim. 1981. "Language Policies in South Korea since 1945 and Their Probable Impact on Education." Ed.D. diss., University of San Francisco.

Bloom, Alfred H. 1981. *The Linguistic Shaping of Thought: A Study of the Impact of*

Language on Thinking in China and the West. Hillsdale, N.J.: Lawrence
   Erlbaum Associates.
Bloomfield, Leonard. 1933. *Language.* New York: Holt, Rinehart and Winston.
Bolinger, Dwight L. 1946. "Visual Morphemes." *Language* 22:333–350.
———. 1968. *Aspects of Language.* New York: Harcourt, Brace, and World.
Boltz, William G. 1985. "Desultory Notes on Language and Semantics in Ancient
   China." *Journal of the American Oriental Society* 105:309–313.
———. 1986. "Early Chinese Writing." *World Archaeology* 17 (3): 420–436.
Boodberg, Peter A. 1937. "Some Proleptical Remarks on the Evolution of Archaic
   Chinese." *Harvard Journal of Asiatic Studies* 2:329–372.
———. 1940. " 'Ideography' or Iconolatry?" *T'oung pao* 35:266–288.
———. 1957. "The Chinese Script: An Essay in Nomenclature (the First Heca-
   ton)." *Bulletin of the Institute of History and Philology Academia Sinica* (Taipei)
   39:113–120.
Bowman, Elizabeth. 1960. "A Note on the Development of Egyptian Writing."
   Journal of Near Eastern Studies 19:46–48.
Boxer, C. R. 1953. *South China in the Sixteenth Century.* London: Hakluyt Society.
Bradley, Henry. 1913. *On the Relationship between Spoken and Written Language, with
   Special Reference to English.* London: Oxford University Press.
Bricker, Victoria R. 1986. Review of John S. Justeson and Lyle Campbell, eds.,
   Phoneticism in Mayan Hieroglyphic Writing. Institute for Mesoamerican Studies
   Publication no. 9. (Albany: State University of New York, 1984). *Language*
   62 (3): 694–697.
Brown, R. A. 1987. "Kyoyo and Multigraphia in Japan." *Asian and Pacific Quarterly
   of Cultural and Social Affairs* 19 (2): 19–30.
Budge, Ernest A. Wallis. 1963. *Egyptian Language. Easy Lessons in Egyptian Hiero-
   glyphics, with Sign List.* London: Kegan Paul, Trench, Trubner & Co.
Bullis, Michael, ed. 1987. *Communication Development in Young Children with Deaf-
   Blindness: Literature Review III.* Monmouth, Ore.: Communication Skills
   Center for Young Children with Deaf-Blindness.
Cajori, Florian. 1928–1929. *A History of Mathematical Notations.* 2 vols. Chicago:
   Open Court.
Callender, John Bryan. 1984. "Egypt. Language and Literature." *Encyclopedia Ameri-
   cana* 10:57–59.
Campbell, Lyle. 1984a. Review of Linda Schele, *Mayan Glyphs. The Verbs* (Austin:
   University of Texas Press, 1982). *Language* 60 (3): 621–623.
———. 1984b. "The Implications of Mayan Historical Linguistics for Glyphic
   Research." In John S. Justeson and Lyle Campbell, eds., *Phoneticism in
   Mayan Hieroglyphic Writing.* Institute for Mesoamerican Studies Publication
   no. 9. Albany: State University of New York.
Chadwick, John. 1967. *The Decipherment of Linear B.* London: Cambridge Univer-
   sity Press.
———. 1987. *Linear B and Related Scripts.* Berkeley: University of California Press.
Champollion, Jean François. 1822. "Letter to M. Dacier Concerning the Alphabet
   of the Phonetic Hieroglyphs." Paris, September 22, 1822. Trans. V. M.
   Conrad. In Kurt W. Marek, *Hands on the Past.* Pp. 162–170. New York:
   Knopf.

Chang, K. C. 1983. "Concluding Remarks." In David N. Keightley, ed., *The Origins of Chinese Civilization*. Pp. 565–581. Berkeley: University of California Press.

——, ed. 1977. *Food in Chinese Culture*. New Haven: Yale University Press.

Chang Te-k'un. 1982. *Studies in Chinese Archaeology*. Hong Kong: Chinese University Press.

Chao, Yuen Ren. 1968. *A Grammar of Spoken Chinese*. Berkeley and Los Angeles: University of California Press.

——. 1976. *Aspects of Chinese Sociolinguistics*. Ed. Answar S. Dil. Stanford: Stanford University Press.

Chen Shilin. 1979. "Guifan Yi wen de shijian xiaoguo he youguan de jige wenti [The practical results of standardizing Yi writing and some related questions]." *Minzu yuwen* 4:241–248.

Cheng, Robert L. 1975. "Phonological Units and the Japanese Syllabary." In M. D. Kinkade et al., eds., *Linguistics and Anthropology, in Honor of C. F. Voegelin*. Pp. 67–85. Lisse: Peter de Ridder.

Cheung Kwong-yue. 1983. "Recent Archaeological Evidence Relating to the Origin of Chinese Characters." In David N. Keightley, ed., *The Origins of Chinese Civilization*. Pp. 323–391. Berkeley: University of California Press.

Chiera, Edward. 1938. *They Wrote on Clay*. Chicago: University of Chicago Press.

Chomsky, Noam, and Morris Halle. 1968. *The Sound Pattern of English*. New York: Harper and Row.

Civil, Miguel. 1973. "The Sumerian System: Some Problems." *Orientalia* 42: 21–34.

Civil, Miguel, and R. D. Biggs. 1966. "Notes sur des textes sumériens archaïques." *Revue d'assyriologie et d'archéologie orientale* 60 (1): 1–16.

Claiborne, Robert. 1974. *The Birth of Writing*. New York: Time-Life Books.

Cohen, Marcel. 1958. *La grande invention de l'écriture et son évolution*. Paris: Imprimerie Nationale.

Comrie, Bernard. 1981. *The Languages of the Soviet Union*. Cambridge: Cambridge University Press.

Coulmas, Florian. 1984. "Arbitrariness and Double Articulation." In Leslie Henderson, ed., *Orthographies and Reading*. Pp. 57–66. London: Lawrence Erlbaum Associates.

Creel, Herrlee Glessner. 1936. "On the Nature of Chinese Ideography." *T'oung pao* 32:85–161.

——. 1938. "On the Ideographic Element in Ancient Chinese." *T'oung pao* 34: 265–294.

Daniels, Harvey A. 1985. "Nine Ideas about Language." In Virginia P. Clark, Paul A. Escholz, and Alfred F. Rosa, eds., *Language. Introductory Readings*. 4th ed. New York: St. Martin's Press. Pp. 18–36. Reprinted from Harvey A. Daniels, *Famous Last Words: The American Language Crisis Reconsidered* (Carbondale: Southern Illinois University Press, 1983).

Davies, W. W. 1987. *Egyptian Hieroglyphics*. Berkeley: University of California Press.

DeFrancis, John. 1947. "Japanese Language Reform. Politics and Phonetics." *Far Eastern Survey* 16 (19): 217–220.

————. 1950. *Nationalism and Language Reform in China.* Princeton: Princeton University Press. Reprint ed. New York: Octagon Books, 1972.

————. 1977. *Colonialism and Language Policy in Viet Nam.* The Hague: Mouton.

————. 1984a. *The Chinese Language: Fact and Fantasy.* Honolulu: University of Hawaii Press.

————. 1984b. "Digraphia." *Word* 35 (1): 59–66.

————. 1985. "China's Literary Renaissance: A Reassessment." *Bulletin of Concerned Asian Scholars* 17 (4): 52–63.

Deregowski, Jan B. 1973. "Illusion and Culture." In R. L. Gregory and E. H. Gombrich, eds., *Illusion in Nature and Art.* Pp. 161–191. New York: Charles Scribner's Sons.

Diakonoff, I. M. 1975. "Ancient Writing and Ancient Written Language: Pitfalls and Peculiarities in the Study of Sumerian." In Stephen J. Lieberman, ed., *Sumerological Studies in Honor of Thorkild Jacobsen on his Seventieth Birthday, June 7, 1974.* Assyriological Studies no. 20. Pp. 99–121. Chicago: University of Chicago Press.

Diringer, David. 1937. *L'alfabeto nella storia della civiltà.* Florence: Barbèra.

————. 1948. *The Alphabet. A Key to the History of Mankind.* London and New York: Hutchinson.

————. 1968. *The Alphabet. A Key to the History of Mankind.* 3d ed. 2 vols. London: Hutchinson.

————. 1984. "Alphabet." *Encyclopedia Americana. International Edition* 1:618–626.

Doblhofer, Ernst. 1961. *Voices in Stone.* Trans. Mervyn Savill. New York: Viking.

Dreyer, June Teufel. 1976. *China's Forty Millions.* Cambridge: Harvard University Press.

Driver, G. R. 1976. *Semitic Writing. From Pictograph to Alphabet.* London: Oxford University Press.

DuPonceau, Peter S. 1838. *A Dissertation on the Nature and Character of the Chinese System of Writing.* Philadelphia: American Philosophical Society.

Eberhard, Wolfram. 1982. *China's Minorities: Yesterday and Today.* Belmont, Calif.: Wadsworth Publishing Co.

EBMIC (Encyclopaedia Brittanica). 1988a. "Akkadian Language." *The New Encyclopaedia Brittanica. Micropaedia.* 15th ed. 1:192.

————. 1988b. "Phoenicia." *The New Encyclopaedia Brittanica. Micropaedia.* 15th ed. 9:392.

Edgerton, William F. 1940. "Egyptian Phonetic Writing, from Its Invention to the Close of the Nineteenth Dynasty." *Journal of the American Oriental Society* 60: 473–506.

————. 1941. "Ideograms in English Writing." *Language* 17:148–150.

————. 1952. "On the Theory of Writing." *Journal of Near Eastern Studies* 11:287–290.

Edzard, D. O. 1980. "Keilschrift." In *Reallexikon der Assyriologie und vorderasiatischen Archäologie.* Vol. 5, pp. 544–568. Berlin: Walter de Gruyter.

Erbaugh, Mary S. 1988. "What Linguists Wish Sinologists Knew about Language: There Are No Primitive Languages and Chinese Is Not One of Them." To appear in *Early China* XI.

Falkenstein, Adam. 1936. *Archaische Texte aus Uruk.* Berlin: Deutsche Forschungsgemeinschaft.

Feeling, Durbin. 1975. *Cherokee–English Dictionary*. Tahlequah, Okla.: Cherokee Nation of Oklahoma.

Février, James G. 1948. *Histoire de l'écriture*. Paris: Payot.

Fischer, Susan D. 1978. "Sign Language and Creoles." In Patricia Siple, ed., *Understanding Language through Sign Language Research*. Pp. 309–331. New York: Academic Press.

Foreman, Grant. 1938. *Sequoya*. Norman: University of Oklahoma Press.

French, M. A. 1976. "Observations on the Chinese Script, and Classification of Writing-Systems." In William Haas, ed., *Writing without Letters*. Pp. 101–129. Manchester: Manchester University Press.

Friberg, Joran. 1984. "Numbers and Measures in the Earliest Written Records." *Scientific American* 250 (2): 110–118.

Friedrich, Johannes. 1957. *Extinct Languages*. New York: Philosophical Library.

———. 1966. *Geschichte der Schrift*. Heidelberg: Carl Winter.

Frishberg, Nancy. 1981. "Code and Culture." In Fred C. C. Peng, ed., *Sign Language and Sign Language Acquistion in Man and Ape. New Dimensions in Comparative Pedolinguistics*. Pp. 45–85. Boulder, Colo.: Westview Press.

Fu Maoxi. 1986a. "Dongbawen [Tomba script]." *Zhongguo da baike quanshu. Minzu.* P. 95. Beijing: Zhongguo Da Baike Quanshu Chubanshe.

———. 1986b. "Gebawen [Geba script]." *Zhongguo da baike quanshu. Minzu.* Pp. 133–134. Beijing: Zhongguo Da Baike Quanshu Chubanshe.

Furth, Hans G. 1966. *Thinking without Language: Psychological Implications of Deafness*. New York: Free Press.

Gadd, C. J. 1924. *A Sumerian Reading-Book*. Oxford: Clarendon Press.

Gardiner, Alan. 1927. *Egyptian Grammar*. Oxford: Clarendon Press.

Gaur, Albertine. 1984. *A History of Writing*. London: The British Library.

Gelb, I. J. 1961. *Old Akkadian Writing and Grammar*. Chicago: University of Chicago Press.

———. 1963. *A Study of Writing*. 2d ed. Chicago: University of Chicago Press.

———. 1974. "Records, Writing, and Decipherment." *Visible Language* 8 (4): 293–318.

———. 1979. "Writing, Forms of." *The New Encyclopaedia Britannica. Macropaedia.* 15th ed. 19:1033–1045.

Geoghegan, Sheila Graves, et al. 1979. *Language Files*. Reynoldsburg, Ohio: Advocate Publishing Group.

George, Alexander. 1987. Review of Roy Harris, *The Origin of Writing*. (London: Duckworth, 1986). *Language* 63 (1): 130–132.

Giedion, S. 1966. "Symbolic Expression in Prehistory and in the First High Civilizations." In Gyorgy Kepes, ed., *Sign Image Symbol*. New York: George Braziller.

Gleason, H. A. 1961. *An Introduction to Descriptive Linguistics*. Rev. ed. New York: Holt, Rinehart and Winston.

Goody, Jack. 1987. *The Interface between the Written and the Oral*. Cambridge: Cambridge University Press.

Goody, Jack, and I. Watt. 1972. "The Consequences of Literacy." In Pier Paolo Giglioli, ed. *Language and Social Context. Selected Readings*. Pp. 311–357. Harmondsworth: Penguin Education. Reprinted from *Comparative Studies in Society and History* 5 (1962–1963): 304–326, 332–345.

Gordon, Cyrus H. 1970. "The Accidental Invention of the Phonemic Alphabet." *Journal of Near Eastern Studies* 29:193–197.

———. 1971. *Before Columbus: Links between the Old World and Ancient America.* New York: Crown Publishers.

———. 1982. *Forgotten Scripts.* Rev. and enl. ed. New York: Basic Books.

Gordon, Raymond C. 1981. "Symbolic Manipulation of Orthography." Ph.D. diss., Cornell University.

Green, M. W. 1981. "The Construction and Implementation of the Cuneiform Writing System." *Visible Language* 15:345–372.

Haas, William. 1970. *Phono-graphic Translation.* Manchester: Manchester University Press.

———. 1976. "Writing: The Basic Options." In idem, ed., *Writing without Letters.* Manchester: Manchester University Press.

———. 1983. "Determining the Level of a Script." In Florian Coulmas and Konrad Ehlich, eds., *Writing in Focus.* Pp. 16–29. Berlin: Mouton.

Hall, Robert King. 1949. *Education for a New Japan.* New Haven: Yale University Press.

Halle, Morris. 1969. "Some Thoughts on Spelling." In Kenneth S. Goodman and J. T. Fleming, eds., *Psycholinguistics and the Teaching of Reading.* Pp. 17–24. Newark, Del.: International Reading Association.

———. 1972. "On a Parallel between Conventions of Versification and Orthography; and on Literacy among the Cherokee." In J. F. Kavanagh and Ignatius G. Mattingly, eds., *Language by Ear and by Eye. The Relationships between Speech and Reading.* Cambridge: MIT Press.

Hansen, Chad. 1983. *Language and Logic in Ancient China.* Ann Arbor: University of Michigan Press.

Harris, Roy. 1986. *The Origin of Writing.* London: Duckworth.

Haugen, Einar. 1973. "The Curse of Babel." *Daedalus* 102 (3): 47–57.

———. 1984. "Danish Language." *Encyclopedia Americana* 8:484–485.

Hawkes, Jaquetta, and Sir Leonard Woolley. 1963. *Prehistory and the Beginnings of Civilization.* New York: Harper and Row.

Heimbach, Ernest E. 1966. *White Meo-English Dictionary.* 2 vols. Chiengmai: Overseas Missionary Fellowship.

Herskovitz, M. J. 1959. "Art and Value." In R. Redfield, M. J. Herskovitz, and G. F. Ekholm, *Aspects of Primitive Art.* Pp. 42–97. New York: Museum of Primitive Art.

Heyd, Uriel. 1954. *Language Reform in Modern Turkey.* Jerusalem: Israel Oriental Society.

Hill, Archibald A. 1967. "The Typology of Writing Systems." In William M. Austin, ed. *Papers in Linguistics in Honor of Leon Dostert.* Pp. 92–99. The Hague: Mouton.

HKNC. 1964. *Without Sight and Sound: Facts about Blindness.* Sands Point, N.Y.: Helen Keller National Center for Deaf-Blind Youths and Adults.

Hockett, Charles F. 1954. "Chinese versus English: An Exploration of the Whorfian Thesis." In Harry Hoijer, ed. *Language in Culture. Conference on the Interrelations of Language and other Aspects of Culture.* Pp. 106–123, 247–262. Chicago: University of Chicago Press.

————. 1963. "The Problem of Universals in Language." In J. H. Greenberg, ed., *Universals of Language*. Pp. 1–22. Cambridge: MIT Press.

————. 1978. "In Search of Jove's Brow." *American Speech* 53 (4): 243–313.

Hodge, Carlton T. 1975. "Ritual and Writing: An Inquiry into the Origin of Egyptian Script." In M. Dale Kinkaid, Kenneth L. Hale, and Oswald Werner, eds., *Linguistics and Anthropology, in Honor of C. F. Voegelin*. Pp. 331–350. Lisse: Peter de Ridder.

————. 1984. Review of Barbara Watterson, *Introducing Egyptian Hieroglyphs*. (Atlantic Heights, N.J.: Scottish Academic Press, 1981.) *Anthropological Linguistics* 26 (2): 240–243.

Holenstein, Elmar. 1983. "Double Articulation in Writing." In Florian Coulmas and Konrad Ehlich, eds., *Writing in Focus*. Pp. 45–62. Berlin: Mouton.

Holmes, Ruth Bradley, and Betty Sharp Smith. 1977. *Beginning Cherokee*. 2d edition. Norman: University of Oklahoma Press.

Horodeck, Richard Alan. 1987. "The Role of Sound in Reading and Writing Kanji." Ph.D. diss., Cornell University.

House, Betty J., Michael J. Hanley, and Deborah F. Magid. 1980. "Logographic Reading in TMR Adults." *American Journal of Mental Deficiency* 85 (2): 161–170.

Householder, Fred. W. 1971. *Linguistic Speculations*. Cambridge: Cambridge University Press.

Hu Qingjun. 1986. "Yizu [Yi nationality]." *Zhongguo da baikeshu. Minzu*. Pp. 500–502. Beijing: Zhongguo Da Baikeshu Chubanshe.

Huang Chuan-sheng. 1939. *Origine et évolution de l'écriture hiéroglyphique et l'écriture chinoise*. Paris: G. Guether.

Huttar, George L. 1985. "The Afaka Script: An Indigenous Creole Syllabary." In Ilah Fleming, ed., *The Thirteenth LACUS Forum 1986*. Pp. 167–177. Lake Bluff, Ill.: Linguistic Association of Canada and the United States.

Iokhel'son, Vladimir Ilich. See Jochelson, Waldemar I.

Isayev, M. I. 1977. *National Languages in the USSR: Problems and Solutions*. Moscow: Progress Publishers.

Istrin, V. A. 1965. *Vozniknovenie i razvitie pis'ma* [*The origin and development of writing*]. Moscow: Nauka. First published in 1961 under the title *Razvitie pis'ma*.

Ivanov, S. V. 1954. *Materialy po izobrazitel'nomu iskusstvu narodov Sibiri XIX-nachala XX v.* [*Materials on the pictorial arts of the peoples of Siberia in the 19th- beginning of the 20th centuries*]. Moscow: Akademiia Nauk SSSR.

Jasim, Sabah Abboud, and Joan Oates. 1986. "Early Tokens and Tablets in Mesopotamia: New Information from Tell Abada and Tell Brak." *World Archaeology* 17 (3): 348–362.

Jeffery, L. H. 1961. *Local Scripts of Archaic Greece*. Oxford: Clarendon Press.

Jensen, Hans. 1969. *Sign, Symbol and Script. An Account of Man's Efforts to Write*. 3d ed., rev. and enl. Trans. George Unwin. New York: G. P. Putnam & Sons.

Jespersen, Otto. 1928. *Monosyllabism in English*. London: H. Milford.

Jochelson, Waldemar I. 1898. "Po rekam Iasachnoi i Korkodonu. Drevnii i sovremennyi Iukagirskii byt i pis'mena [Along the Yassachnaya and Korkodon rivers. Ancient and modern Yukaghir life and writing]." *Izvestiia imperatorskogo Russkogo geograficheskogo obshchestva* 34 (3): 255–293.

———. 1899. "Über die Sprache und Schrift der Jukagiren." *Sitzungsberichte der Geographischen Gesellschaft (Bern)* 17:49–63.

———. 1926. *The Yukaghir and the Yukaghirized Tungus* = Memoirs of the American Museum of Natural History, vol. 13. New York.

———. 1928. *Peoples of Asiatic Russia.* New York: Museum of Natural History.

———. 1934. "Odul'skii (Iukagirskii) iazyk [The Odul (Yukaghir) language]." In I. P. Al'kor, ed., *Iazyki i pis'mennost' narodov severa.* Vol. 3, pp. 149–180. Moscow: Gosudarstvennoe uchebno-pedagogicheskoe izdatel'stvo.

Justeson, John S., and Lyle Campbell. 1984. *Phoneticism in Mayan Hieroglyphic Writing.* Institute for Mesoamerican Studies Publication no. 9. Albany: State University of New York.

Justeson, John S., et al. 1985. *The Foreign Impact on Lowland Mayan Language and Script.* Middle American Research Institute Publication 53. New Orleans: Tulane University.

Kahn, David. 1967. *The Codebreakers: The Story of Secret Writing.* New York: Macmillan.

Karlgren, Bernhard. 1923. *Analytic Dictionary of Chinese and Sino-Japanese.* Paris: P. Geuthner.

———. 1929. *Sound and Symbol in Chinese.* London: Oxford University Press.

———. 1940. *Grammata Serica: Script and Phonetics in Chinese and Sino-Japanese.* Reprinted from *Bulletin of the Museum of Far Eastern Antiquities,* no. 12. Stockholm: Museum of Far Eastern Antiquities.

Keightley, David N. 1978. *Sources of Shang History.* Berkeley: University of California Press.

Keller, Helen. 1959. *The Story of My Life.* New ed., rev. and enl. London: Hodder & Stoughton.

Kelley, David H. 1962. "A History of the Decipherment of the Maya Script." *Anthropological Linguistics* 4 (8): 1–48.

———. 1976. *Deciphering the Maya Script.* Austin: University of Texas Press.

Kennedy, George A. 1953. *ZH Guide. An Introduction to Sinology.* New Haven: Far Eastern Publications.

———. 1964. *Selected Works.* Ed. Tien-yi Li. New Haven: Far Eastern Publications.

Kim Ilsong. 1972. *On Revolutionary Literature and the Arts.* London: Africa Ltd.

Kim-Renaud, Young-Key. 1974. "Korean Consonantal Phonology." Ph.D. diss., University of Hawaii.

Klima, Edward S. 1975. "Sound and Its Absence in the Linguistic Symbol." In J. F. Kavanagh and J. E. Cutting, eds., *The Role of Speech in Language.* Pp. 249–270. Cambridge: MIT Press.

Klima, Edward S. and Ursula Bellugi. 1979. *The Signs of Language.* Cambridge: Harvard University Press.

Klingenheben, A. 1933. "The Vai Script." *Africa* 6 (2): 158–171.

Knorozov, Y. V. 1958. "The Problem of the Study of the Maya Hieroglyphic Writing." Trans. by Sophie D. Coe. *Antiquity* 23:284–291.

Knowlson, James. 1975. *Universal Language Schemes in England and France, 1600–1800.* Toronto: Toronto University Press.

Kokugogakkai [National language association]. 1966. *Kokugogaku jiten* [Dictionary of national language study]. Tokyo: Tokyodo.

Kolers, Paul A. 1969. "Some Formal Characteristics of Pictograms." *American Scientist* 57 (3): 348–363.

Kōno, Rokuro. 1969. "The Chinese Writing and Its Influence on the Scripts of the Neighboring Peoples with Special Reference to Korea and Japan." *Memoirs of the Research Department of the Toyo Bunko* 27:84–140.

Krahmer, Gustav. 1896. "Über jukagirische Briefe." *Globus* 69:208–211.

Kramer, Samuel Noah. 1961. *Sumerian Mythology.* New York: Harper & Brothers.

———. 1963. *The Sumerians.* Chicago: University of Chicago Press.

———. 1986. *In the World of Sumer.* Detroit: Wayne State University Press.

Kreinovich, E. A. 1968. "Iukagirskii iazyk [The Yukaghir language]." *Iazyki narodov SSSR* 5:435–452.

Krishnamurti, Bh. and J. P. L. Gwynn. 1985. *A Grammar of Modern Telugu.* Delhi: Oxford University Press.

Langdon, Stephen. 1928. *Pictographic Inscriptions from Jemdet Nasr.* Oxford Editions of Cuneiform Texts 7. London: Oxford University Press.

Lash, Joseph. 1980. *Helen and Teacher: The Story of Helen Keller and Anne Sullivan.* New York: Delacorte Press.

Laufer, Berthold. 1914. "Some Fundamental Ideas of Chinese Culture." *Journal of Race Development* 5:160–174.

Ledyard, Gari Keith. 1975. *The Korean Language Reform of 1446: The Origin, Background, and Early History of the Korean Alphabet.* Ann Arbor, Mich.: University Microfilms.

Lee Sung-nyŏng. 1972. "On the Need of Teaching Chinese Characters." *Korea Journal* 12 (4): 49–52.

Lehmann-Haupt, Christopher. 1986. Review of Robert K. Logan, *The Alphabet Effect* (New York: William Morrow and Co., 1986). *New York Times,* July 31, 1986.

Li Lincan. 1957. *Mosuo jingdian yizhu liuzhong [Translations and annotations of six Moso (Naxi) classics].* Taipei: China Series Publishing Committee.

Li Lincan, Zhang Kun, and He Cai. 1953. *Mosuo xiangxing wenzi zidian [Dictionary of Moso (Naxi) pictographs].* Hong Kong: Shuowenshe.

Li Min. 1979. "Yi wen [Yi writing]." *Minzu yuwen* 4:304–306.

Liddell, Scott K. 1978. "Nonmanual Signals and Relative Clauses in American Sign Language." In Patricia Siple, ed., *Understanding Language through Sign Language Research.* Pp. 59–90. New York: Academic Press.

Lieberman, S. J. 1980. "Of Clay Tablets, Hollow Clay Balls, and Writing: A Sumerian View." *American Journal of Archaeology* 84:339–358.

Lin Tao. 1988. "Hanyu yuyin [Chinese phonetics]." *Zhongguo da baike quanshu. Yuyan wenzi.* Pp. 183–189. Beijing: Zhongguo Da Baike Quanshu Chubanshe.

Lin Xingren. 1983. "Mantan guangbo de yuyan tedian [Informal comments on the linguistic peculiarities of broadcast scripts]." *Yuwen xuexi* 1:54–56.

Logan, Robert K. 1986. *The Alphabet Effect. The Impact of the Phonetic Alphabet on the Development of Western Civilization.* New York: William Morrow and Co.

LPLP. 1985. "Ending 'Capital Punishment.' " *Language Problems & Language Planning* 9 (3): 284–285.

Ma Xueliang. 1962. "New Scripts for China's Minorities." *China Reconstructs* 11 (8): 24–27.

————. 1981. "Yiwen he Yiwen jingshu [Yi writing and Yi scriptures]." *Minzu yuwen* 1:8–15.

Mair, Victor H. 1988. [Miscellaneous Reviews.] Sino-Platonic Papers No. 8. Philadelphia: Department of Oriental Studies, University of Pennsylvania.

Mallery, Garrick. 1893. *Picture Writing of the American Indians.* Washington: Government Printing Office. Reprint ed., 2 vols. New York: Dover Publications, 1972.

Marcus, Joyce. 1976. "The Origins of Mesoamerican Writing." *Annual Review of Anthropology* 5:35–67.

Marek, Kurt W. 1966. *Hands on the Past: Pioneer Archaeologists Tell Their Own Story.* New York: Knopf.

Margouliès, Georges. 1957. *La Langue et l'écriture chinoises.* Paris: Payot.

Marshack, Alexander. 1964. "Lunar Notation on Upper Paleolithic Remains." *Science* 146:743–745.

————. 1972. *The Roots of Civilization: The Cognitive Beginning of Man's First Art, Symbol, and Notation.* New York: McGraw-Hill.

Marshman, Joshua. 1814. *Clavis Sinica. Elements of Chinese Grammar.* Serampore: Mission Press.

Martin, Samuel E. 1967. *A Korean–English Dictionary.* New Haven: Yale University Press.

————. 1968. "Korean Standardization: Problems, Observations, and Suggestions." *Ural-Altaische Jahrbücher* 40 (1–2): 85–114.

————. 1972. "Non-Alphabetic Writing Systems: Some Observations." In J. F. Kavanagh and Ignatius G. Mattingly, eds., *Language by Ear and by Eye. The Relationships between Speech and Reading.* Pp. 81–102. Cambridge: MIT Press.

Martinet, André. 1962. *A Functional View of Language.* Oxford: Clarendon Press.

————. 1964. *Elements of General Linguistics.* Trans. Elisabeth Palmer. Chicago: University of Chicago Press.

Mason, William A. 1920. *A History of the Art of Writing.* New York: Macmillan.

Mathews, Peter. 1984. "A Maya Hieroglyphic Syllabary." In John S. Justeson and Lyle Campbell, eds., *Phoneticism in Mayan Hieroglyphic Writing.* Institute for Mesoamerican Studies no. 9. Pp. 311–314. Albany: State University of New York.

McIntosh, Angus, and M. A. K. Halliday. 1966. *Patterns of Language.* Bloomington: Indiana University Press.

Mead, Margaret, and Rudolph Modley. 1968. "Communication among All People, Everywhere." *Natural History* 77 (7): 55–63.

Meltzer, E. S. 1980. "Remarks on Ancient Egyptian Writing with Emphasis on Its Mnemonic Aspects." In Paul A. Kolers, Merald E. Wrolstad, and Herman Bouma, eds., *Processing of Visible Language 2.* Pp. 43–66. New York: Plenum Press.

Mickel, Stanley Lewis. 1986. "Literary Aspects of Shang Bone Inscriptions" and "Literary Aspects of Bronze Inscriptions." In William H. Niehauser, Jr., ed., *The Indiana Companion to Traditional Chinese Literature.* Pp. 255–257 and 295–297. Bloomington: Indiana University Press.

Miller, Casey, and Kate Swift. 1980. *The Handbook of Nonsexist Writing.* New York: Lippincott and Crowell.

Miller, Roy Andrew. 1967. *The Japanese Language.* Chicago: University of Chicago Press.

Modley, Rudolf. 1966. "Graphic Symbols for World-Wide Communication." In Gyorgy Kepes, ed., *Sign Image Symbol.* New York: George Braziller.

Moorhouse, A. C. 1953. *The Triumph of the Alphabet. A History of Writing.* New York: Henry Schuman.

Moran, Hugh A., and David H. Kelley. 1969. *The Alphabet and the Ancient Calendar Signs.* 2d ed. Palo Alto: Daily Press.

Morohashi, Tetsuji. 1955–1960. *Dai kan-wa jiten* [*Great Chinese–Japanese Dictionary*]. 13 vols. Tokyo: Taishukan Shoten.

Mowat, Farley. 1972. *The Siberians.* Baltimore: Penguin Books.

Naveh, Joseph. 1982. *Early History of the Alphabet. An Introduction to West Semitic Epigraphy and Paleography.* Leiden: E. J. Brill.

Needham, Joseph. 1964. "Glories and Defects of the Chinese Scientific and Technical Tradition." In Elisabeth Charlotte Welskopf, ed. *Neue Beitrage zur Geschichte der Alten Welt.* 1:87–109. Berlin: Akademie-Verlag.

Neustupný, J. V. 1984. *Introduction to Japanese Writing.* Melbourne: Japanese Studies Center.

Nissen, Hans J. 1986. "The Archaic Texts from Uruk." *World Archaeology* 17 (3): 318–334.

Oldfield, R. C. 1963. "Individual Vocabulary and Semantic Currency." *British Journal of Social and Clinical Psychology* 2:122–130.

d'Ollone, Henri Marie Gustave. 1912. *Ecritures des peuples non chinois de la Chine.* Paris: Leroux.

Oppenheim, A. Leo. 1977. *Ancient Mesopotamia.* Rev. ed. completed by Erica Reiner. Chicago: University of Chicago Press.

Pak Tae-Yong. 1971. "Convertibility between Distinctive Features and Phonemes." *Linguistics* 66:97–114.

Paper, Herbert A. 1982. "Language Spread: The Ancient Near Eastern World." In Robert L. Cooper, ed., *Language Spread. Studies in Diffusion and Social Change.* Pp. 107–117. Bloomington: Indiana University Press.

Paradis, Michel, Hiroko Haguwara, and Nancy Hildebrandt. 1985. *Neurolinguistic Aspects of the Japanese Writing System.* New York: Academic Press.

Park Nahm-sheik. 1985. "Language Purism in Korea Today." Paper presented at the Conference on the Politics of Language Purism: A Rhetoric of Authentication, held at the East-West Center in Honolulu, September 8–14, 1985.

Pedersen, H. 1931. *Linguistic Science in the Nineteenth Century. Methods and Results.* Trans. John Webster Spargo. Cambridge: Harvard University Press.

Pelliot, Paul. 1904. "Deux itinéraires de Chine en Inde." *Bulletin de l'Ecole Française d'Extrême Orient* 4:131–428.

Pike, Kenneth L. 1947. *Phonemics.* Ann Arbor: University of Michigan Press.

Pope, Maurice. 1966. "The Origin of Writing in the Near East." *Antiquity* 40:17–23.

———. 1975. *The Story of Archaeological Decipherment: From Egyptian Hieroglyphics to Linear B.* New York: Charles Scribner's Sons.

Powell, M. A. 1981. "Three Problems in the History of Cuneiform Writing: Origins, Direction of the Script, Literacy." *Visible Language* 15:419–440.

PR. 1958. "Written Languages for All." *Peking Review* 11 (11): 16–17.

Prem, Hanns J., and Berthold Riese. 1983. "Autochthonous American Writing Systems: The Aztec and Maya Examples." In Florian Coulmas and Konrad Ehlich, eds., *Writing in Focus.* Pp. 167–186. Berlin: Mouton.

Ramsey, S. Robert. 1987. *The Languages of China.* Princeton: Princeton University Press.

Rao, Patricia Walsh. 1977. "Conditioning." In Judy E. Pickens, Patricia Walsh Rao, and Linda Cook Roberts, eds., *Without Bias: A Guidebook for Nondiscriminatory Communication.* P. 21. San Francisco: International Association of Business Communicators.

Ray, John D. 1986. "The Emergence of Writing in Egypt." *World Archaeology* 17 (3): 308–316.

Reischauer, Edwin O., and John King Fairbank. 1960. *East Asia. The Great Tradition.* Boston: Houghton Mifflin.

Rimsky-Korsakoff, Svetlana. 1967. "Soviet Dungan: The Chinese Language of Central Asia." *Monumenta Serica* 26:352–421.

Rimsky-Korsakoff Dyer, Svetlana. 1987. "Sulian Dungan minzu yuyan, xianzhuang ji qi shi'eryue ge [The language, present condition, and twelve-months poems of the Soviet Dungan nationality]. In *Wang li xiansheng jinian lunwen.* Pp. 233–280. Hong Kong: Zhongguo Yuwen Xuehui.

Rosemont, H., Jr. 1974. "On Representing Abstraction in Archaic Chinese." *Philosophy East and West* 24:71–88.

Sampson, Geoffrey. 1980. *Making Sense.* Oxford: Oxford University Press.

———. 1985. *Writing Systems. A Linguistic Approach.* London: Hutchinson.

Sanders, Robert M. 1987. *The Four Languages of "Mandarin."* Sino-Platonic Papers No. 4. Philadelphia: Department of Oriental Studies, University of Pennsylvania.

Sansom, George B. 1928. *An Historical Grammar of Japanese.* Oxford: Clarendon Press.

Saussure, Ferdinand de. 1959. *Course in General Linguistics.* Trans. Wade Baskin. New York: Philosophical Society.

Schenkel, W. 1976. "The Structure of Hieroglyphic Script." *Royal Anthropological Institute News* 15 (August): 4–7.

Schmandt-Besserat, Denise. 1978. "The Earliest Precursor of Writing." *Scientific American* 238 (6): 50–59.

———. 1979. "An Archaic Recording System in the Uruk–Jemdet Nasr Period." *American Journal of Archaeology* 83:19–48.

———. 1981. "From Tokens to Tablets: A Re-Evaluation of the So-Called 'Numerical Tablets.' " *Visible Language* 15 (4): 321–344.

———. 1984. "Before Numerals." *Visible Language* 18 (1): 48–60.

———. 1986. "Tokens: Facts and Interpretation." *Visible Language* 20 (3): 250–273.

Schoolcraft, Henry Rowe. 1851–1857. *Information Respecting the History, Condition and Prospects of the Indian Tribes of the United States.* 6 vols. Philadelphia: Lippincott, Grambo.

Schuessler, Axel. 1987. *A Dictionary of Early Zhou Chinese.* Honolulu: University of Hawaii Press.

Scinto, Leonard M. 1986. *Written Language and Psychological Development.* New York: Academic Press.

Scribner, Sylvia, and Michael Cole. 1981. *The Psychology of Literacy.* Cambridge: Harvard University Press.

Searle, John R. 1980. "Minds, Brains, and Programs." *The Behavioral and Brain Sciences* 3:417–457.

Seashore, R. H., and L. D. Eckerson. 1940. "The Measurement of Individual Differences in General English Vocabularies." *Journal of Educational Psychology* 31:14–38.

Segall, Marshall H., Donald T. Campbell, and Melville Herskovitz. 1966. *Influence of Culture on Visual Perception.* Indianapolis: Bobbs-Merrill.

Serruys, Paul L.-M. 1974. "The Language of the Shang Oracle Bone Inscriptions." *T'oung pao* 60 (1–3): 12–120.

Shargorodskii, S. 1895. "Ob Iukagirskikh pis'menakh [On Yukaghir writing]." *Zemlevedenie* 2/3: 135–148.

Siple, Patricia, ed. 1978. *Understanding Language through Sign Language Research.* New York: Academic Press.

Sivin, N. 1982. "Why the Scientific Revolution Did Not Take Place in China—Or Didn't It?" *Chinese Science* 5:45–66.

Slaughter, Mary. 1982. *Universal Language and Scientific Taxonomy in the 17th Century.* Cambridge: Cambridge University Press.

Smalley, William A., Chia Koua Vang, and Gnia Yee Yang. Forthcoming. *Mother of Writing. The Origin and Development of a Hmong Messianic Script.* Chicago: University of Chicago Press.

Smith, Richard J. 1983. *China's Cultural Heritage. The Ch'ing Dynasty, 1644–1912.* Boulder, Colo.: Westview Press.

Sohn Ho-min. 1988. *Korean.* Cambridge: Cambridge University Press.

Soothill, W. E. 1942. *The Student's Four Thousand Character and Pocket Dictionary* (preface dated 1889). 16th ed. London: Kegan Paul, Trench, Trubner & Co.

Spencer, H. 1969. *The Visible Word.* New York: Hastings House.

Stevenson, Harold W., et al. 1982. "Reading Disabilities: The Case of Chinese, Japanese, and English." *Child Development* 53:1164–1181.

Stokoe, William C., Jr. 1974. "Classification and Description of Sign Languages." In Thomas A. Sebeok, ed., *Current Trends in Linguistics* 12 (1): 345–371. The Hague: Mouton.

———. 1975. "The Shape of Soundless Language." In J. F. Kavanagh and J. E. Cutting, eds., *The Role of Speech in Language.* Pp. 207–228. Cambridge: MIT Press.

Stremel-Campbell, Kathleen, and Jimmie Matthews. 1987. "Development of Emergent Language." In Michael Bullis, ed., *Communication Development in Young Children with Deaf-Blindness: Literature Review III.* Pp. 141–183. Monmouth, Ore.: Communication Skills Center for Young Children with Deaf-Blindness.

Suzuki, Takao. 1975. "On the Twofold Phonetic Realization of Basic Concepts: In Defense of Chinese Characters in Japanese." In Fred C. C. Peng, ed., *Language in Japanese Society.* Pp. 175–192. Tokyo: University of Tokyo Press.

Taylor, Allan. 1975. "Nonverbal Communication Systems in Native North America." *Semiotica* 13:329–374.

Taylor, Insup. 1980. "The Korean Writing System: An Alphabet? A Syllabary? A Logography?" In Paul A. Kolers, Merald E. Wrolstad, and Herman Bouma, eds., *Processing of Visible Language 2.* Pp. 67–82. New York: Plenum Press.

Taylor, Isaac. 1899. *The History of the Alphabet.* 2 vols. New York: Scribner's.

Taylor, Jared. 1983. *Shadows of the Rising Sun.* New York: William Morrow and Co.

Thompson, John Eric S. 1962. *A Catalogue of Maya Hieroglyphs.* Norman: University of Oklahoma Press.

Thomsen, Marie-Louise. 1984. *The Sumerian Language.* MESOPOTAMIA. Copenhagen Studies in Assyriology. Vol. 10. Copenhagen: Akademisk Forlag.

Trager, George. 1974. "Writing and Writing Systems." In Thomas A. Sebeok, ed., *Current Trends in Linguistics* 12 (1): 373–496. The Hague: Mouton.

Trnka, B. 1968. *Phonological Analysis of Present-Day Standard English.* University, Ala.: University of Alabama Press.

Tsao, Yao-Chung, and Tsai-Guey Wang. 1983. "Information Distribution in Chinese Characters." *Visible Language* 17 (4): 357–364.

Tyumenev, A. I. 1969. "The State Economy in Ancient Sumer." In I. M. Diakonoff, ed. *Ancient Mesopotamia. Socio-Economic History. A Collection of Studies by Soviet Scholars.* Pp. 70–87. Moscow: Nauka Publishing.

Tzeng, Ovid J. L., Daisy L. Hung, and Wiliam S.-Y. Wang. 1977. "Speech Recoding in Reading Chinese Characters." *Journal of Experimental Psychology: Human Learning and Memory* 3 (6): 621–630.

Tzeng, Ovid J. L., Daisy L. Hung, and Linda Garro. 1978. "Reading the Chinese Characters: An Information Processing View." *Journal of Chinese Linguistics* 6 (2): 287–305.

Umiker, Donna Jean. 1974. "Speech Surrogates: Drum and Whistle Systems." In Thomas A. Sebeok, ed., *Current Trends in Linguistics* 12 (1): 497–536. The Hague: Mouton.

Unger, J. Marshall. 1980. "The Etymology of the Japanese Word /kana/." *Papers in Japanese Linguistics* 7:173–184.

———. 1984. "Japanese Braille." *Visible Language* 18 (3): 254–266.

———. 1987. *The Fifth Generation Fallacy.* New York: Oxford University Press.

———. 1988. *Computers and Japanese Literacy.* Sino-Platonic Papers No. 6. Philadelphia: Department of Oriental Studies, University of Pennsylvania.

Untermeyer, Louis, ed. 1942. *Modern British Poetry.* Vol. 2. New York: Harcourt, Brace and Company.

Vachek, Josef. 1945–1949. "Some Remarks on Writing and Phonetic Transcription." *Acta Linguistica* 5:86–93. Reprinted in Josef Vachek, ed., *Praguiana. Some Basic and Less Known Aspects of the Prague Linguistic School.* Pp. 199–209. Amsterdam: John Benjamins, 1983.

———. 1973. *Written Language. General Problems and Problems of English.* The Hague: Mouton.

———. 1976. "Two Chapters on Written English." In Josef Vachek, *Selected Writings in English and General Linguistics.* Pp. 408–441. The Hague: Mouton. Reprinted from *Brno Studies in English* 1 (1959): 7–34.

————. 1979. "Some Remarks on the Stylistics of Written Language." In D. J. Allerton and David Holdcraft, eds., *Context in Linguistic Analysis. A Festschrift for William Haas.* Pp. 206–215. Cambridge: Cambridge University Press.

Vaiman, A. A. 1974. "Über die protosumerische Schrift." *Acta Antiqua Academiae Scientiarum Hungaricae* 22:15–27.

Vallins, G. H. 1965. *Spelling.* Rev. ed. London: André Deutsch.

Vanstiphout, H. L. J. 1979. "How Did They Learn Sumerian?" *Journal of Cuneiform Studies* 31 (2): 118–126.

Venezky, Richard L. 1970. *The Structure of English Orthography.* The Hague: Mouton.

Voegelin, C. F., and F. M. Voegelin. 1961. "Typological Classification Systems with Included, Excluded, and Self-Sufficient Alphabets." *Anthropological Linguistics* 3 (1): 55–96.

Walker, W. n.d. "An Experiment in Programmed Cross-Cultural Education: The Import of the Cherokee Primer for the Behavioral Sciences." Mimeograph.

Waller, Robert H. W. 1980. "Graphic Aspects of Complex Texts: Typography as Macro-Punctuation." In Paul A. Kolers, Merald E. Wrolstad, and Herman Bouma, eds., *Processing of Visible Language 2.* Pp. 241–253. New York: Plenum Press.

Wang Hongdao. 1986. "Naxizu [Naxi nationality]." *Zhongguo da baike quanshu. Minzu.* Pp. 345–348. Beijing: Zhongguo Da Baike Quanshu Chubanshe.

Wang, William S.-Y. 1979. Review of J. F. Kavanagh and J. E. Cutting, eds., *The Role of Speech in Language.* (Cambridge: MIT Press, 1975). *Language* 55 (4): 941–945.

————. 1980. Review of Winfred P. Lehman, ed. *Language and Linguistics in the People's Republic of China.* (Austin: University of Texas Press, 1975). *Language* 56 (1): 197–202.

————. 1981. "Language Structure and Optimal Orthography." In Ovid J. L. Tzeng and Harry Singer, eds., *Perception of Print. Reading Research in Experimental Psychology.* Pp. 223–236. Hillside, N.J.: Lawrence Erlbaum Associates.

Weule, Karl. 1915. *Vom Kerbstock zum Alphabet.* Stuttgart: Kosmos.

Whorf, Benjamin Lee. 1933. *The Phonetic Value of Certain Characters in Maya Writing.* Papers of the Peabody Museum of American Archaeology and Ethnology, vol. 13, no. 2. Cambridge: Harvard University.

————. 1935. "Maya Writing and Its Decipherment." *Maya Research* 2:367–382.

————. 1942. "Decipherment of the Linguistic Portion of the Maya Hieroglyphs." *Annual Report of the Smithsonian Institution for 1941.* Pp. 479–502. Washington.

Wieger, Leon. 1965. *Chinese Characters.* Reprint of 1915 ed. New York: Paragon Reprint Corp.

Wijk, Axel. 1959. *Regularized English.* Stockholm: Almquist & Wiksell.

Wilbur, Ronnie. 1976. "The Linguistics of Manual Language and Manual Systems." In L. Lloyd, ed., *Communication Assessment and Intervention Strategies.* Pp. 423–500. Baltimore: University Park Press.

Wilhelm, Gernat. 1983. "Reconstructing the Phonology of Dead Languages." In Florian Coulmas and Konrad Ehlich, eds., *Writing in Focus.* Pp. 157–166. Berlin: Mouton.

Winnington, Alan. 1959. *The Slaves of Cool Mountain.* London: Lawrence & Wishart.

Woodcock, Richard W. 1968. *Rebus as a Medium in Beginning Reading Instruction.* IMRID Papers and Reports, vol. V, no. 4. Nashville.

Woodcock, Richard, Charlotte R. Clark, and Cornelia Oakes Davies. 1967–1969. *The Peabody Rebus Reading Program.* 7 vols. Circle Pines, Minn.: American Guidance Service.

Yamagiwa, Joseph. 1969. "From Chinese to the Korean, Japanese, and Vietnamese Systems of Writing: Three Cases of Linguistic Nationalism." In Denis Sinor, ed., *American Oriental Society, Middle West Branch, Semicentennial Volume.* Pp. 233–267. Bloomington, Ind.

Yi Ki-moon. 1975. "Language and Writing Systems in Traditional Korea." In Peter H. Lee, ed., *The Traditional Culture and Society of Korea: Art and Literature.* Occasional Papers of the Center for Korean Studies, no. 4. Pp. 15–32. Honolulu: University of Hawaii.

Yin Bin-yong. 1984. "Hanyu yusu de dingliang yanjiu [A quantitative study of Chinese morphemes]." *Zhongguo yuwen* 5:338–347.

Young Ching-chi. 1935–1936. "L'écriture et les manuscrits lolos." *Orient et Occident* 1 (11): 1–18, 1 (12): 1–13, 2 (1): 1–11, 2 (2): 43–56.

Yushmanov, N. V. 1961. *The Structure of the Arabic Language.* Washington: Center for Applied Linguistics.

Zachrisson, R. E. 1931. "Four Hundred Years of English Spelling Reform." *Studia Neophilologica* 4:1–68.

Zhou Youguang. 1988. "Ni Haishu tongzhi he Ladinghua yundong [Comrade Ni Haishu and the Latinization movement]." *Yuwen jianshe* 3:46–47.

ZSM. 1981. *Zhongguo shaoshu minzu [China's minority nationalities].* Beijing: Renmin Chubanshe.

Nyikos, Julius. 1988. "A Linguistic Perspective of Illiteracy." In Sheila Empleton, ed., *The Fourteenth LACUS Forum 1987.* Pp. 146–163. Lake Bluff, Ill.: Linguistic Association of Canada and the United States.

The preceding item came to my attention just as this book approached the final stage of production. It is worth tacking on at the end in this way because it is a valuable study, one of the most detailed that I have encountered, of the phoneme-grapheme relationship in English. The author surveys and criticizes other works dealing with English phonemes and their graphemes and notes that his own research found 80 graphemes for the back vowel phoneme /u/ (as in *truancy*), 1,120 graphemes for the 40 phonemes in a survey of "common words," and 1,768 for those in a survey of "practically all dictionary words." Nyikos finds here the primary reason for the high rate of functional illiteracy in the United States.

INDEX